AF574206

THE METALWORKER'S ART

A PICTORIAL CELEBRATION

BOSTON ARCHITECTURAL CLUB

DOVER PUBLICATIONS, INC.
MINEOLA, NEW YORK

Bibliographical Note

This Dover edition, first published in 2011, is an unabridged republication of *The Year Book of the Boston Architectural Club Containing Examples of Metal Work,* originally published by the Boston Architectural Club, Boston, in 1930.

Library of Congress Cataloging-in-Publication Data

Year book of the Boston Architectural Club containing examples of metal work.
The metalworker's art : a pictorial celebration.
p. cm.
"Boston Architectural Club."
"This Dover edition, first published in 2011, is an unabridged republication of The Year Book of the Boston Architectural Club Containing Examples of Metal Work, originally published by the Boston Architectural Club, Boston, in 1930."
ISBN-13: 978-0-486-47313-0
ISBN-10: 0-486-47313-9
1. Art metal-work. 2. Architectural metal-work. I. Boston Architectural Club. II. Title.

NK6405.Y43 2011
739—dc22

2010026499

Manufactured in the United States by Courier Corporation
47313901
www.doverpublications.com

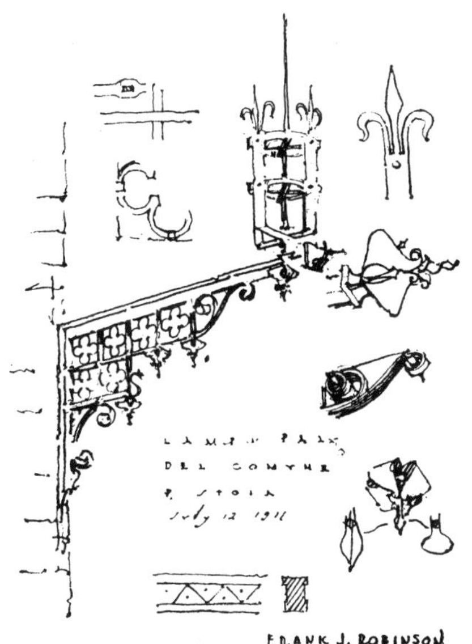

FOREWORD

IT is obvious that metal is entering with new importance into architectural design. The contribution of bronze is particularly notable. The faculty of this aristocratic material to enhance the nobility of building has always been understood. At the hands of the modern designer, however, it is revealing unexpected versatility. One is impressed by the nervous grace and delicacy with which it is made to assist the swift lines of the new architecture and by the felicity with which it articulates the reticent surfaces. Joined with its capacity for the gracious rendering of ambitious sculptural form, it is difficult to put a limit on its availability as an architectural resource. Were it possible to develop for it a permanent patine in its relation to the statuary of outdoors, this superbly capable metal would be relieved of its single disability. The genius of iron is more limited but its traditions are rich and venerable. Hand-wrought iron is capable of a naïve charm which will probably always appeal over the impersonality of bronze to the romantic designer. A wealth of beautiful precedent in this field has come down to us from the patient and primitive processes of the mediaeval smithy and from the Renaissance craftsman of Spain, Italy and England.

The dullness of lead seems uninspiring, and Shakespeare employs it symbolically in the Merchant of Venice as the humblest of metals. And yet its decorative possibilities are exemplified by many charming details of the architecture of the English Tudors. Its encroachment of late in the field occupied by copper in our building is to be noted, as is the favor which copper itself is finding in fresh directions. The new resources which have come to the designer by the addition of aluminum, chromium and monel are making for larger and more varied exploitation of metal and in associations which had never engaged it before.

The tendency of the modern sophisticated methods, however, to eliminate the historic figure of the craftsman is not to be ignored in the consideration of this subject. William Morris and Burne-Jones and the Arts and Crafts Societies fought valiantly for the tradition, but the pressure of mass production through the enlarged resources of the machine is now felt to be more or less inexorable. It is a dictum of the new artistic philosophy, moreover, that the genius of the individual material need no longer influence its design or its technique. Against the validity of this idea sufficiently eloquent matter may be found in these pages in the contrast between the gates of the Palais de Justice and those of St. John's College, Cambridge. Style and material are not separable. Besides, the exigencies of a strenuous age may tolerate certain compromises of principle, but there is reverent place always in the world for those things which are sincerely and intelligently wrought by hand.

Charles D. Maginnis

Index to Illustrations

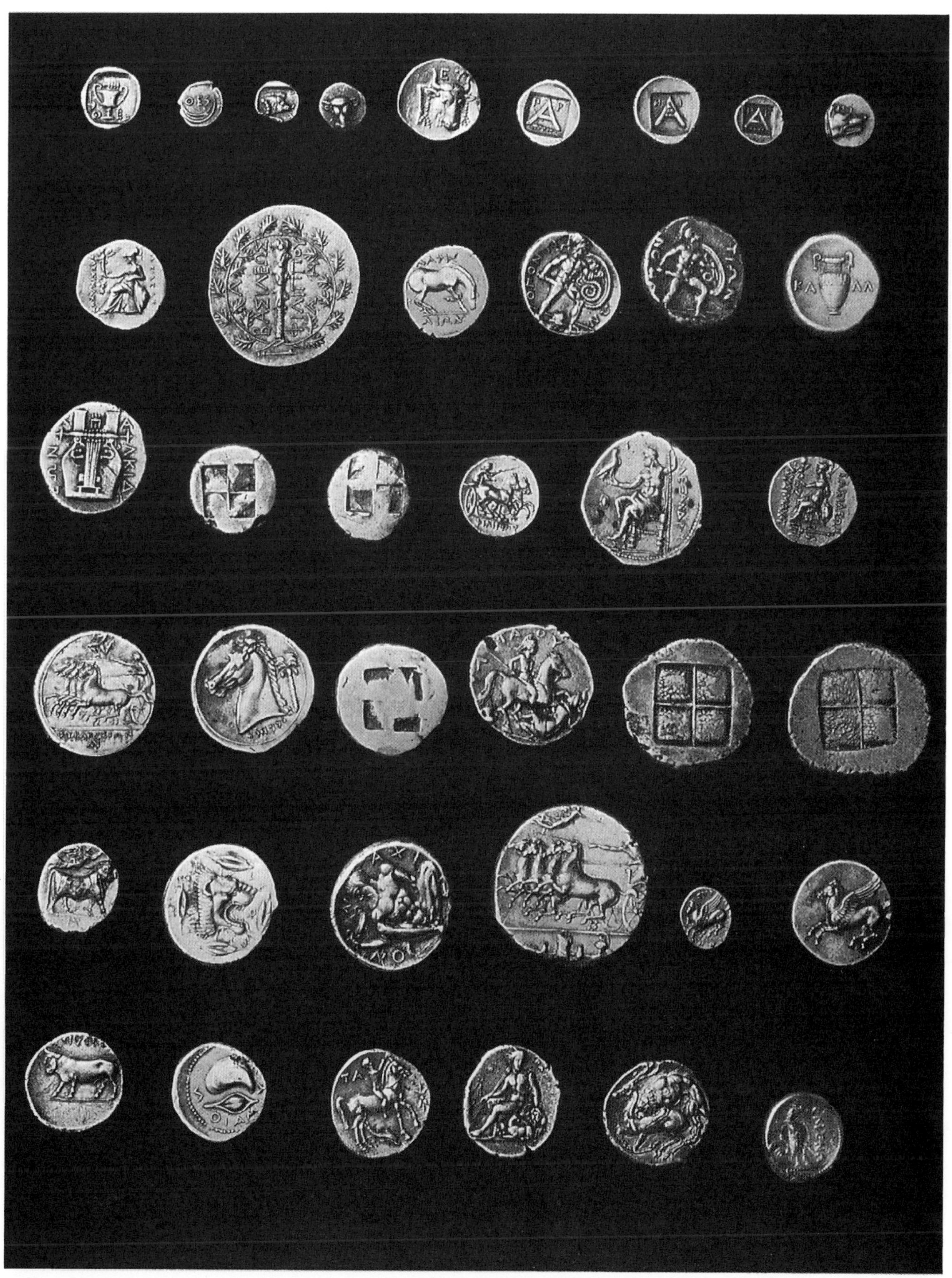

Greek Coins

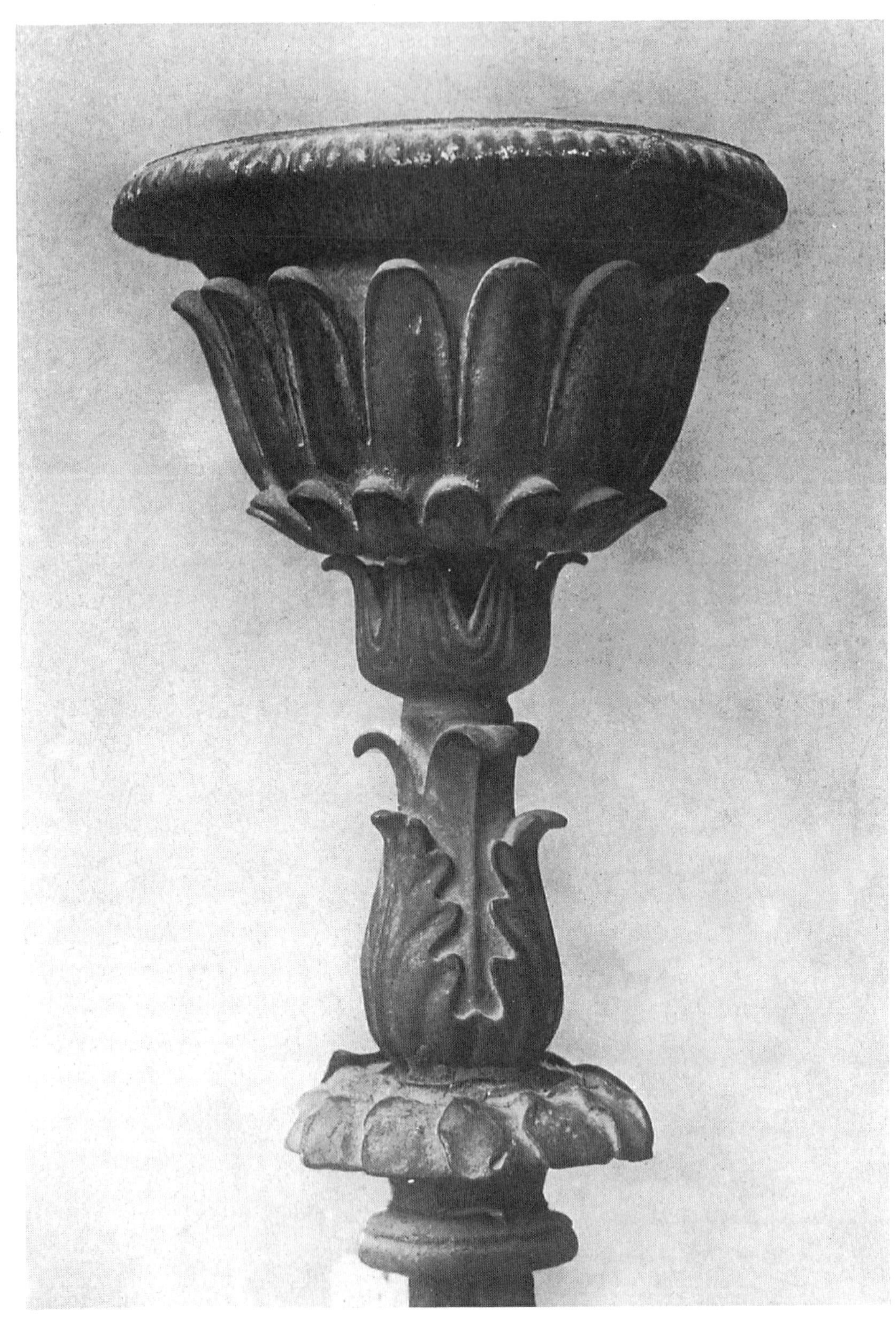

Pompeian Lamp Standard

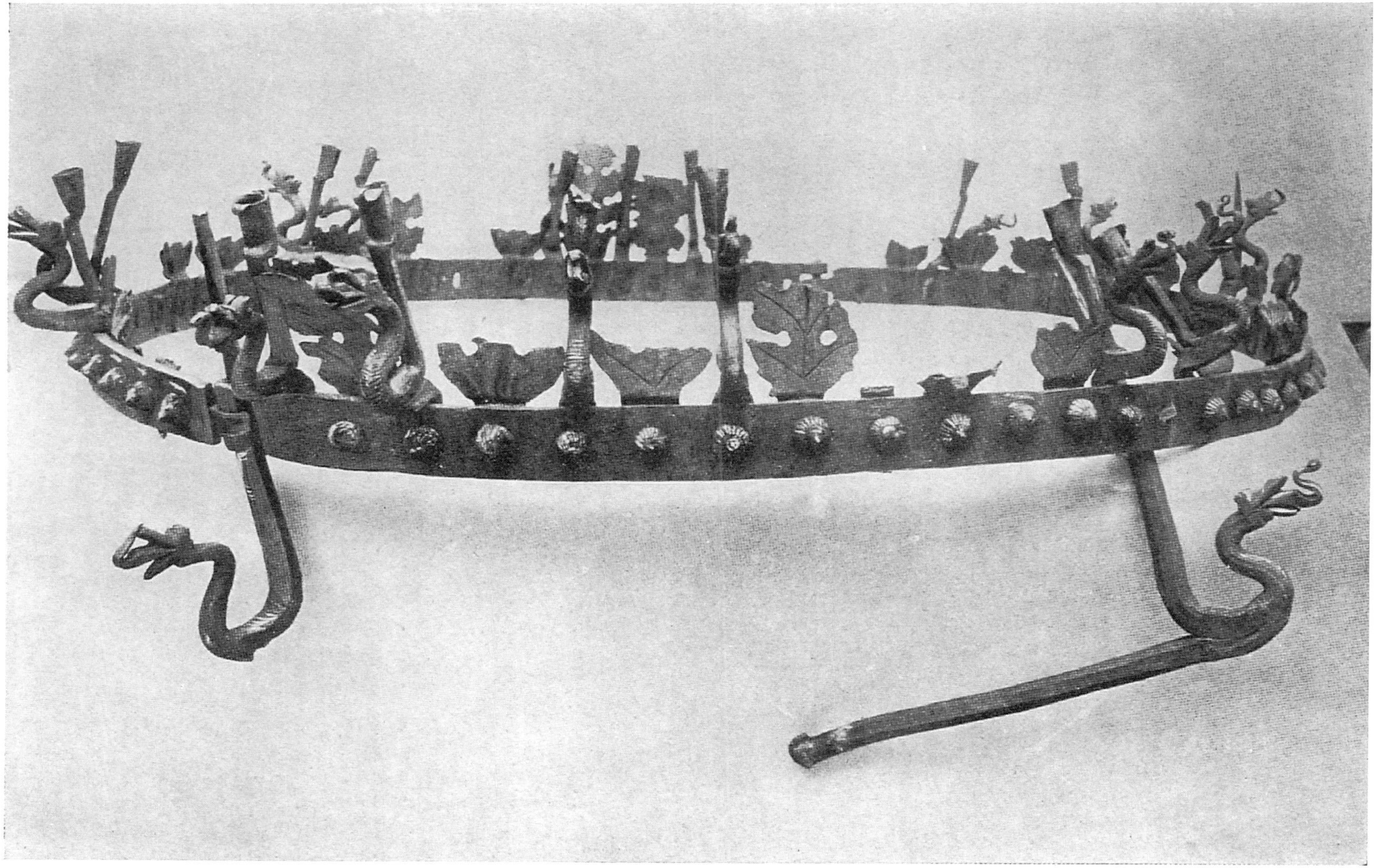

Crown on Column of S. Zanobi, Florence, 13th Century

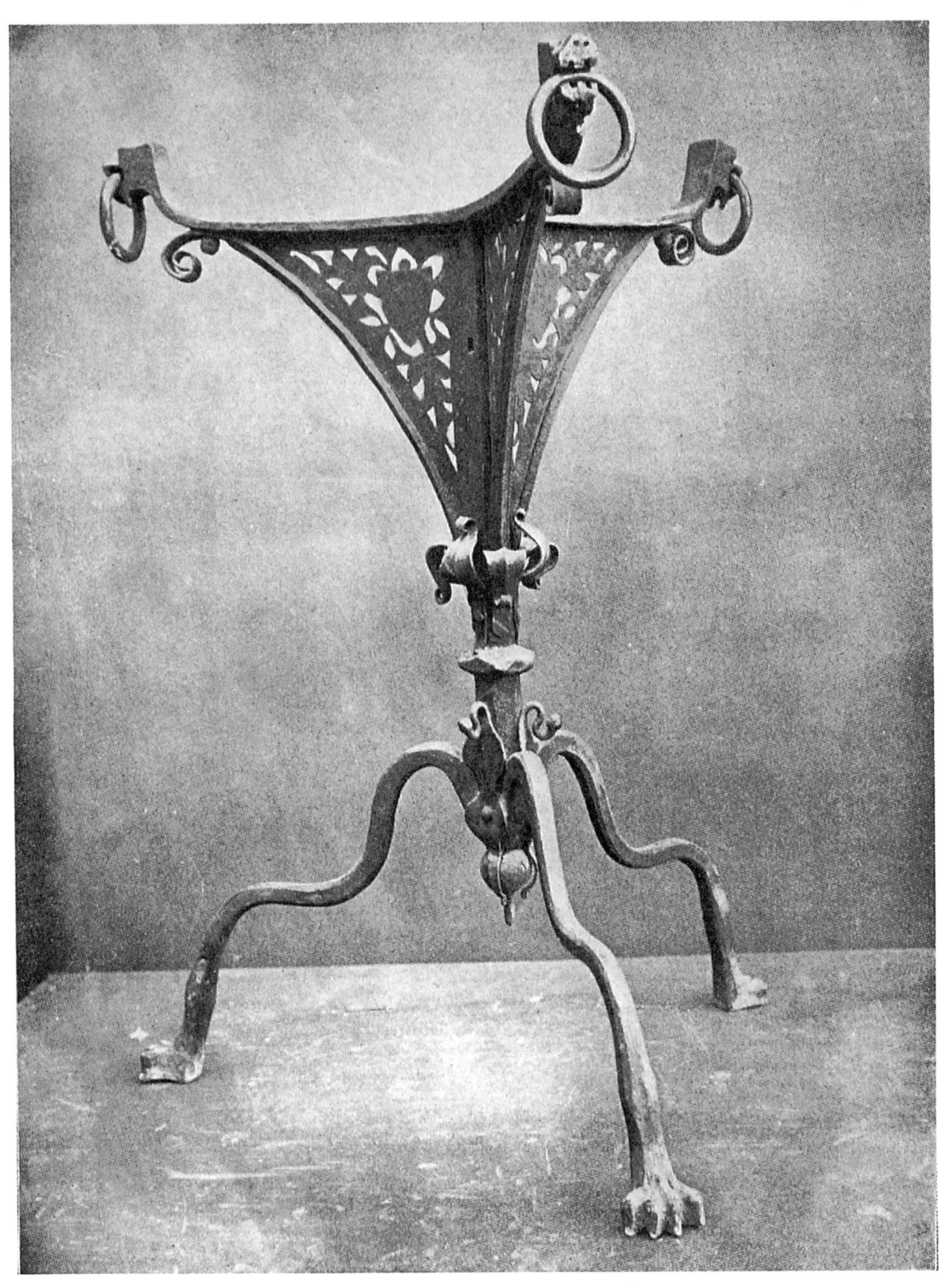

Tripod, Museo del Duomo, Siena, 13th Century

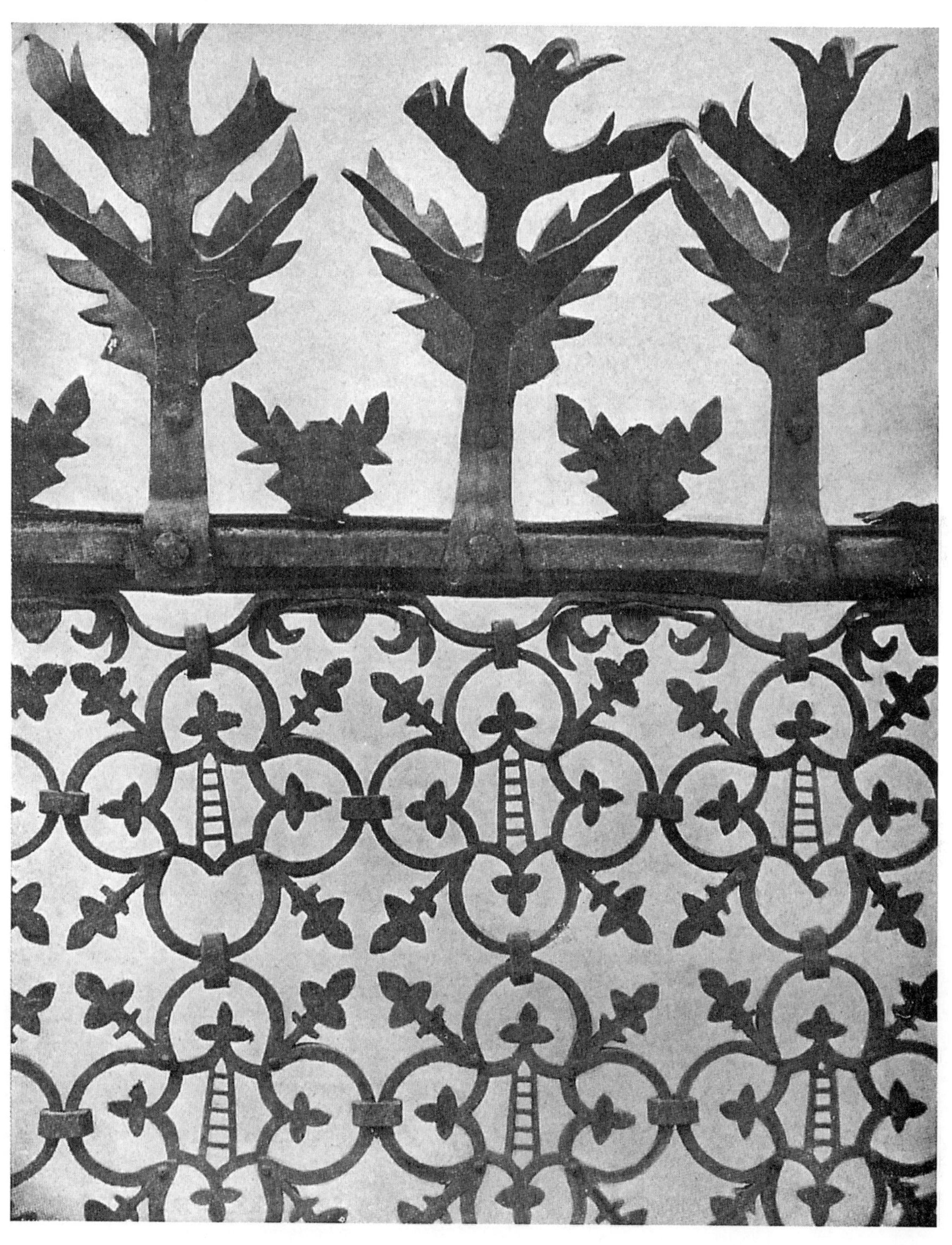

Grille on Tomb of Cansignorio, Verona 13th Century

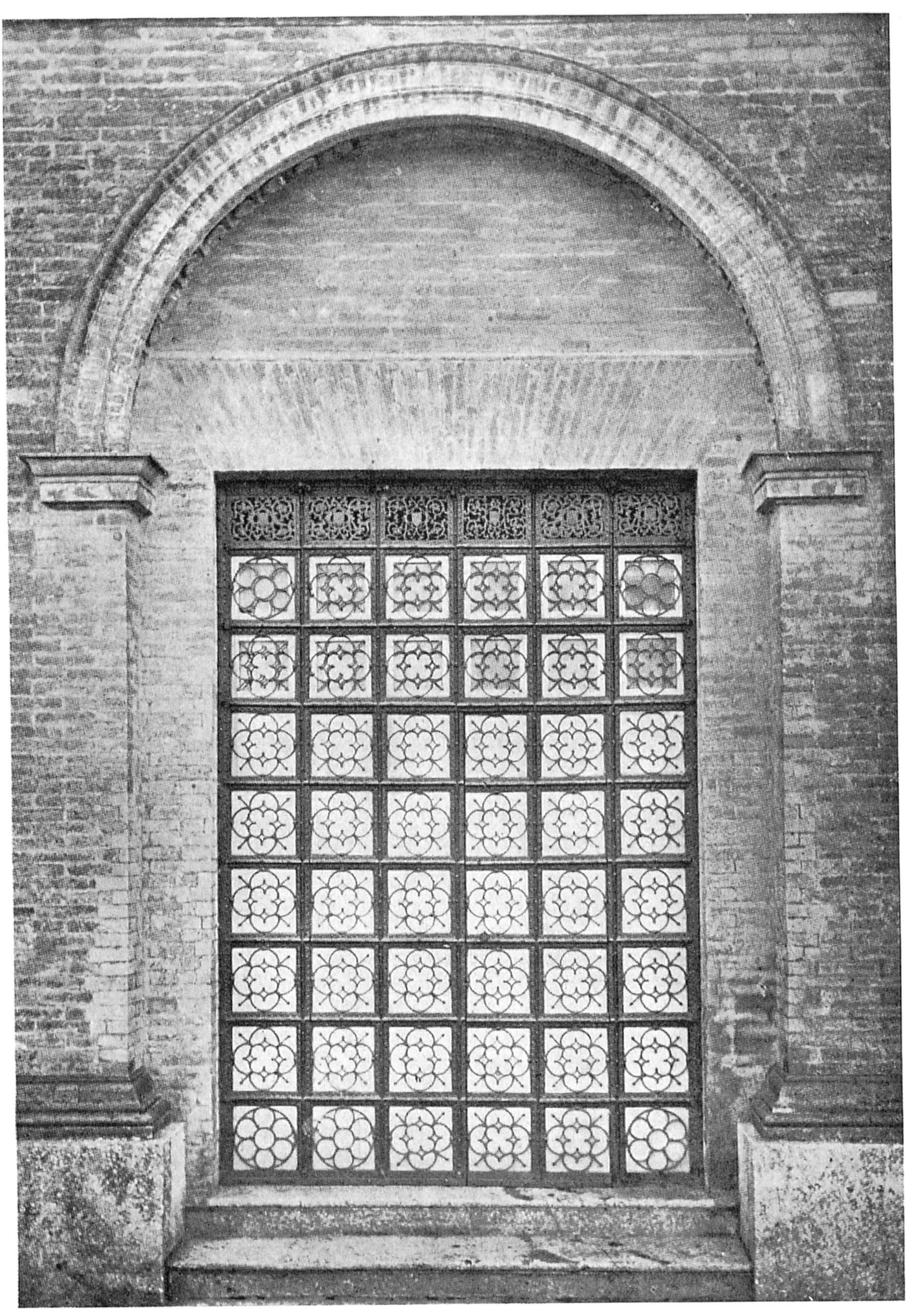

Gate in Church, Palazzo, dei Diavoli, Siena, 13th Century

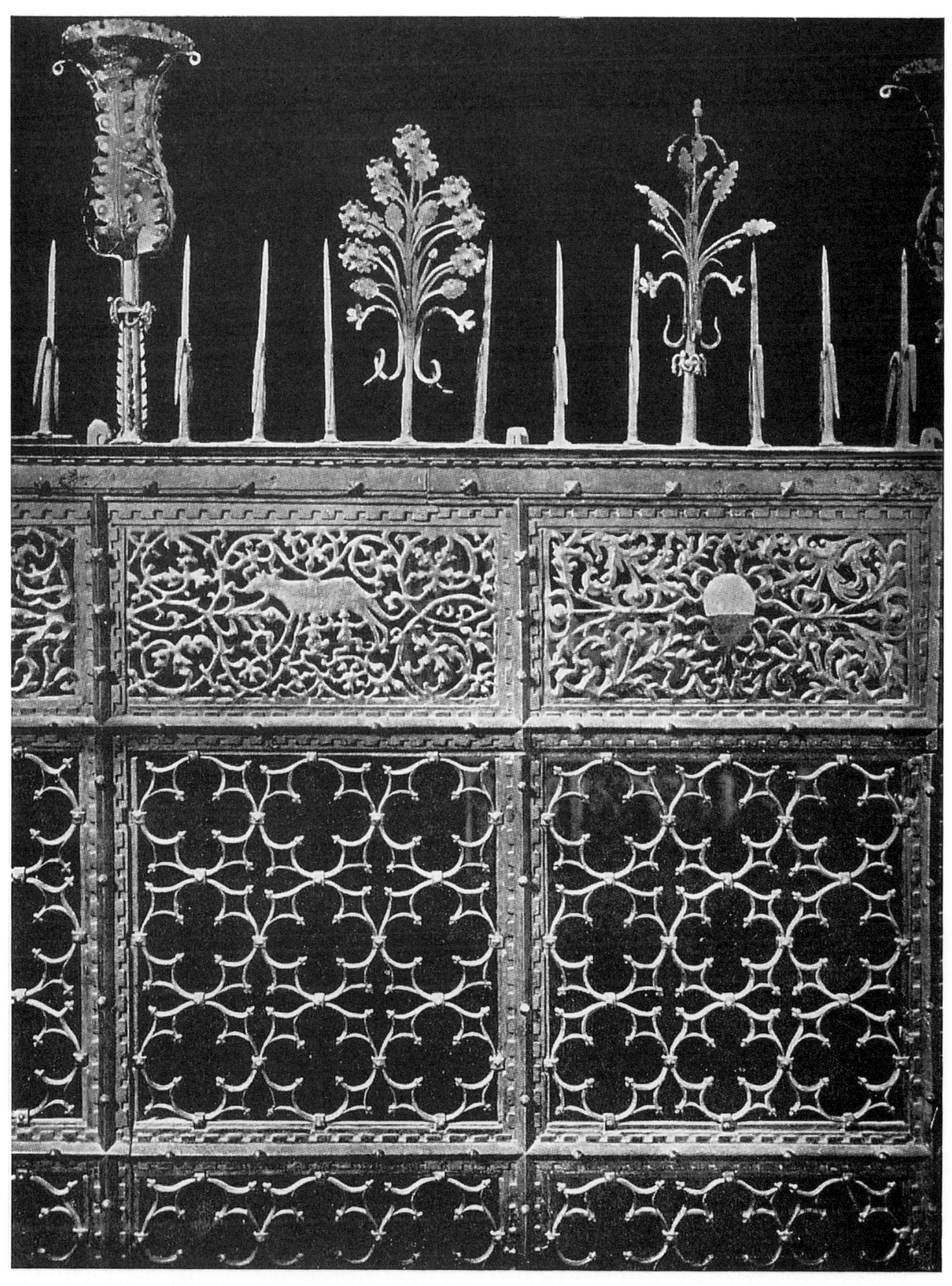

Detail of Gate in Chapel, Palazzo Comunale, Siena 1445

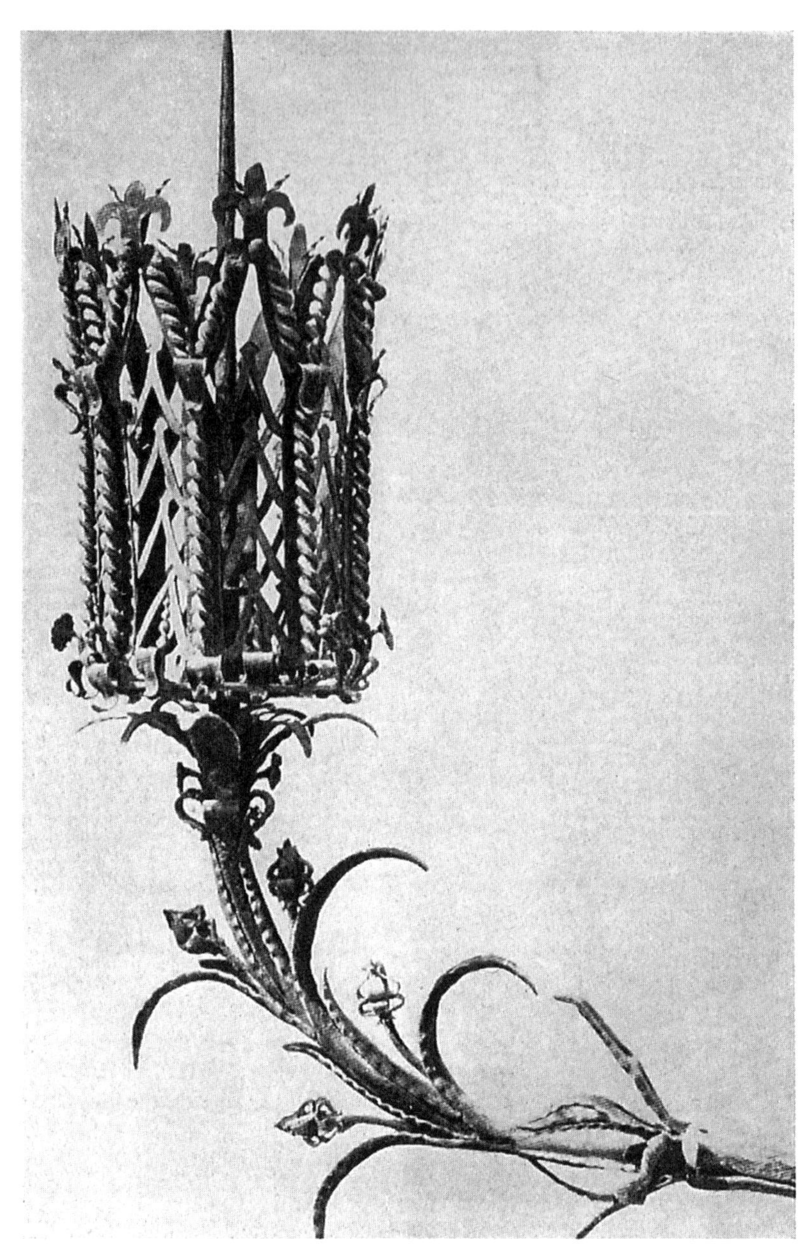

Torch, Palazzo Boccella, Lucca, 16th Century

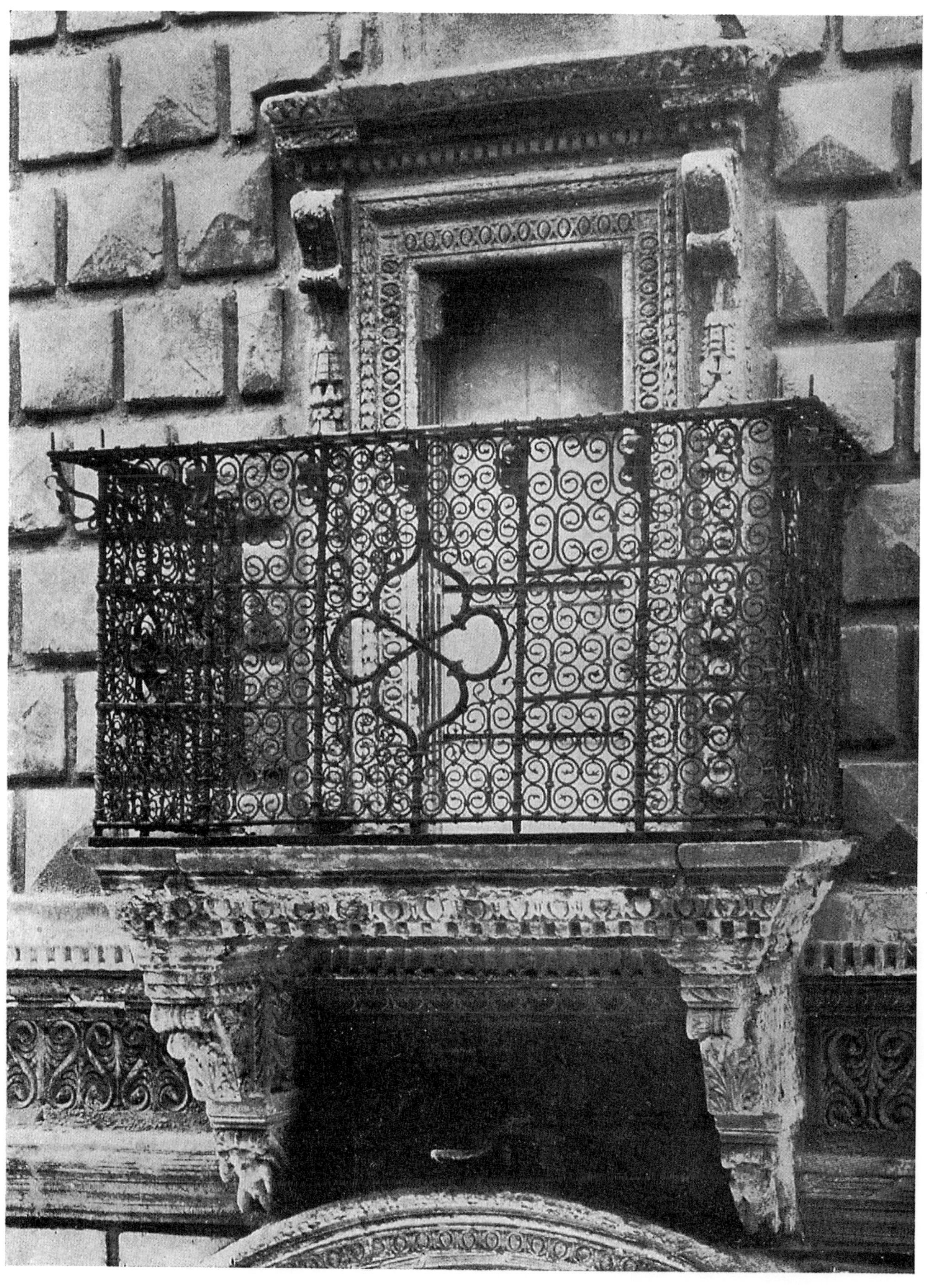

Balcony, Palazzo Bevilacqua, Bologna, 16th Century

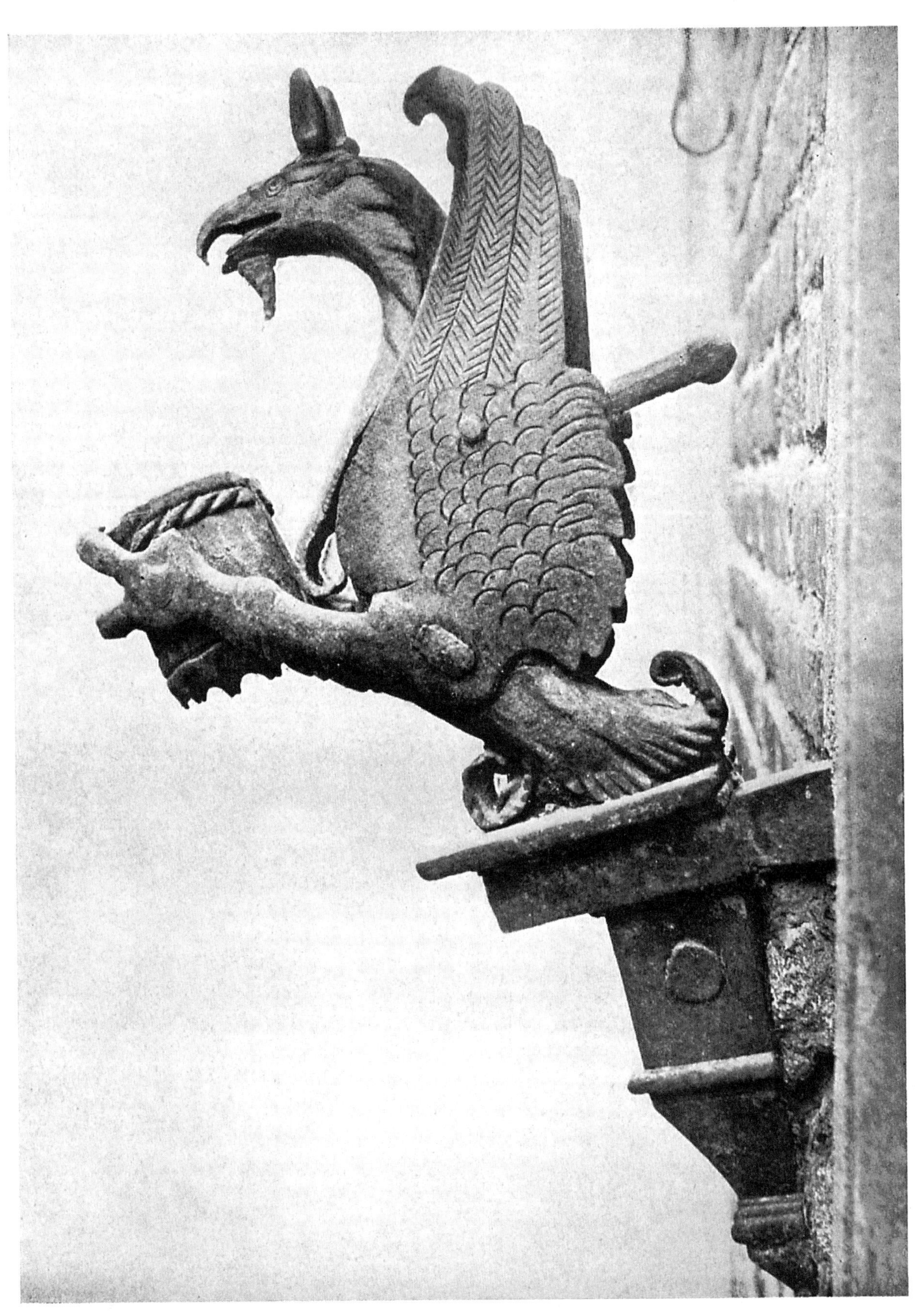

Flag Socket, Palazzo Grisoli, Siena, 16th Century

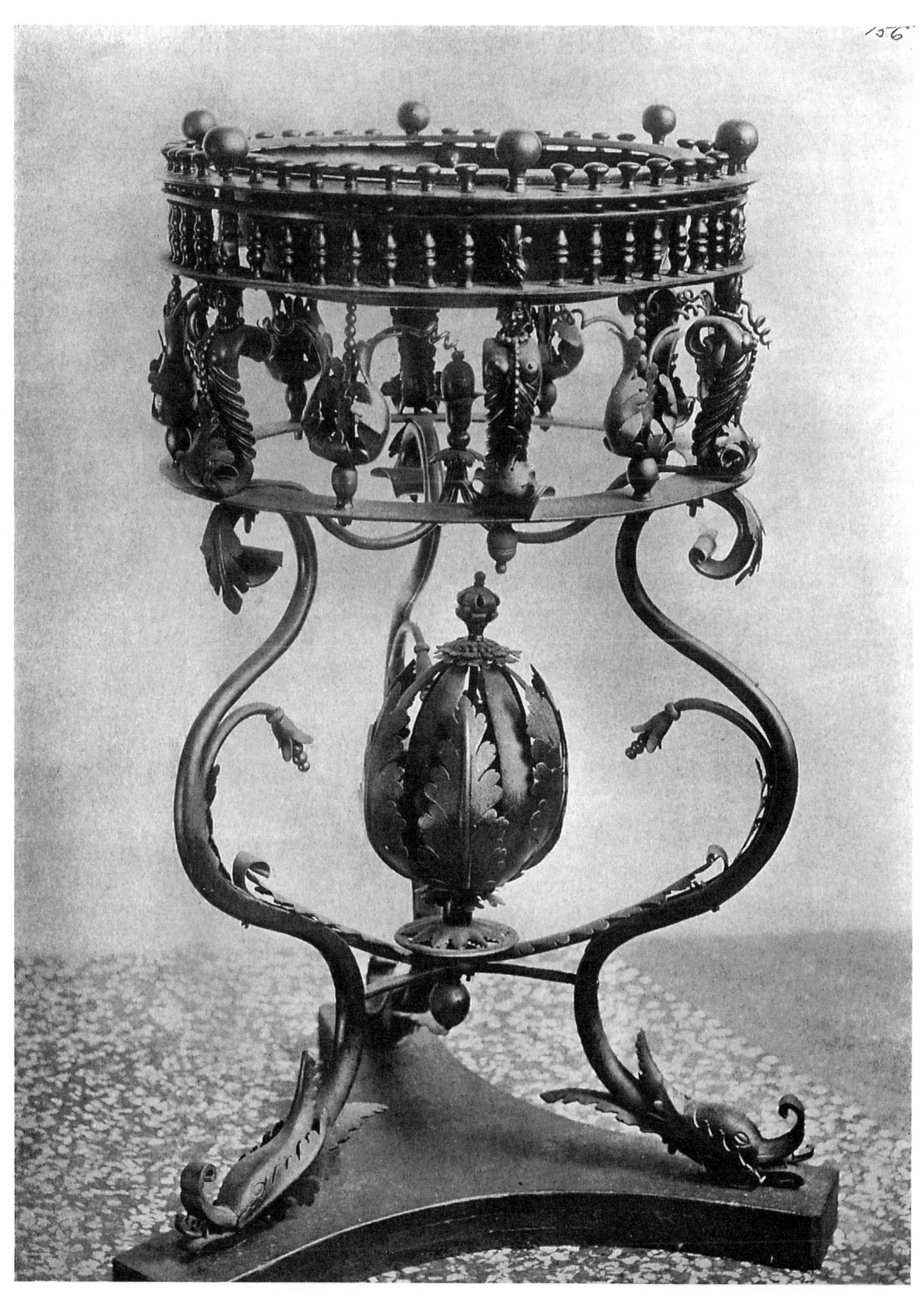

Brassier, Museo Civico Correr, Venice

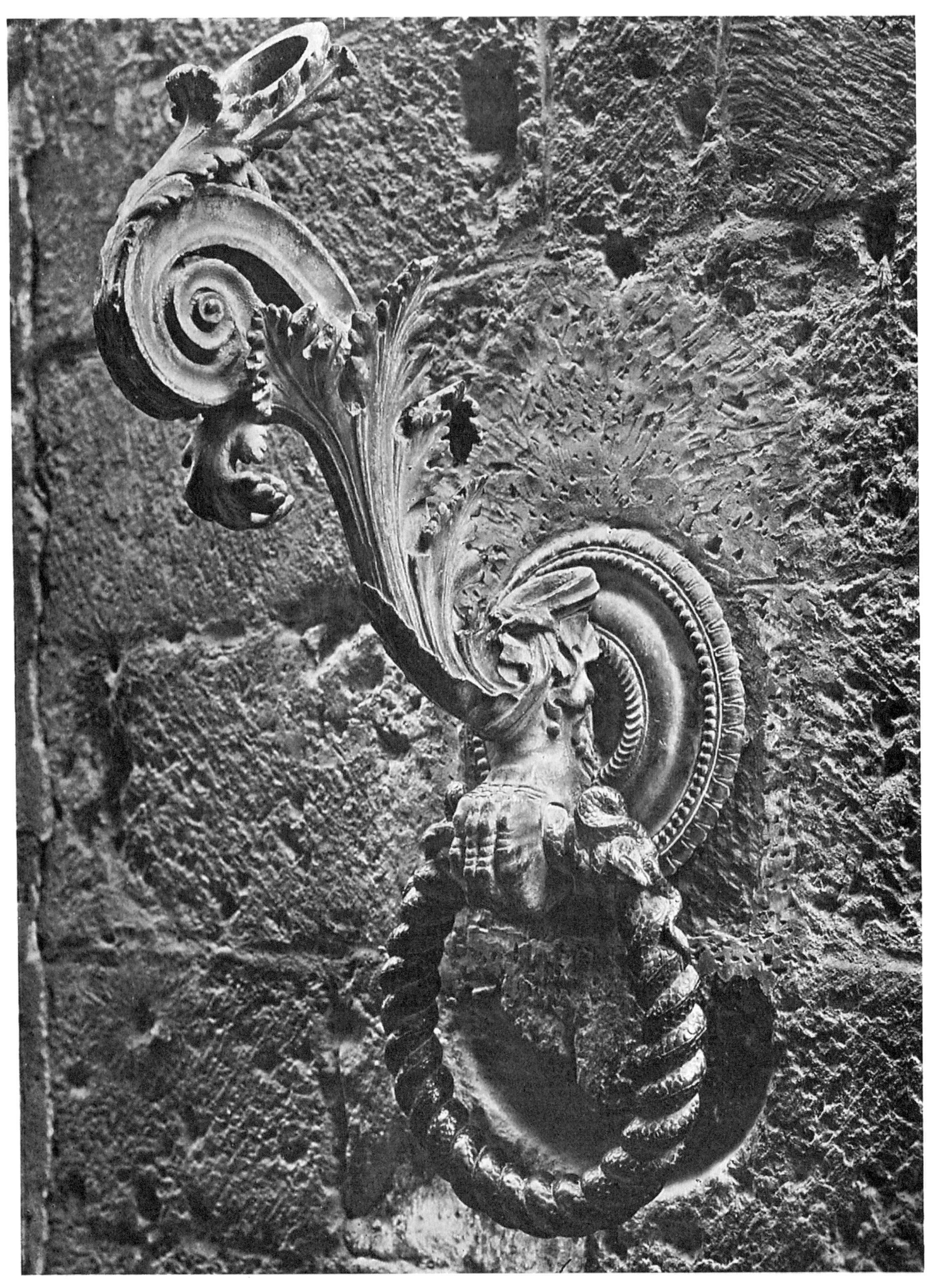

Flag Socket, Palazzo del Magnifico, Siena, 1508

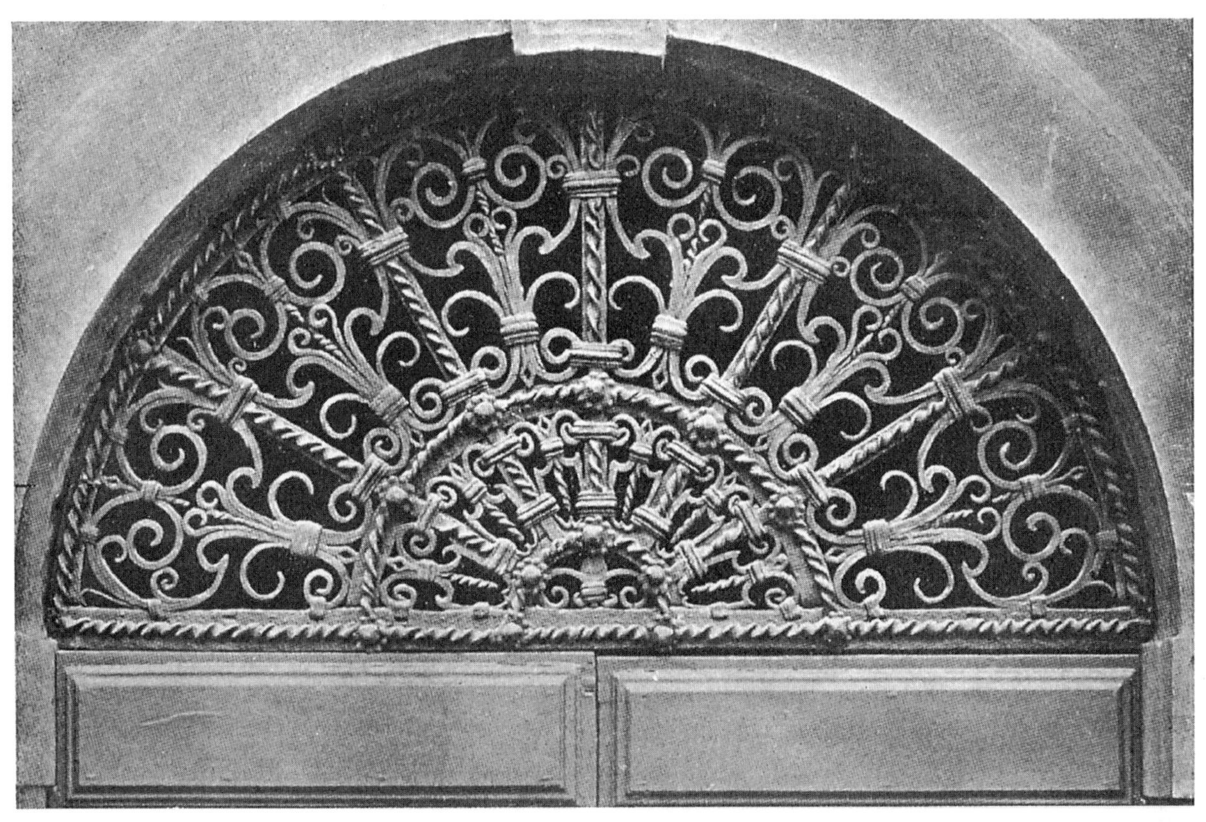

Grille Over Door, Lucca, 16th Century

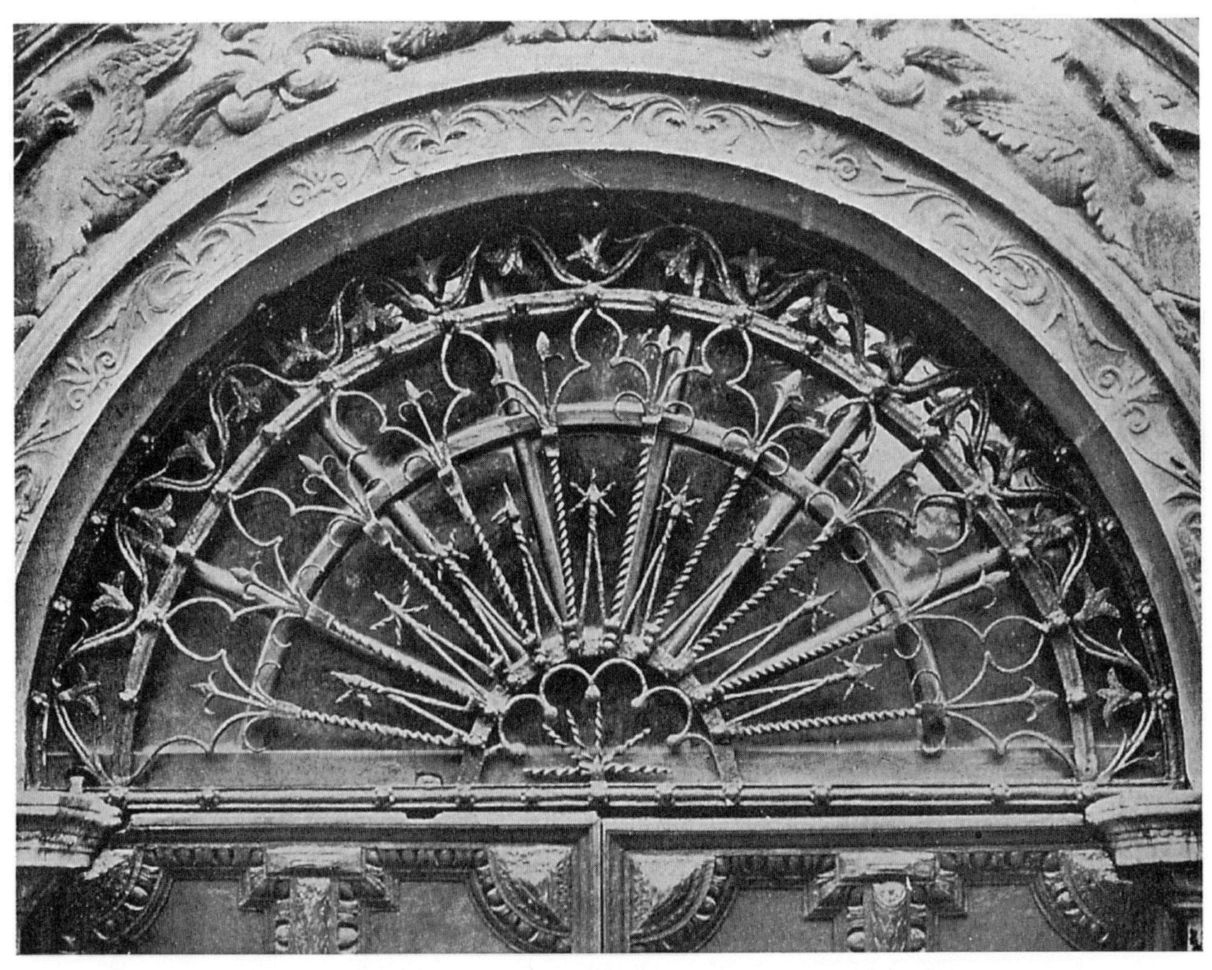

Grille Over Door, Palazzo Orsetti, Lucca, 16th Century

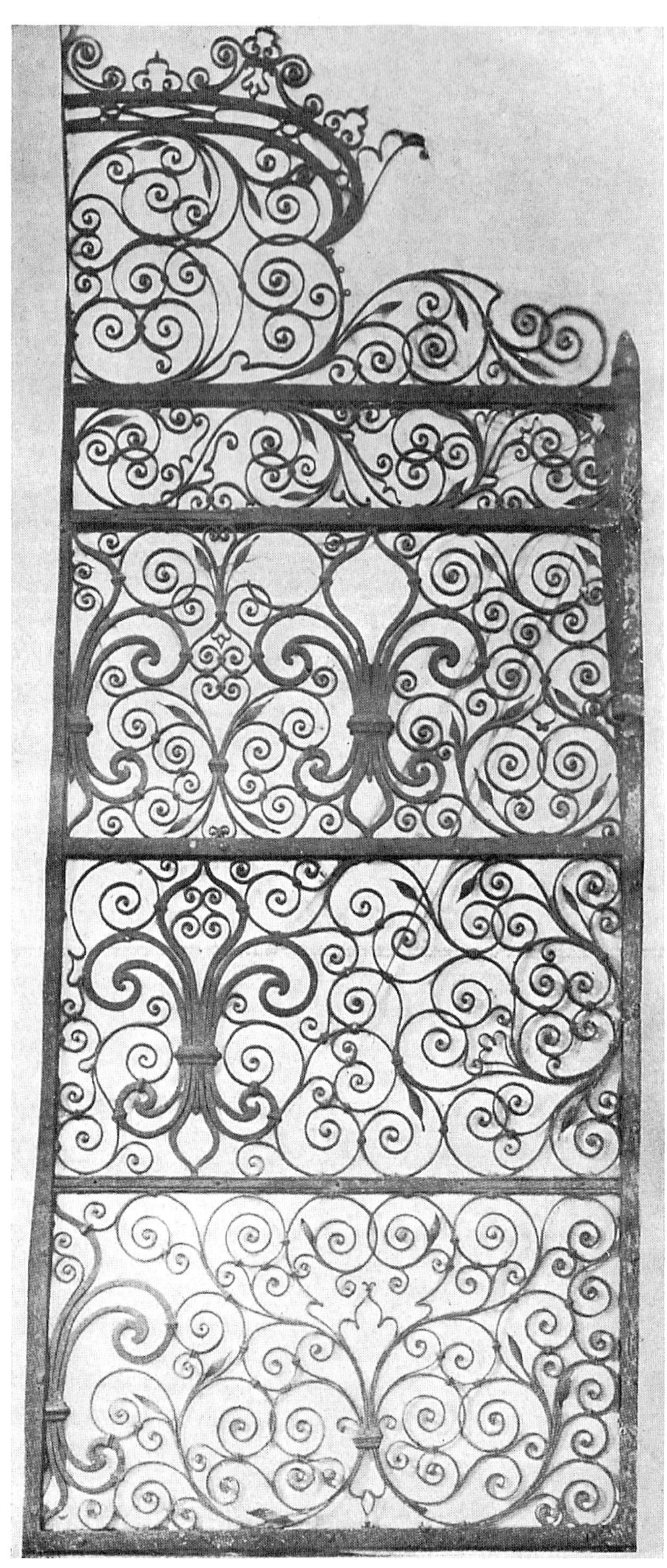

Gate, Palazzo Farnese, Piacenza, 16th Century

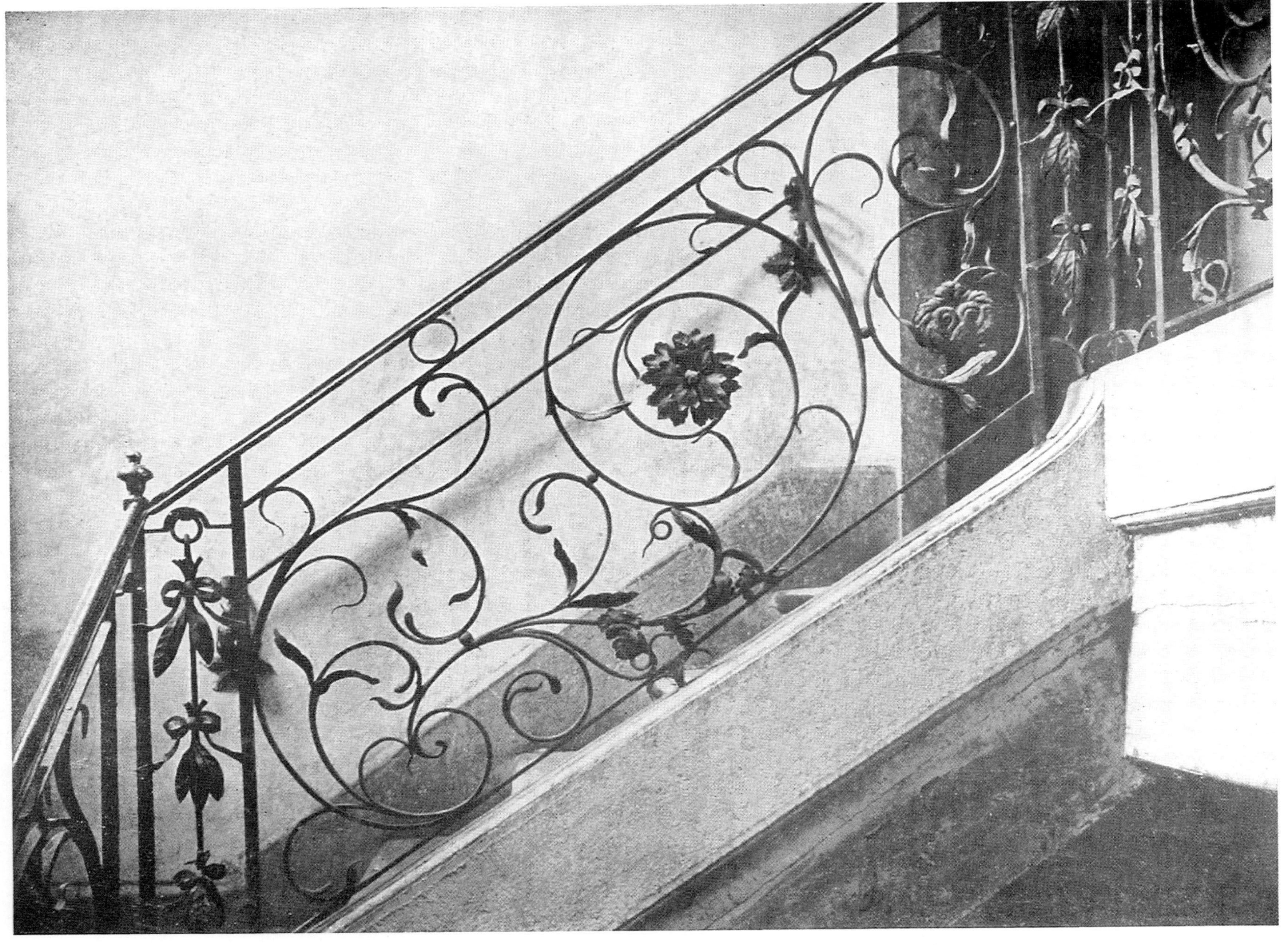

Stair Rail, Arezzo, 17th Century

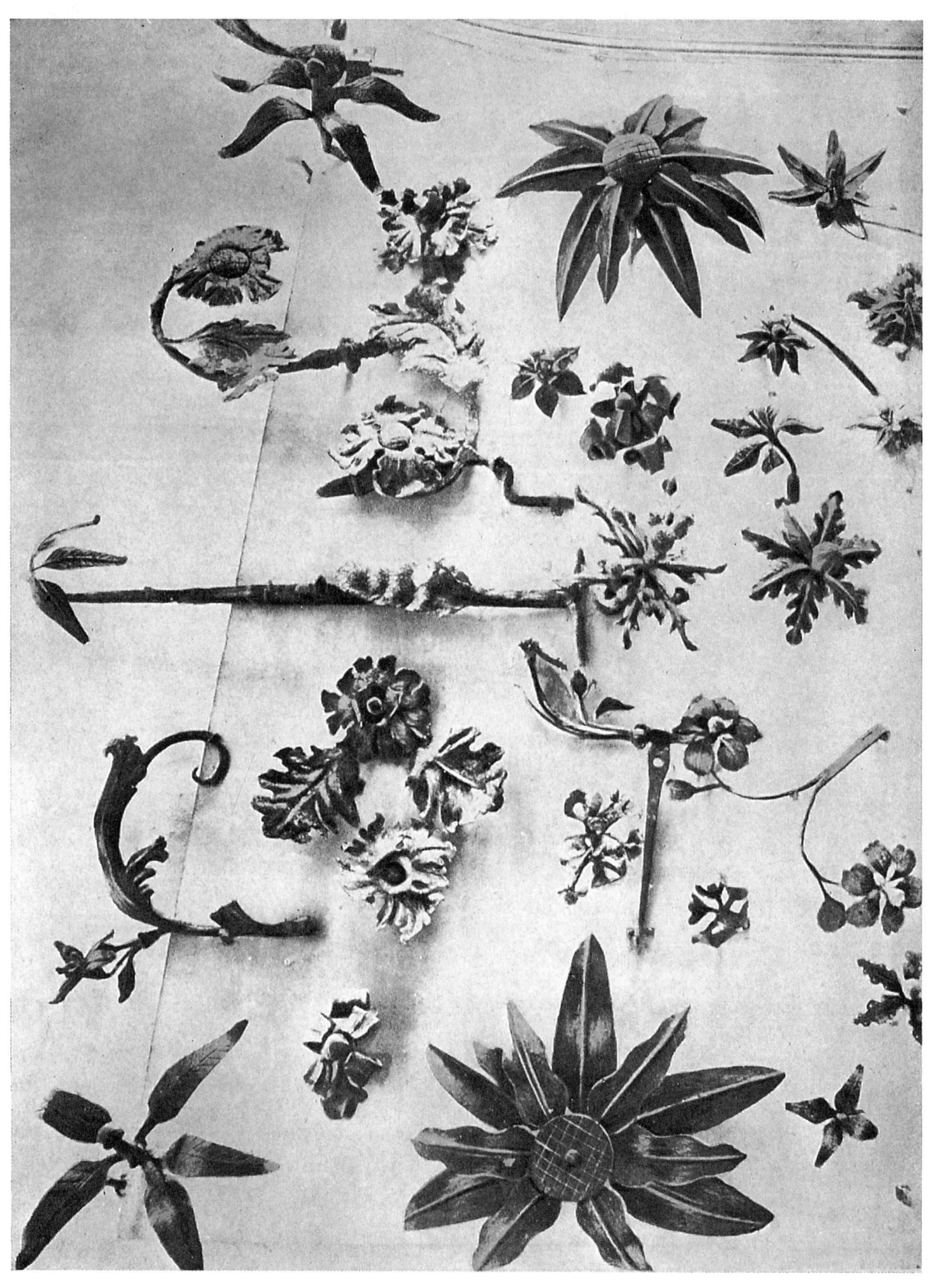

Fragments, Museo, Palermo, 18th Century

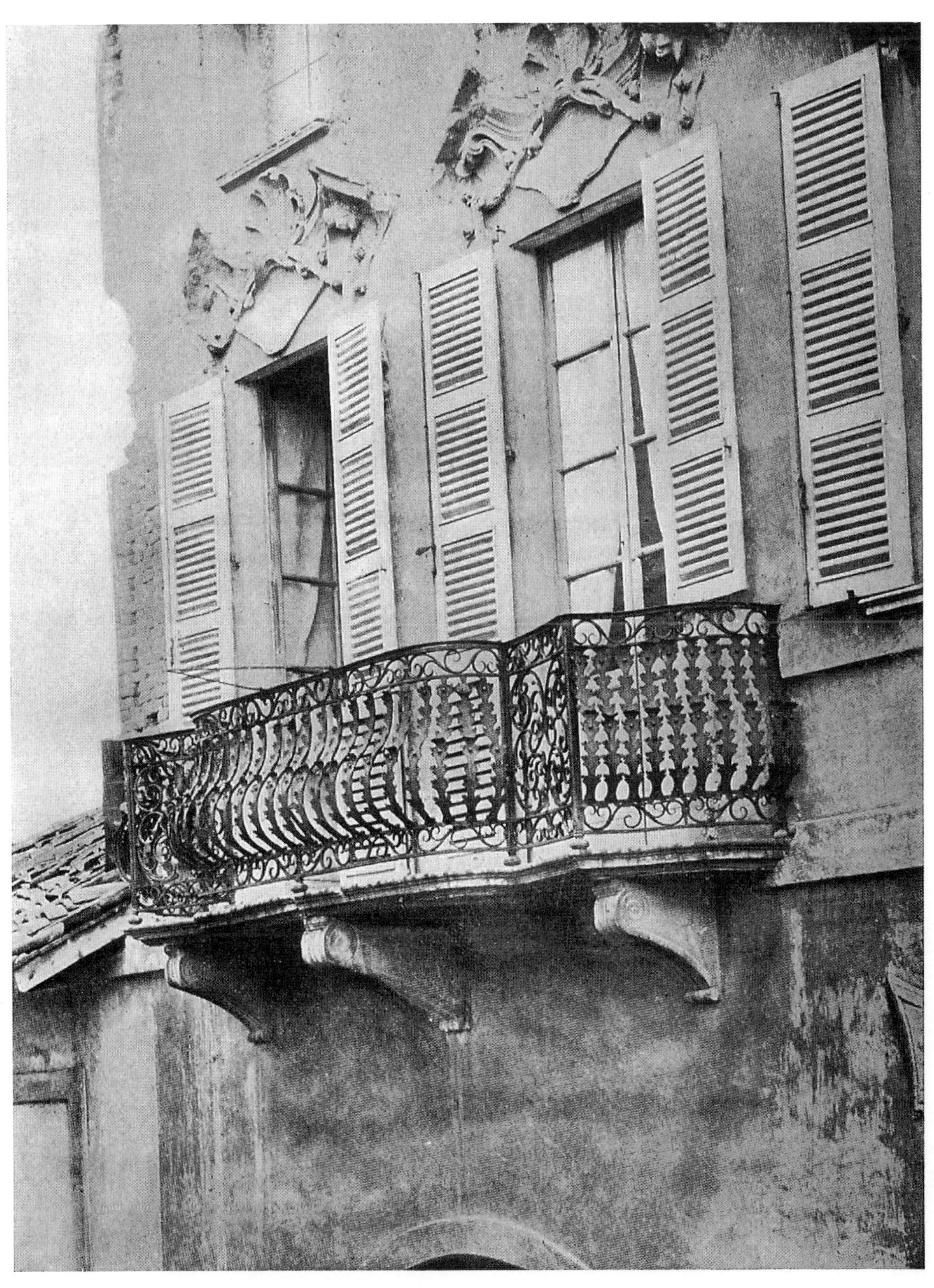

Balcony Casa Fraganeschi, Cremona, 17th Century

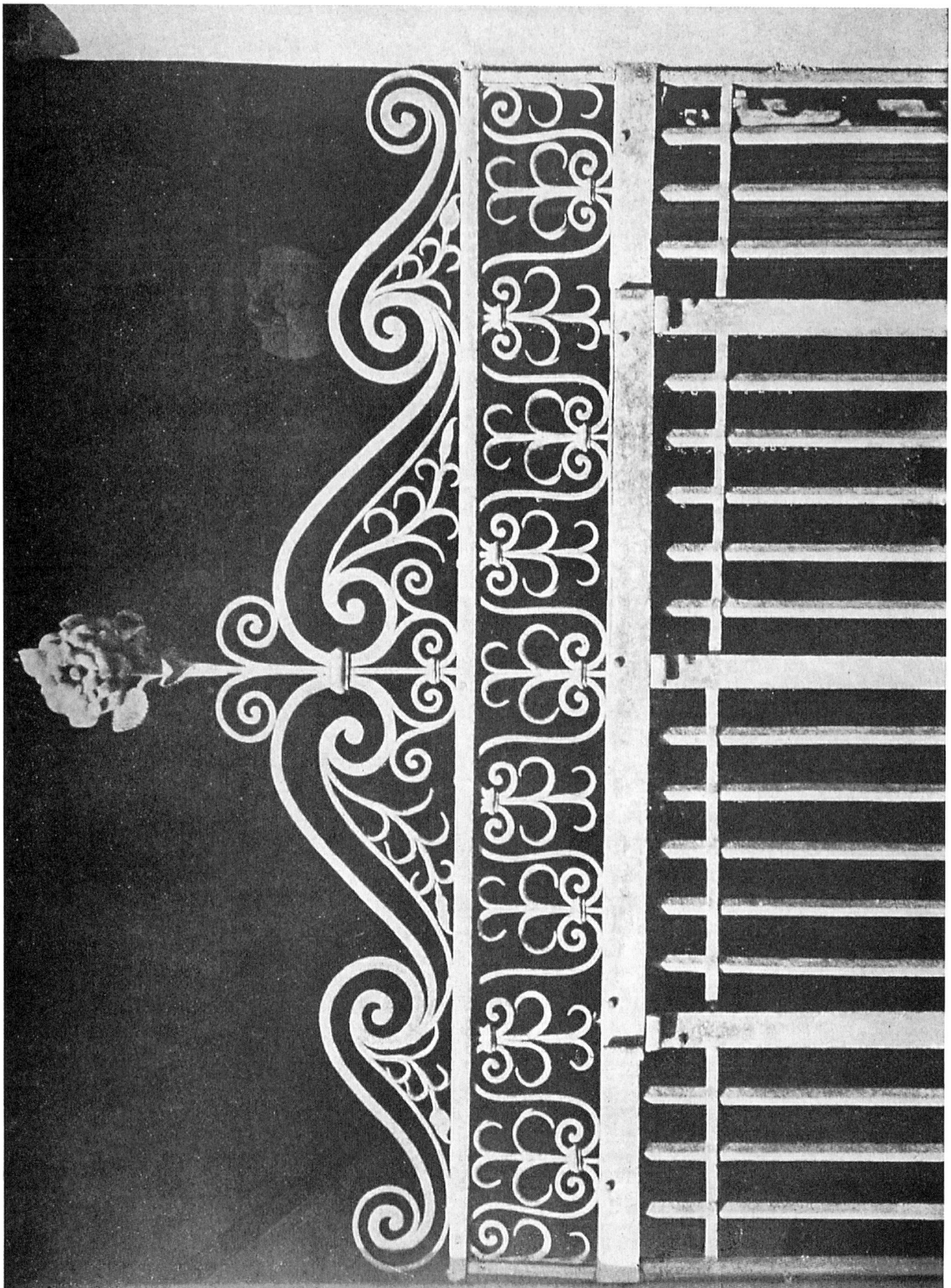

Gate, Church of S. Giovanni e Paolo, Rome, 17th Century

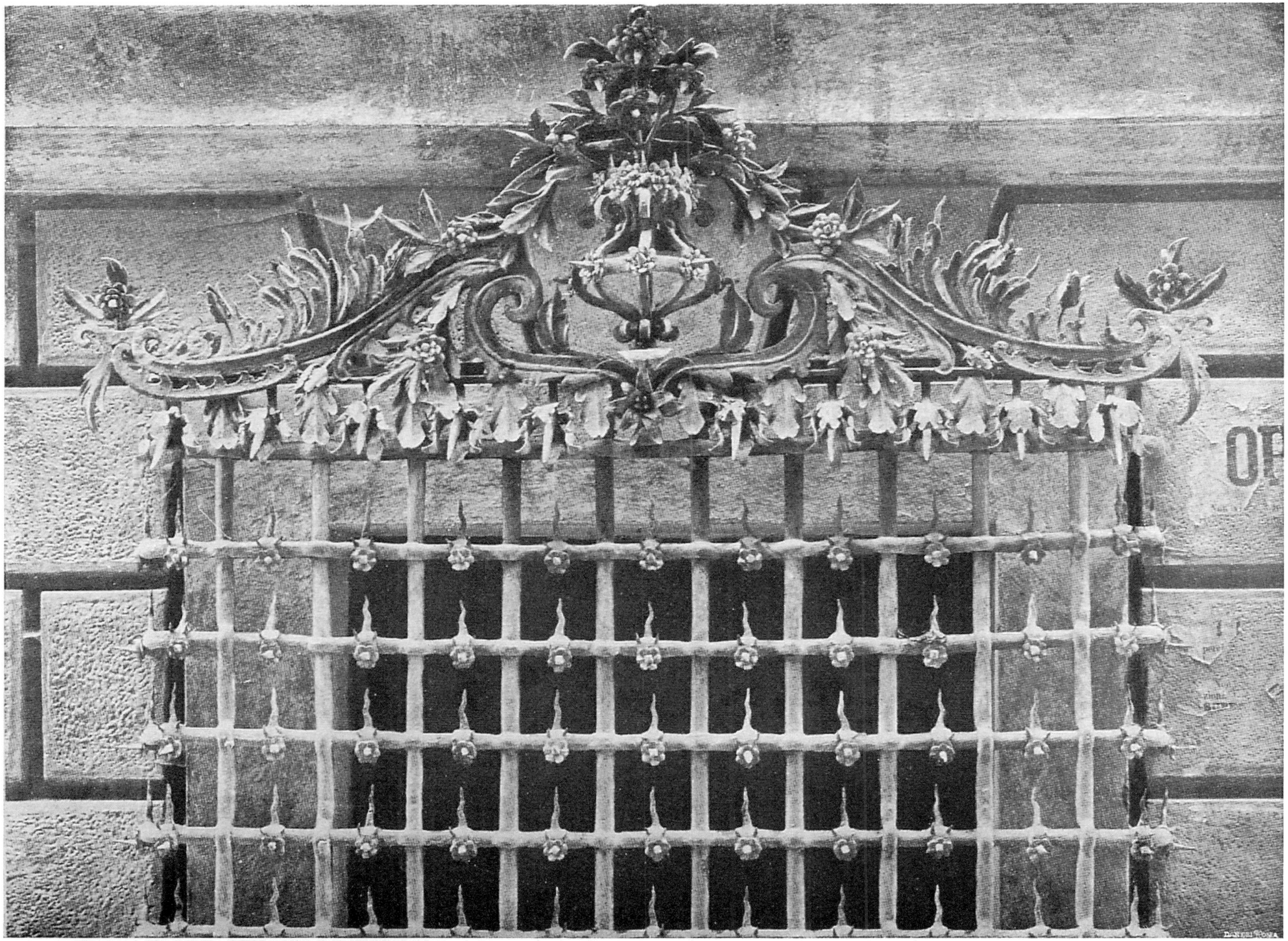

Window Grille, Palazzo Piccioli, Sarzana, 17th Century

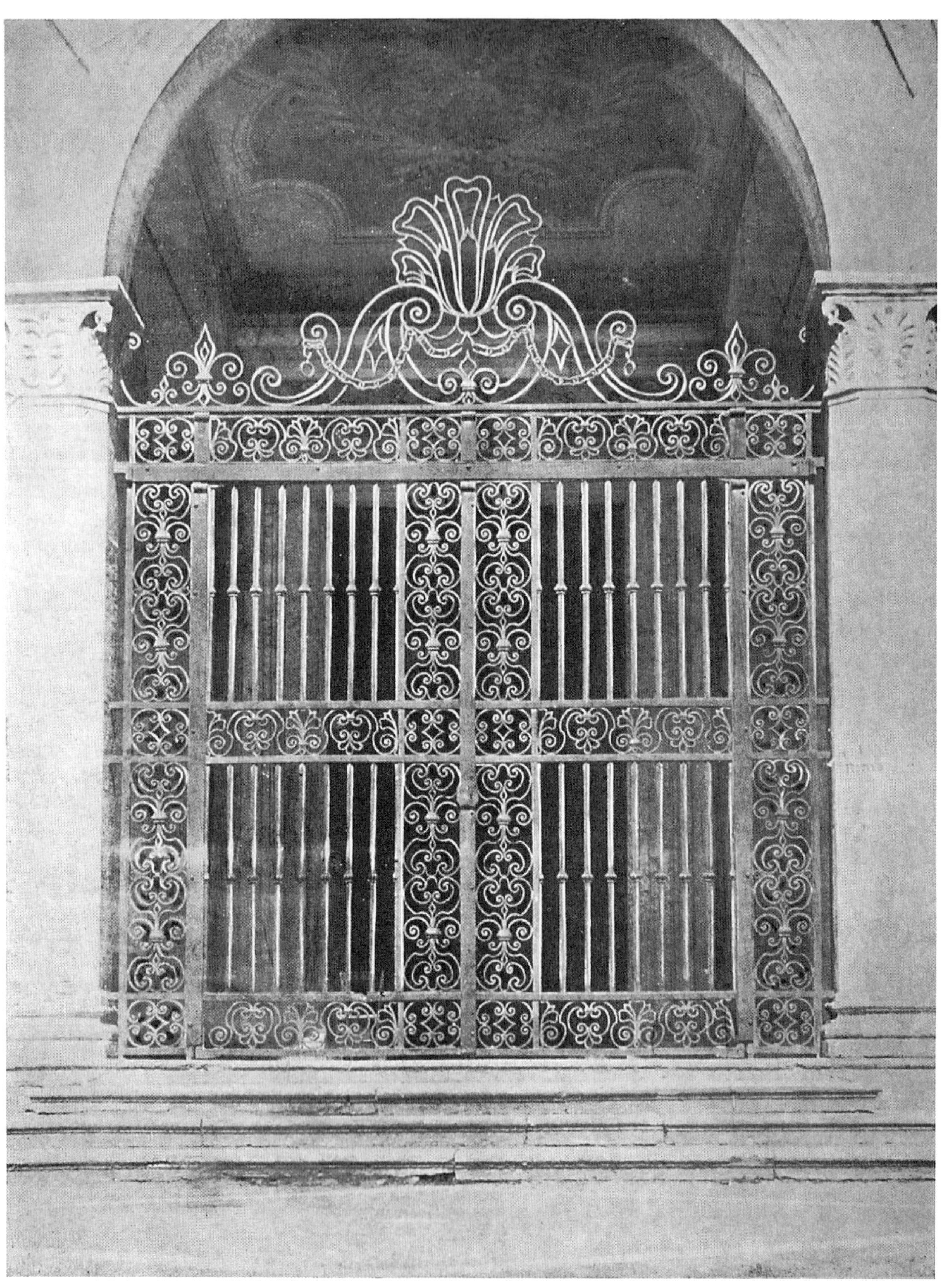

Gate in Church of S. Pietro, Vincoli, Rome, 17th Century

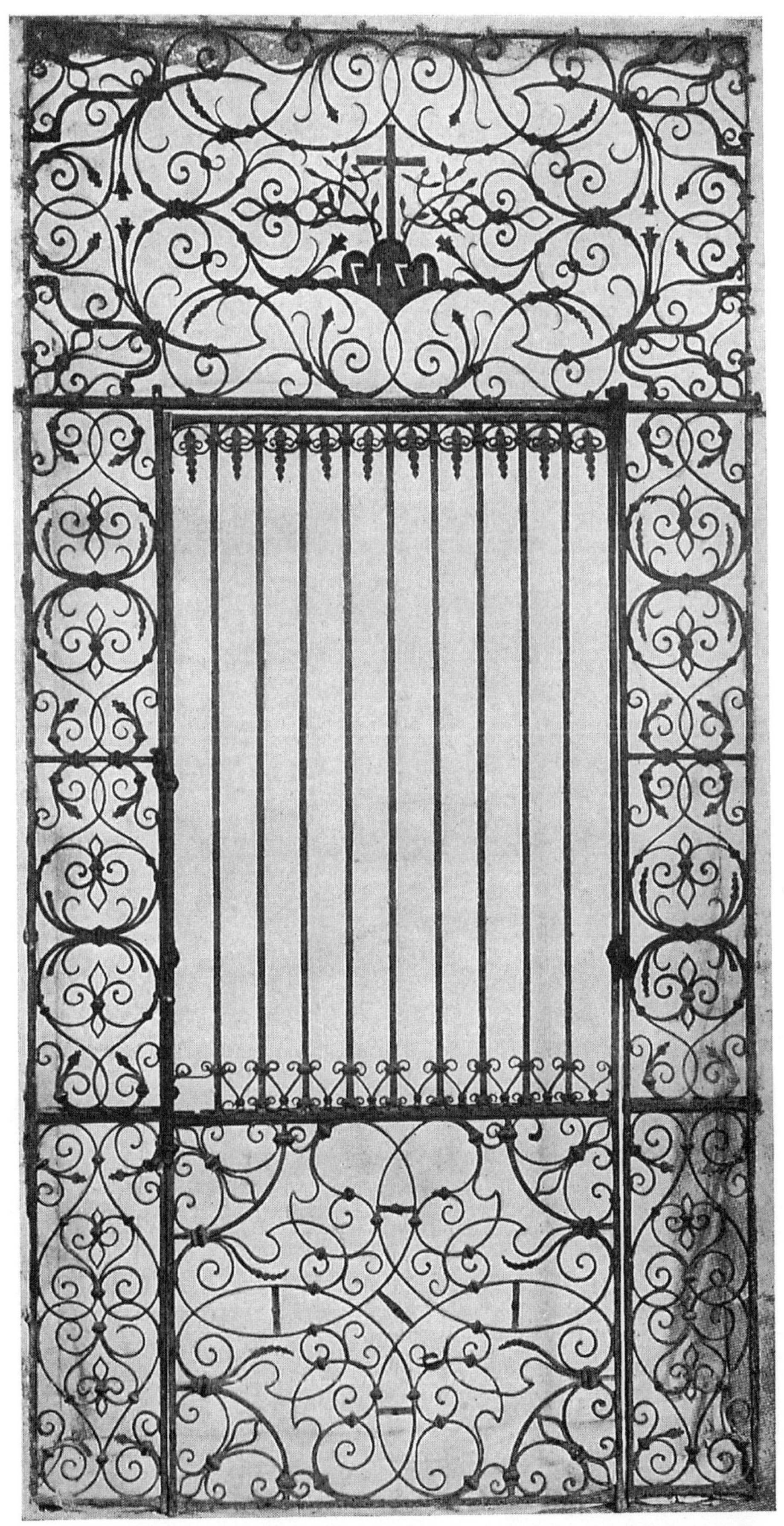

Gate in Museo, Piacenza, 1717

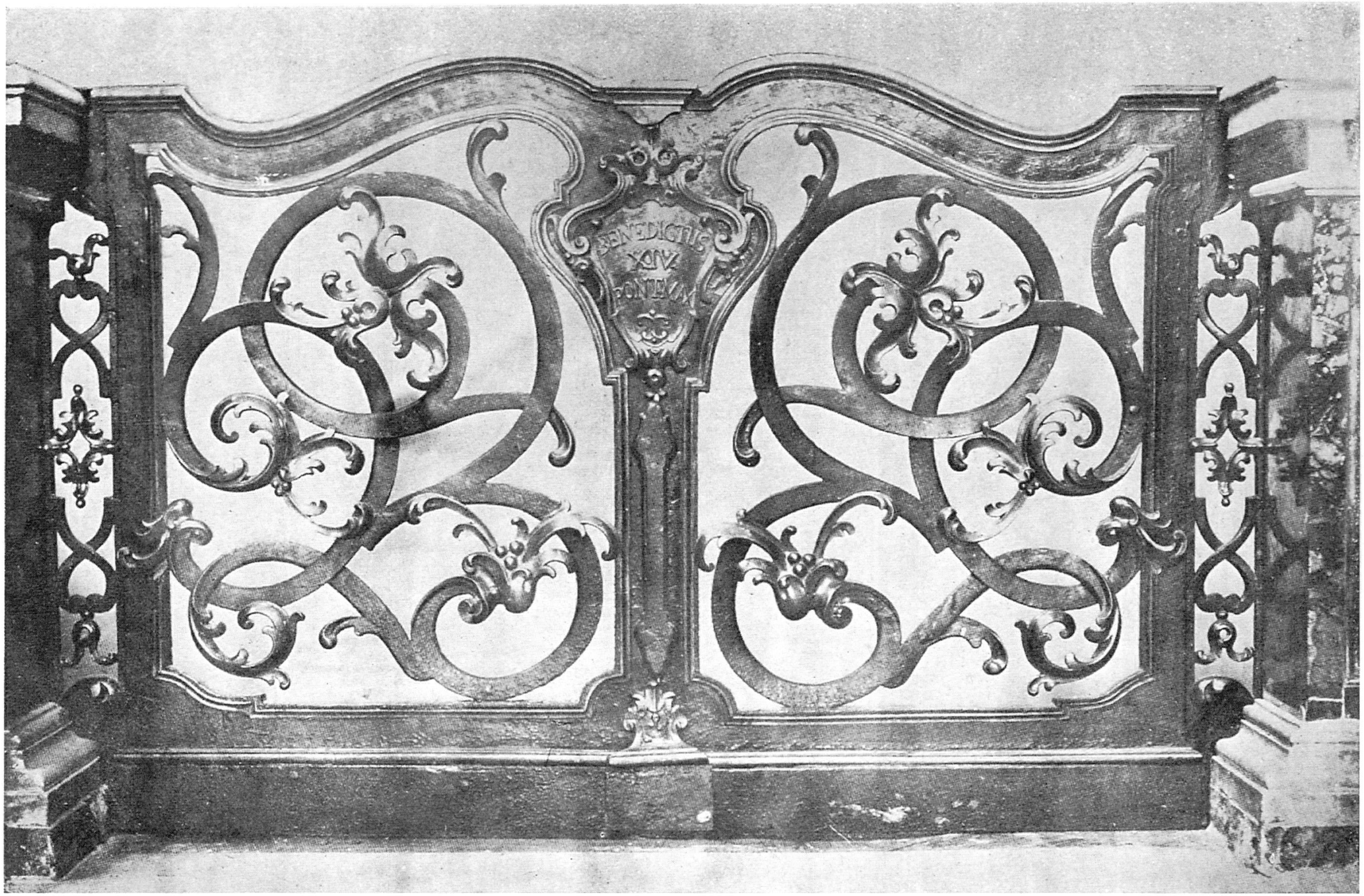

Balustrade of Iron in S. Pietro, Bologna, 18th Century

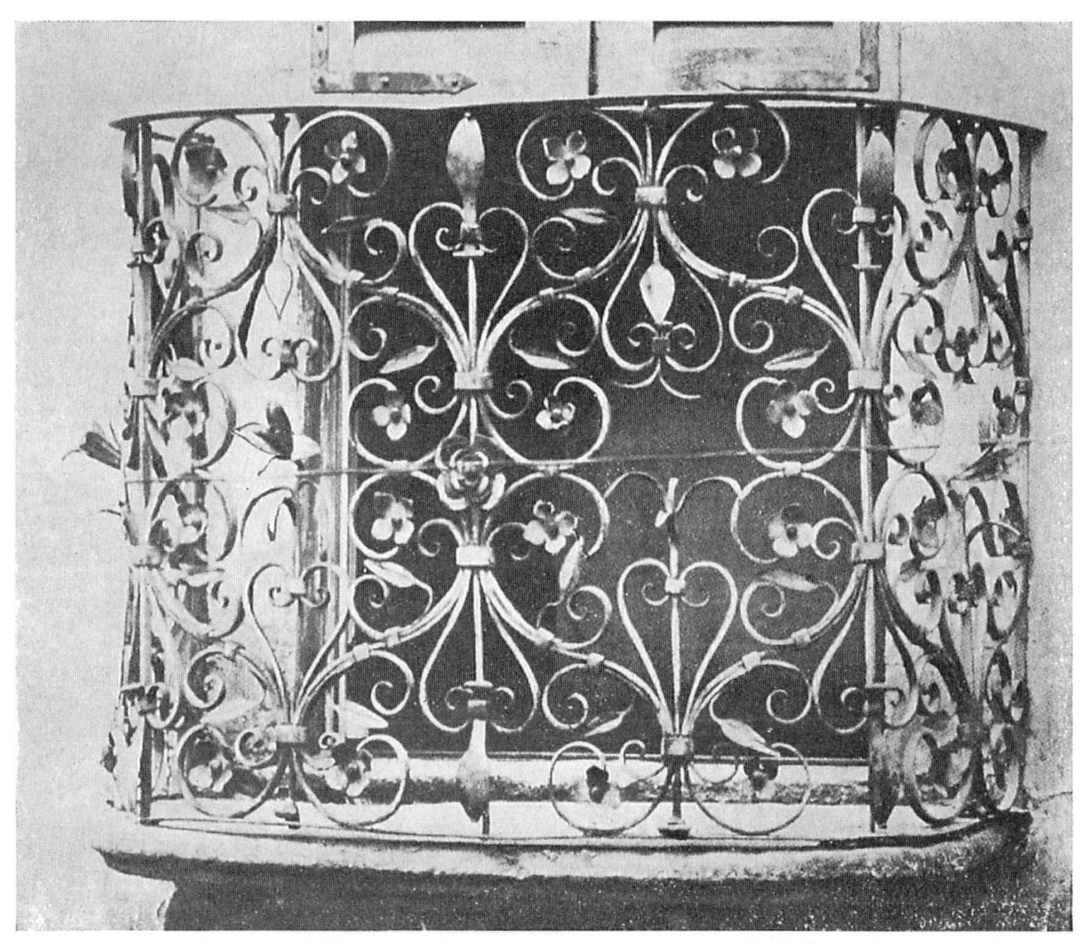

Balcony, Varallo Sesia, 17th Century

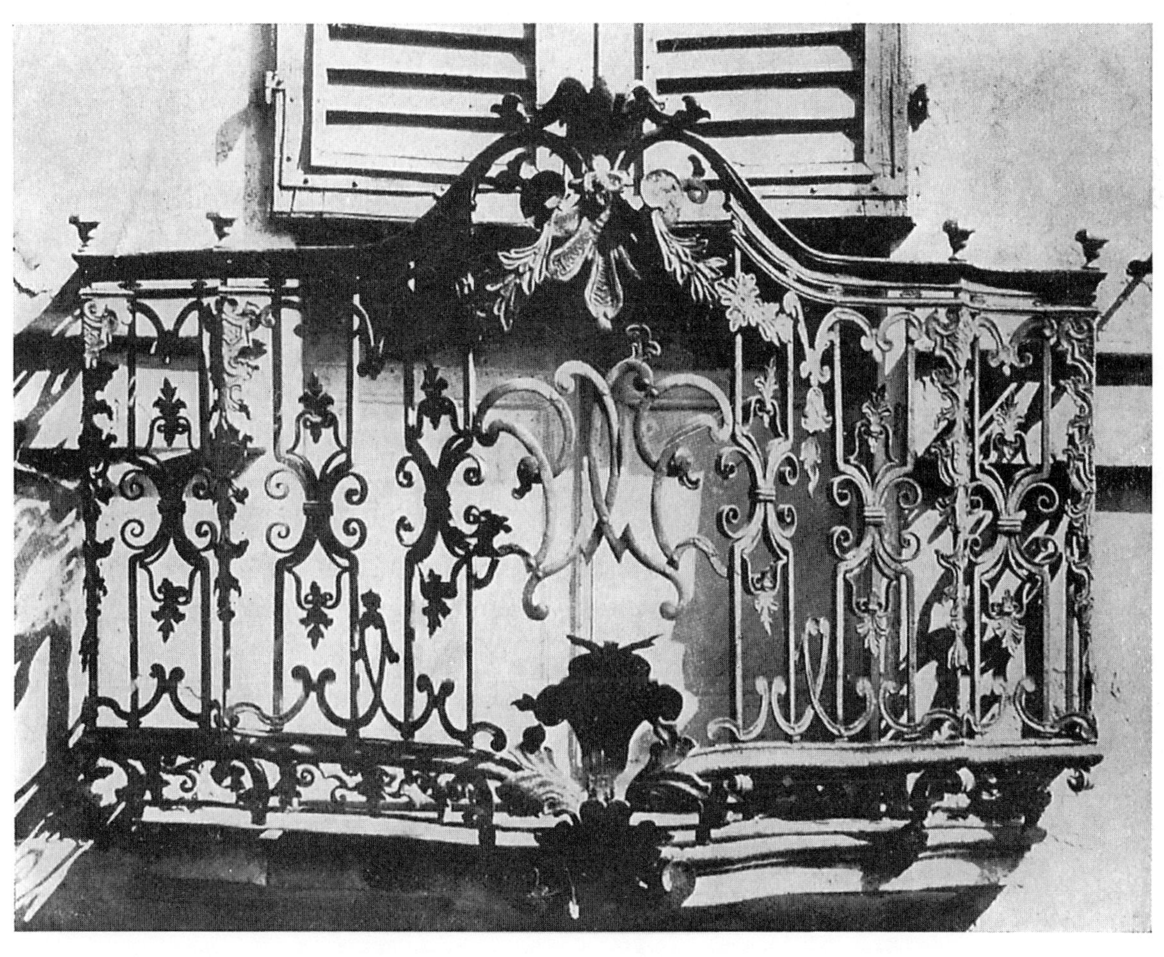

Balcony, Cremona, 18th Century

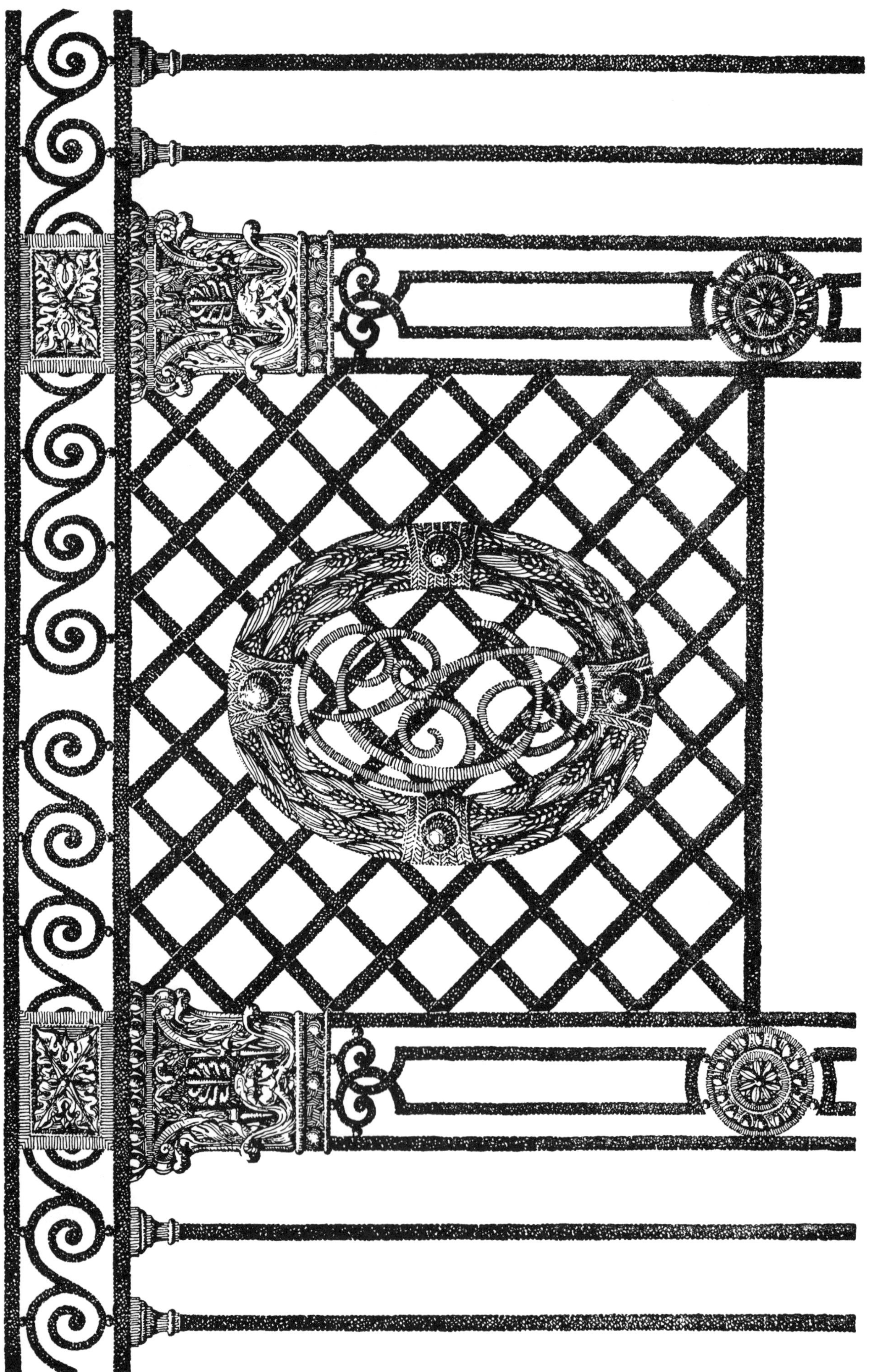

Baker's Sign, Paris

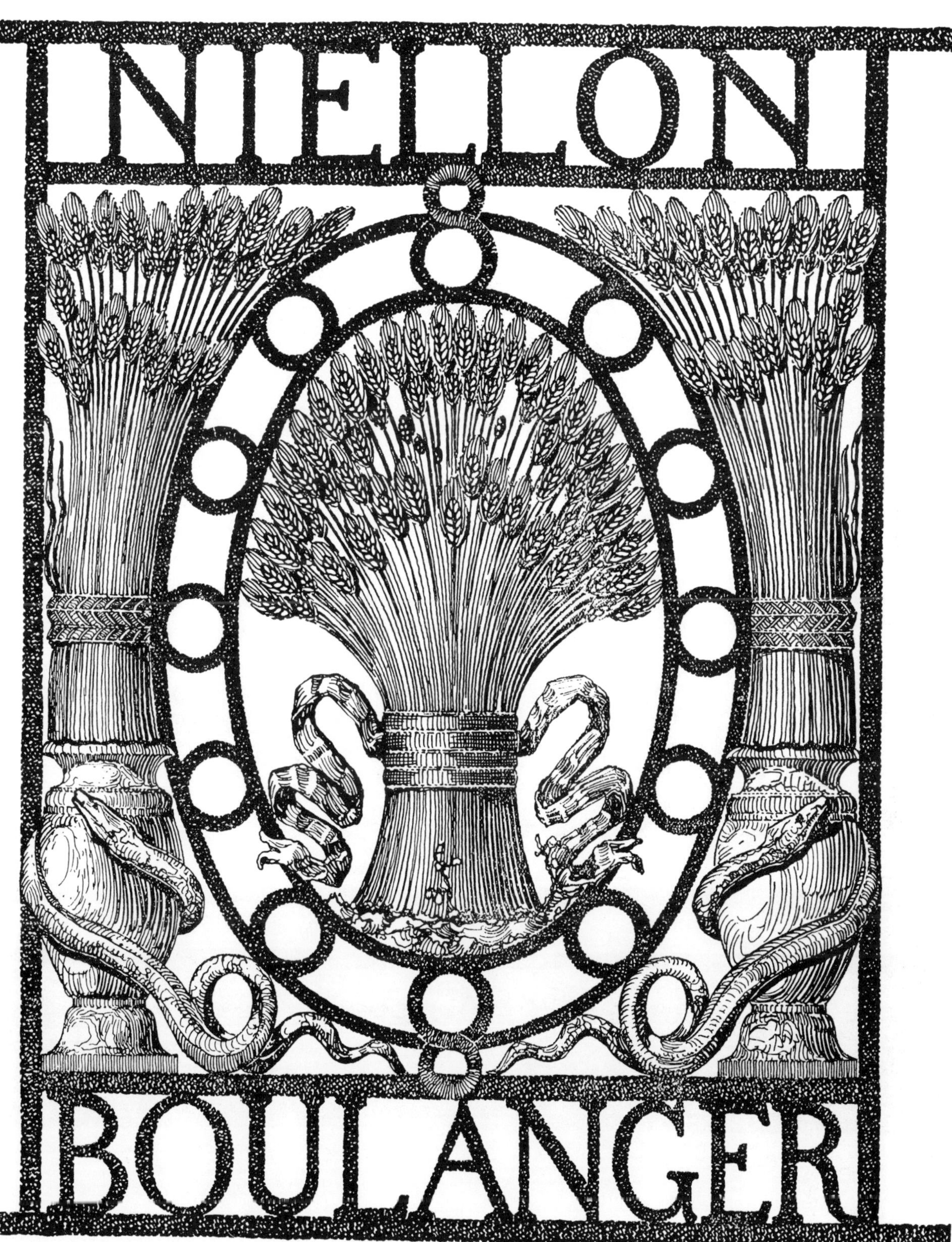

Baker's Sign, Paris

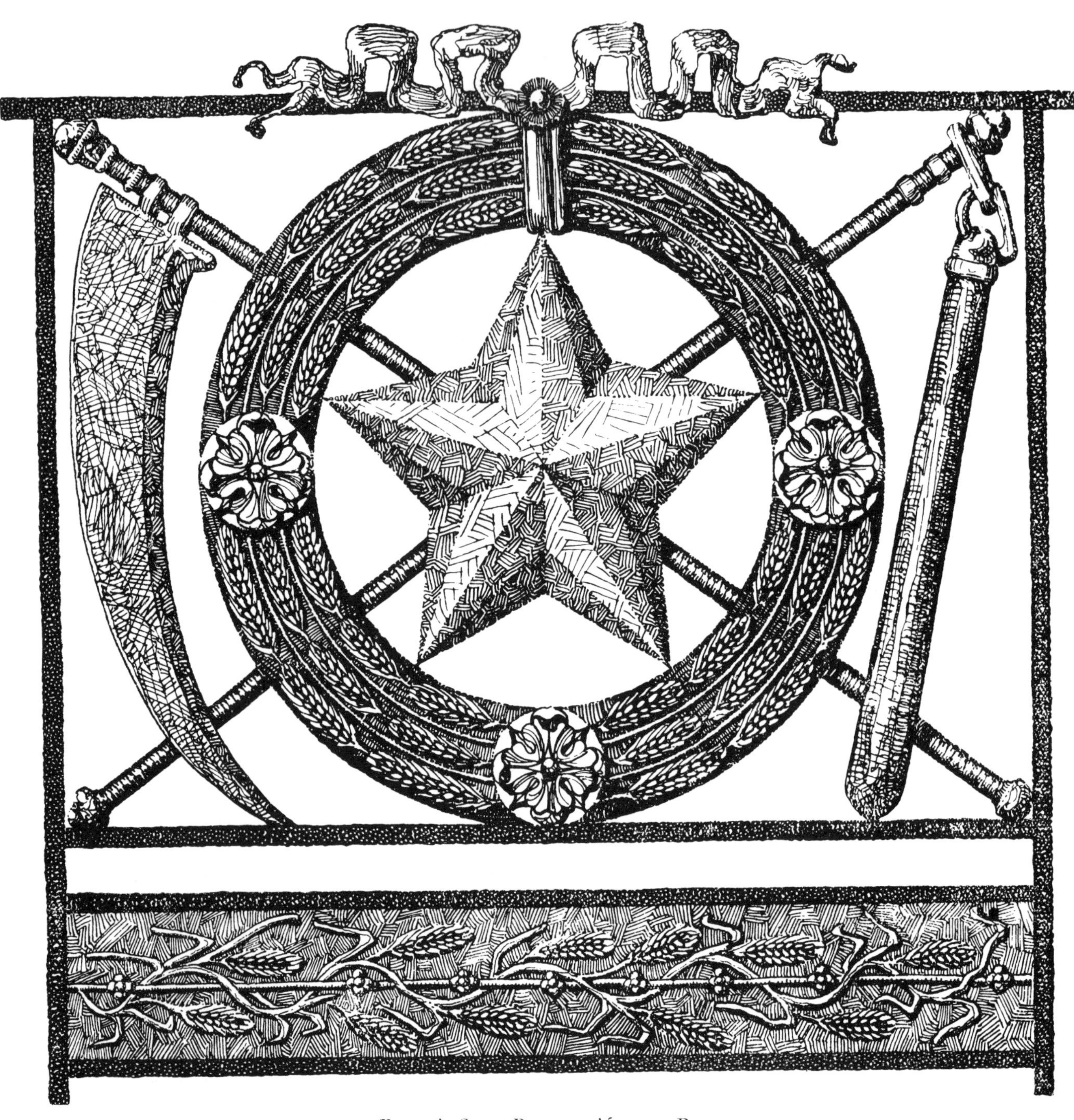

Baker's Sign, Rue de l'Étoile, Paris

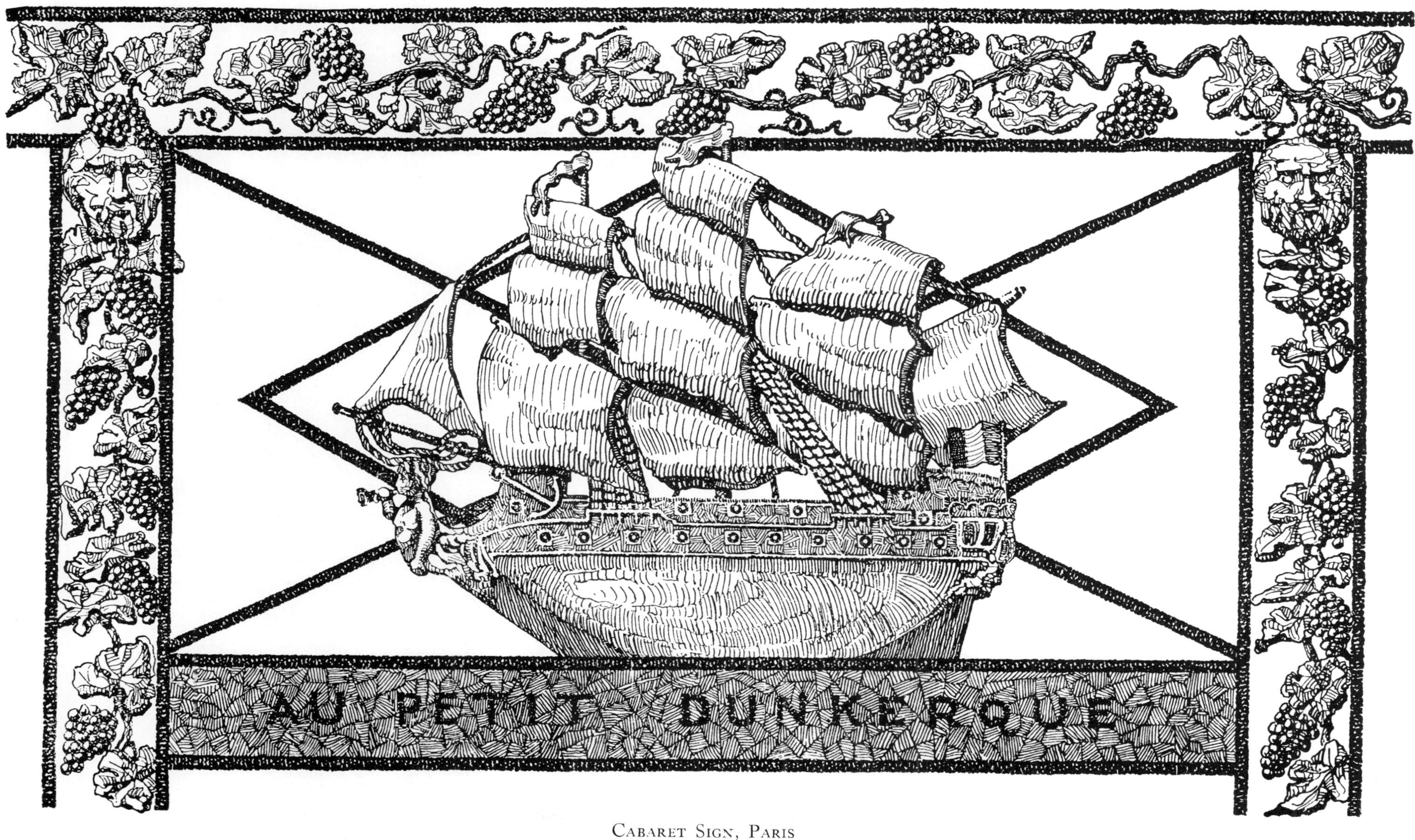

Cabaret Sign, Paris

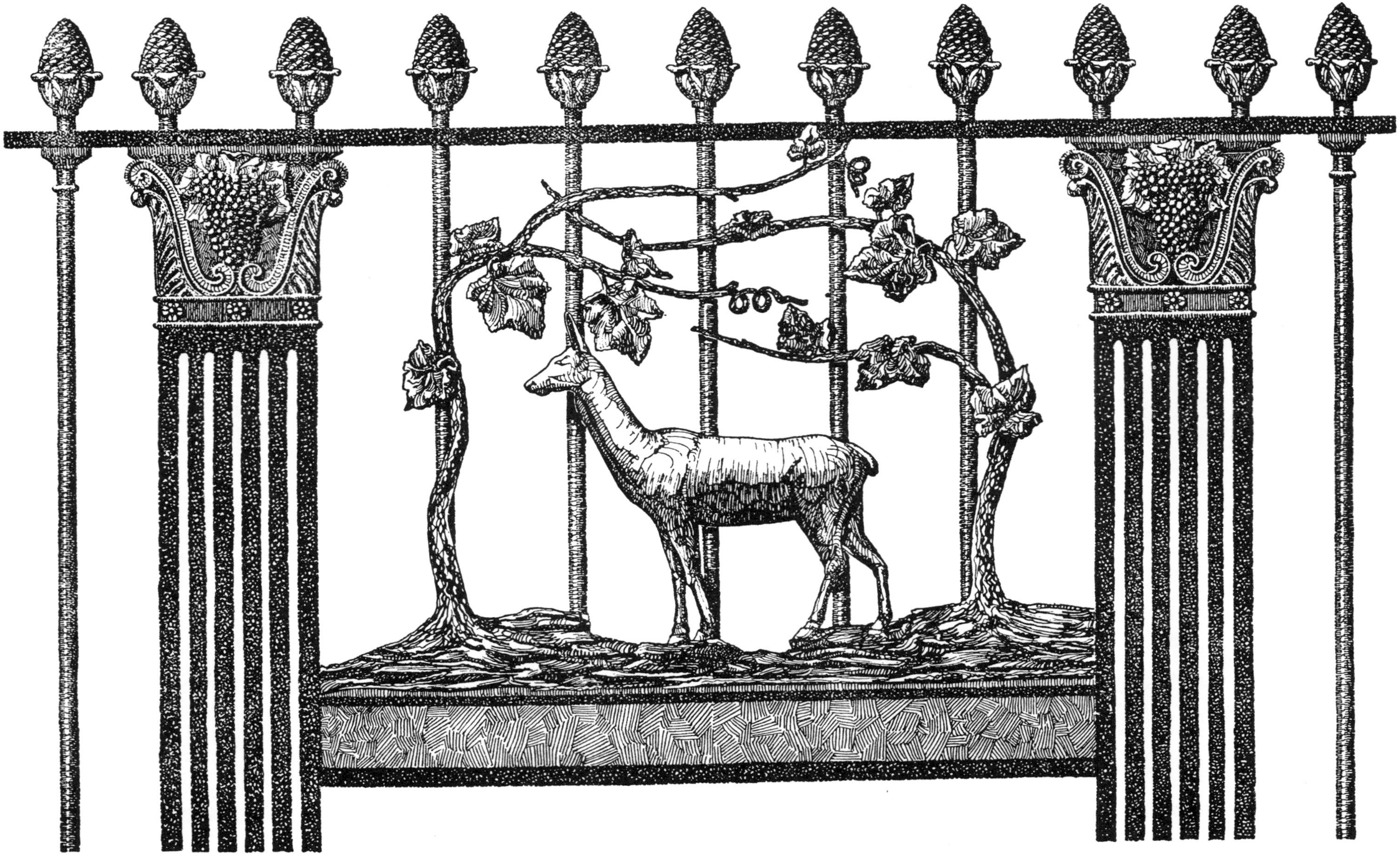

Cabaret Sign, 35 Rue Geoffroy-St. Hilaire, Paris

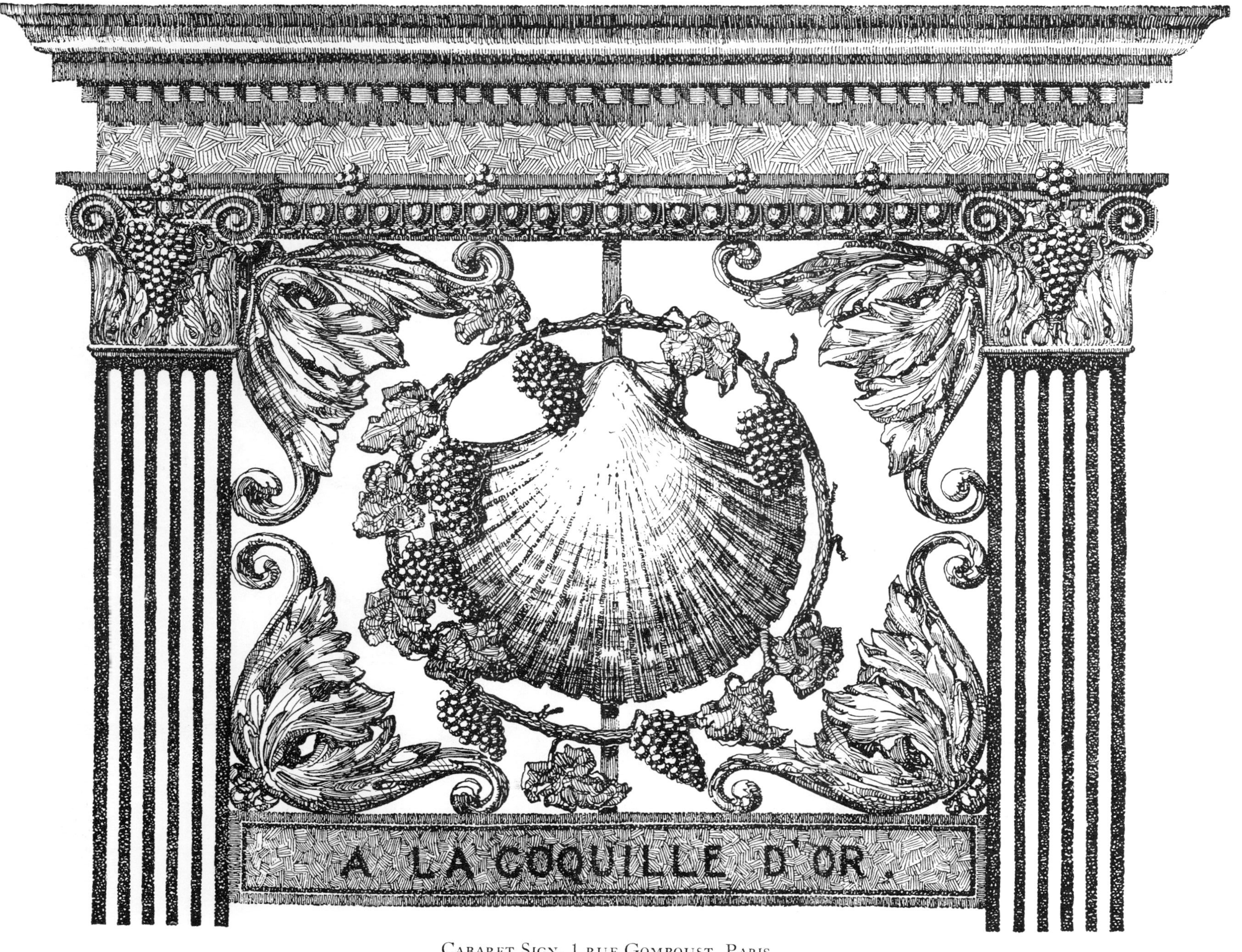

Cabaret Sign, 1 rue Gomboust, Paris

Cabaret Sign, 1 quai Bourbon, Paris

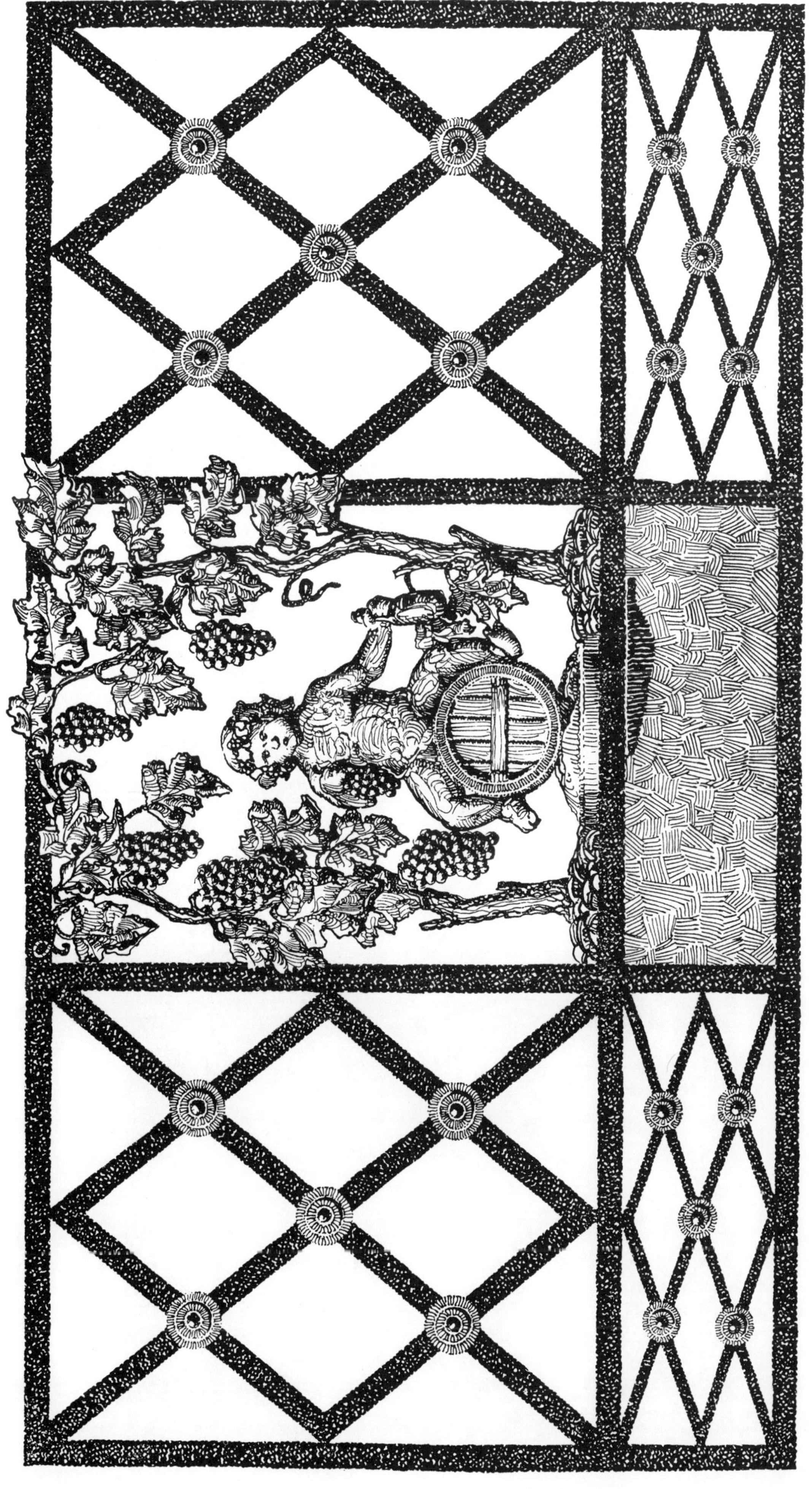

Cabaret Sign, 61 rue Saint-Louis-en-l'Isle, Paris

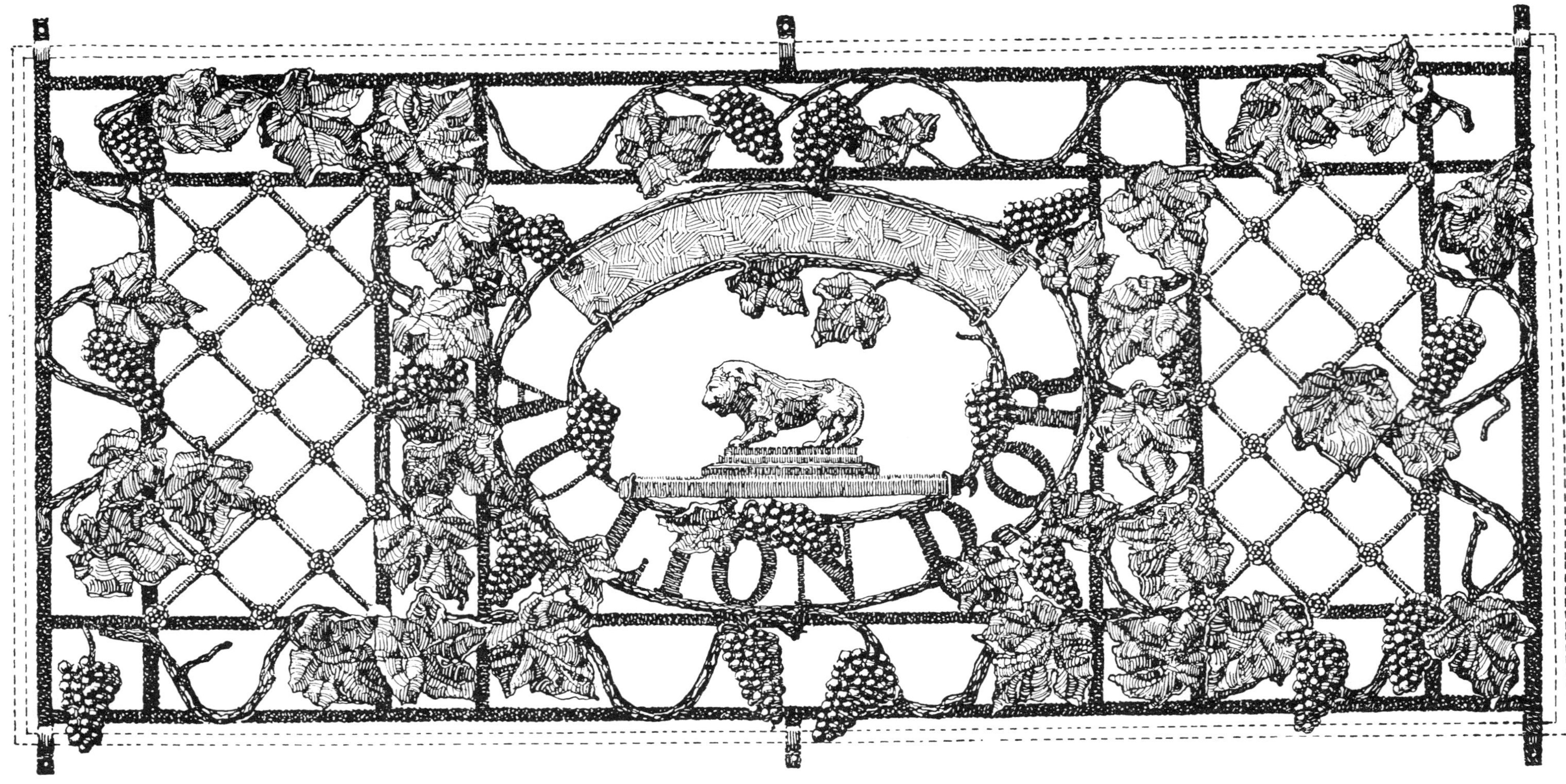

Cabaret Sign, 26 rue St.-Benoît, Paris

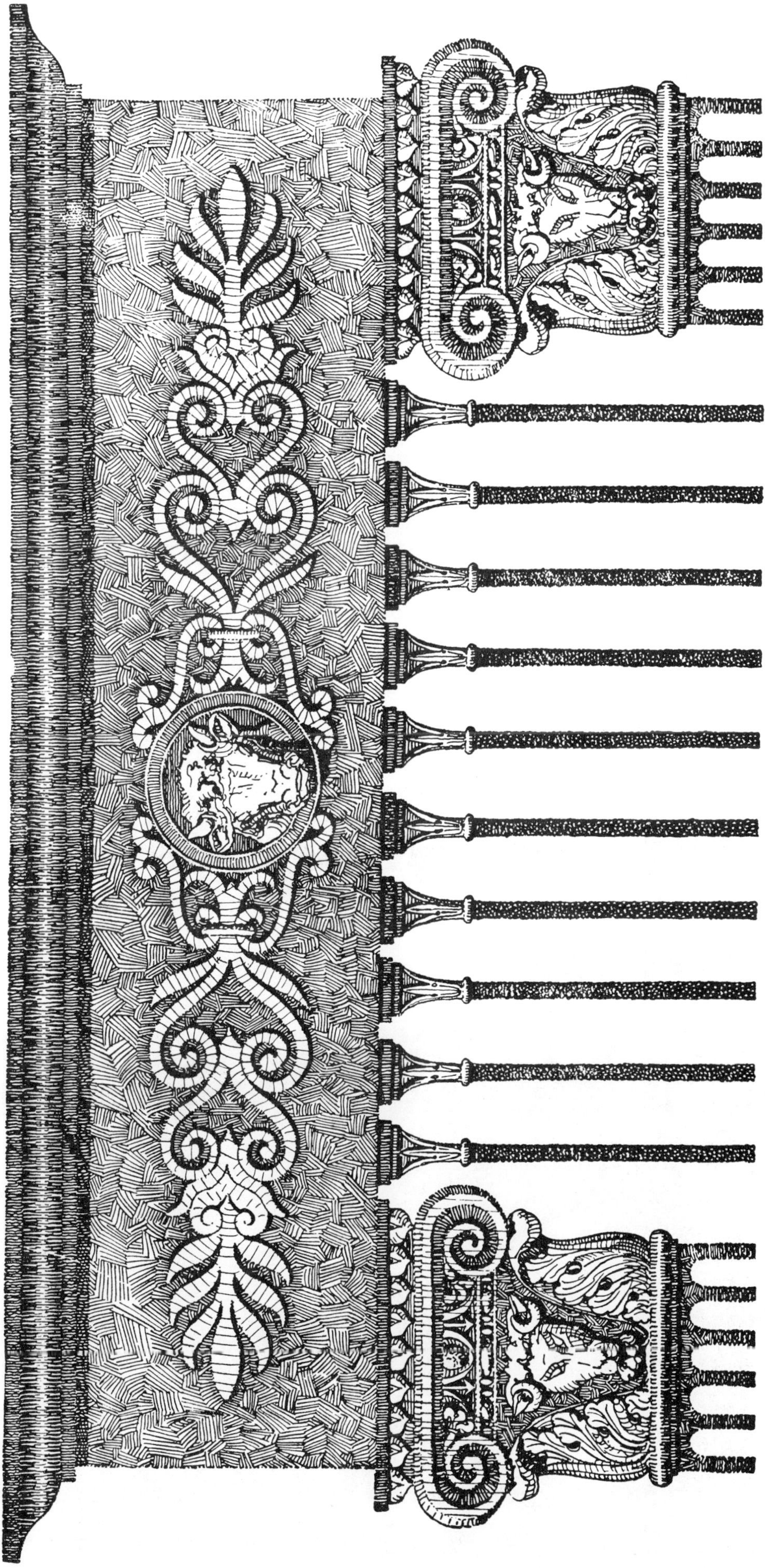

Butcher Shop, Paris

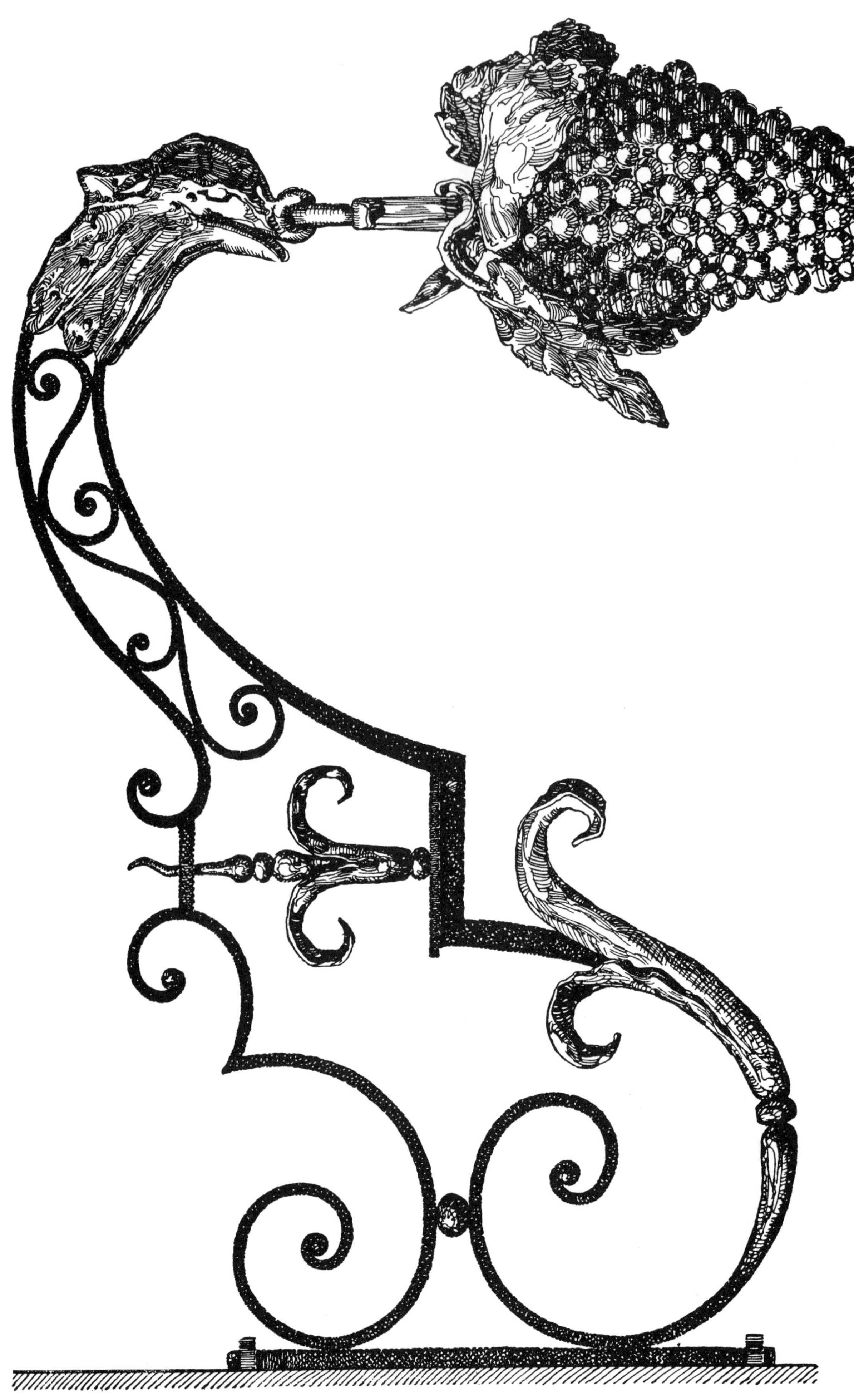

Cabaret Sign, Musée Lesecq des Tournelles, Rouen

Wine Dealer's Sign, Musée Carnavalet, Paris

Cabaret Sign, Paris

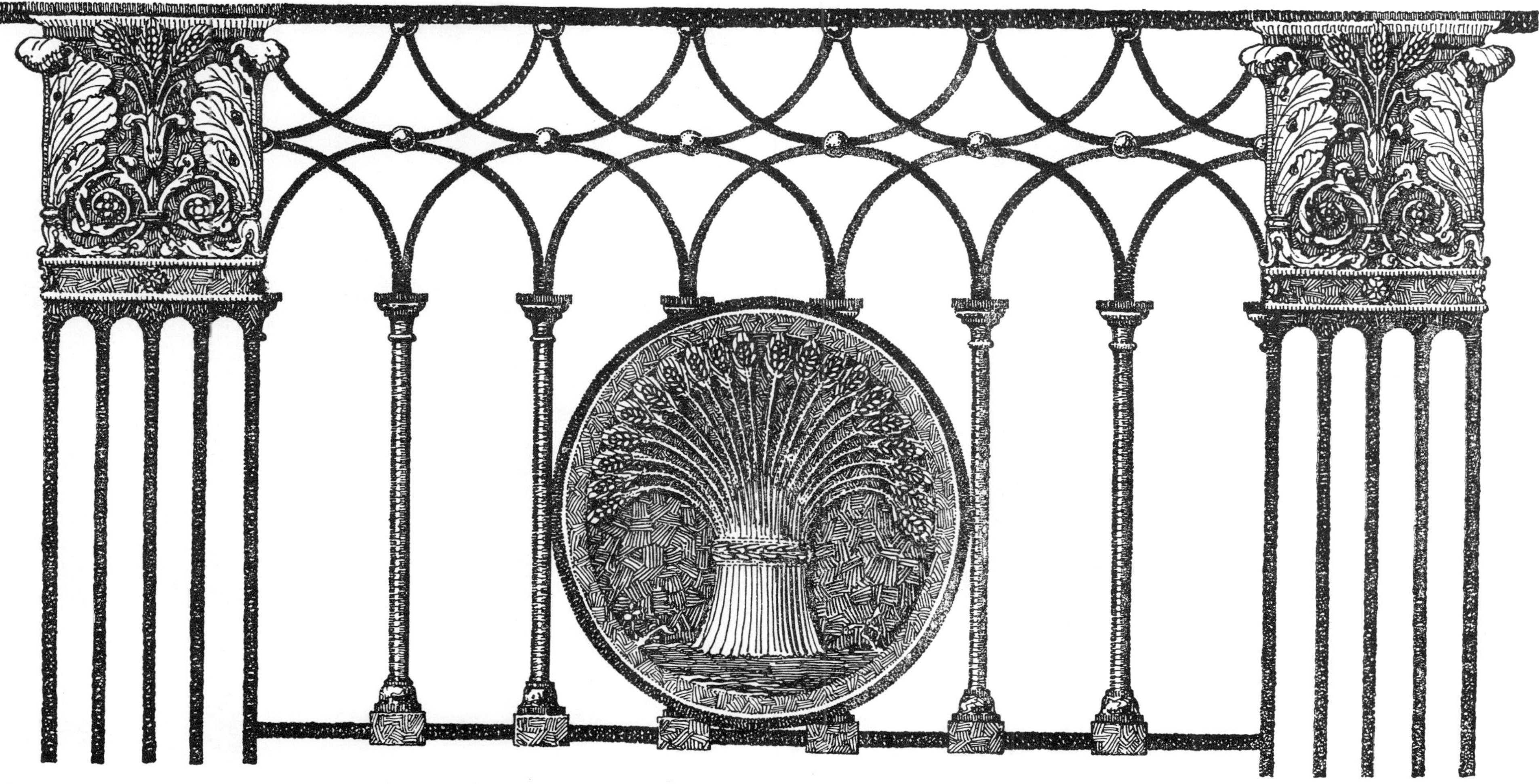

Baker's Sign, Paris

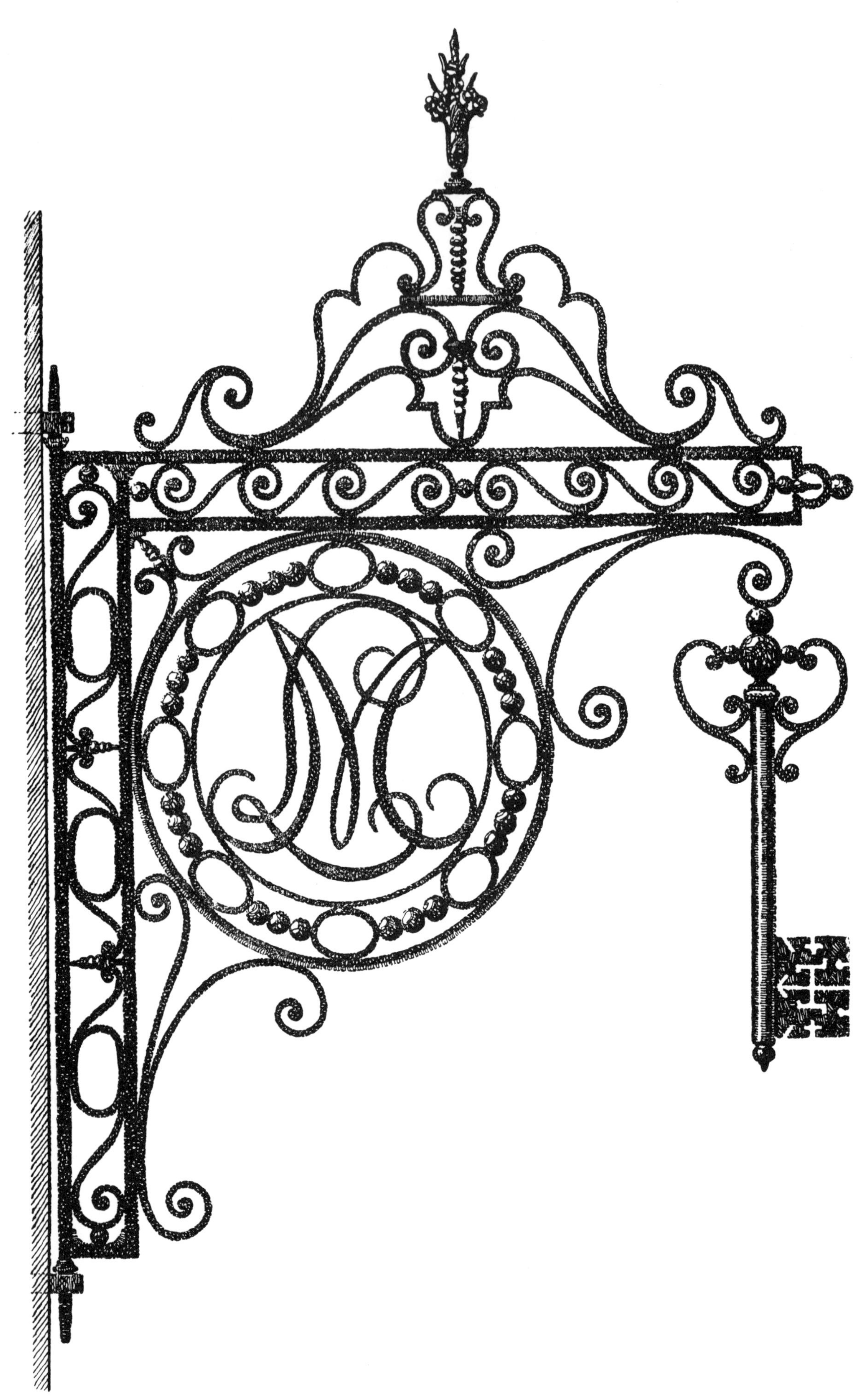

Locksmith's Sign, Musée Lesecq des Tournelles, Rouen

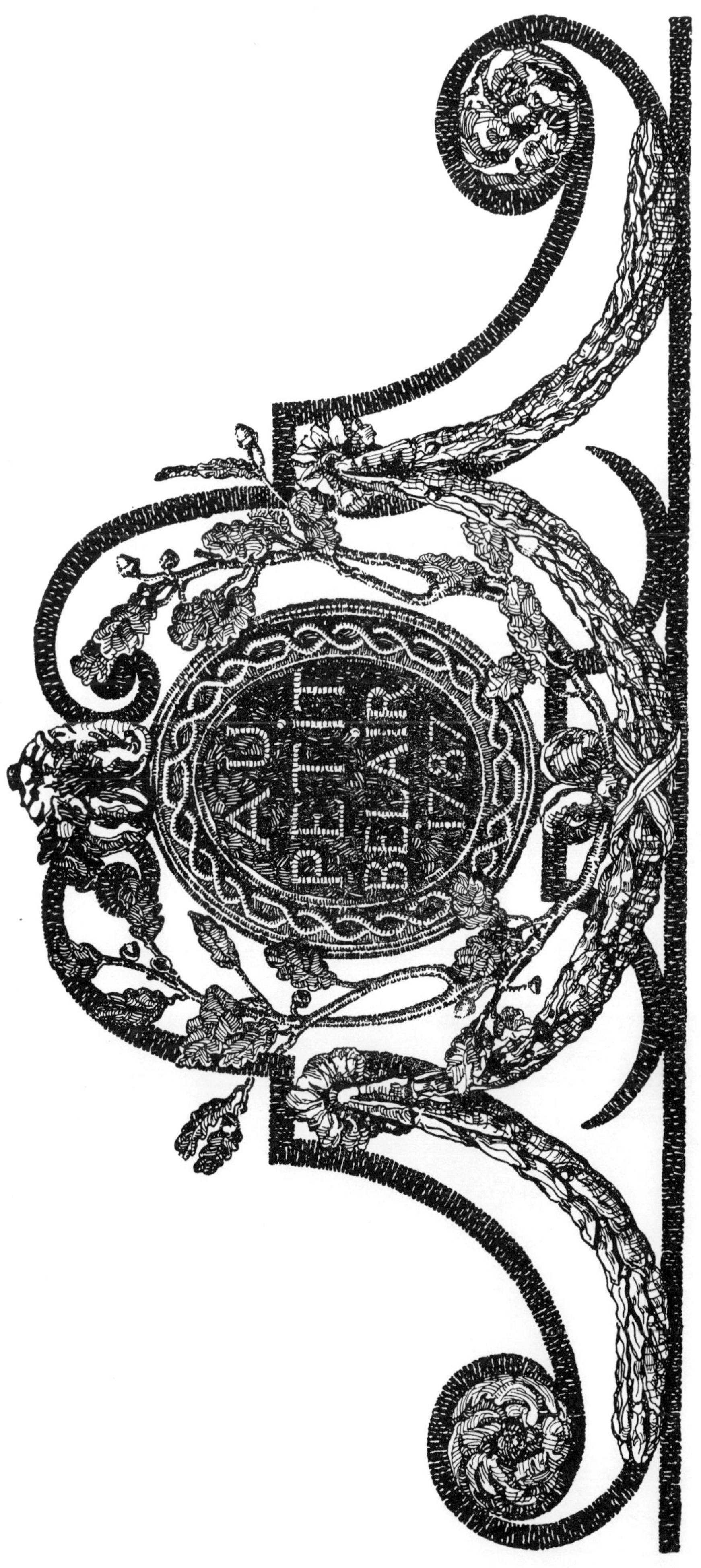

Inn Sign, Musée Carnavalet, Paris

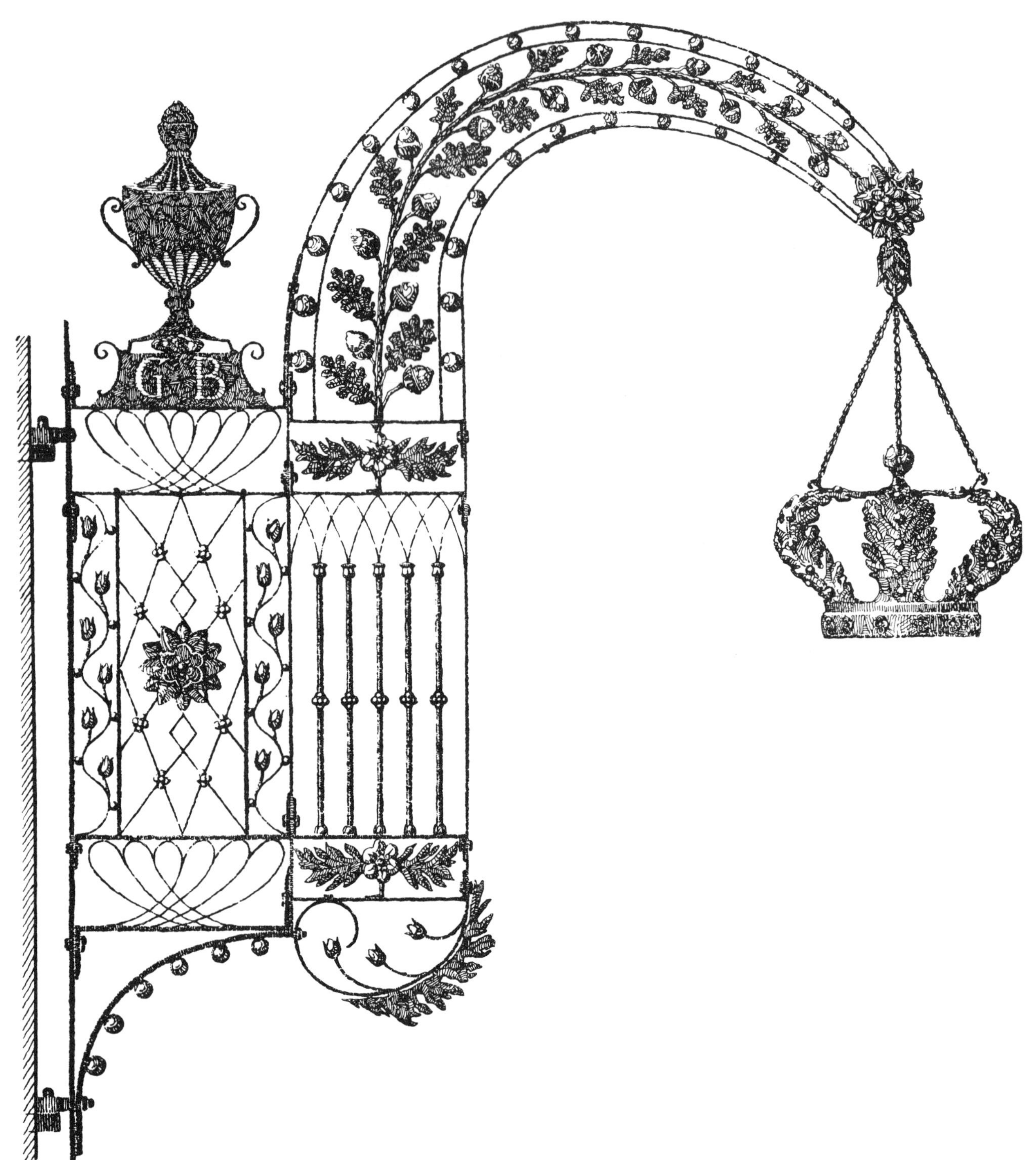

Inn Sign, Musée Carnavalet, Paris

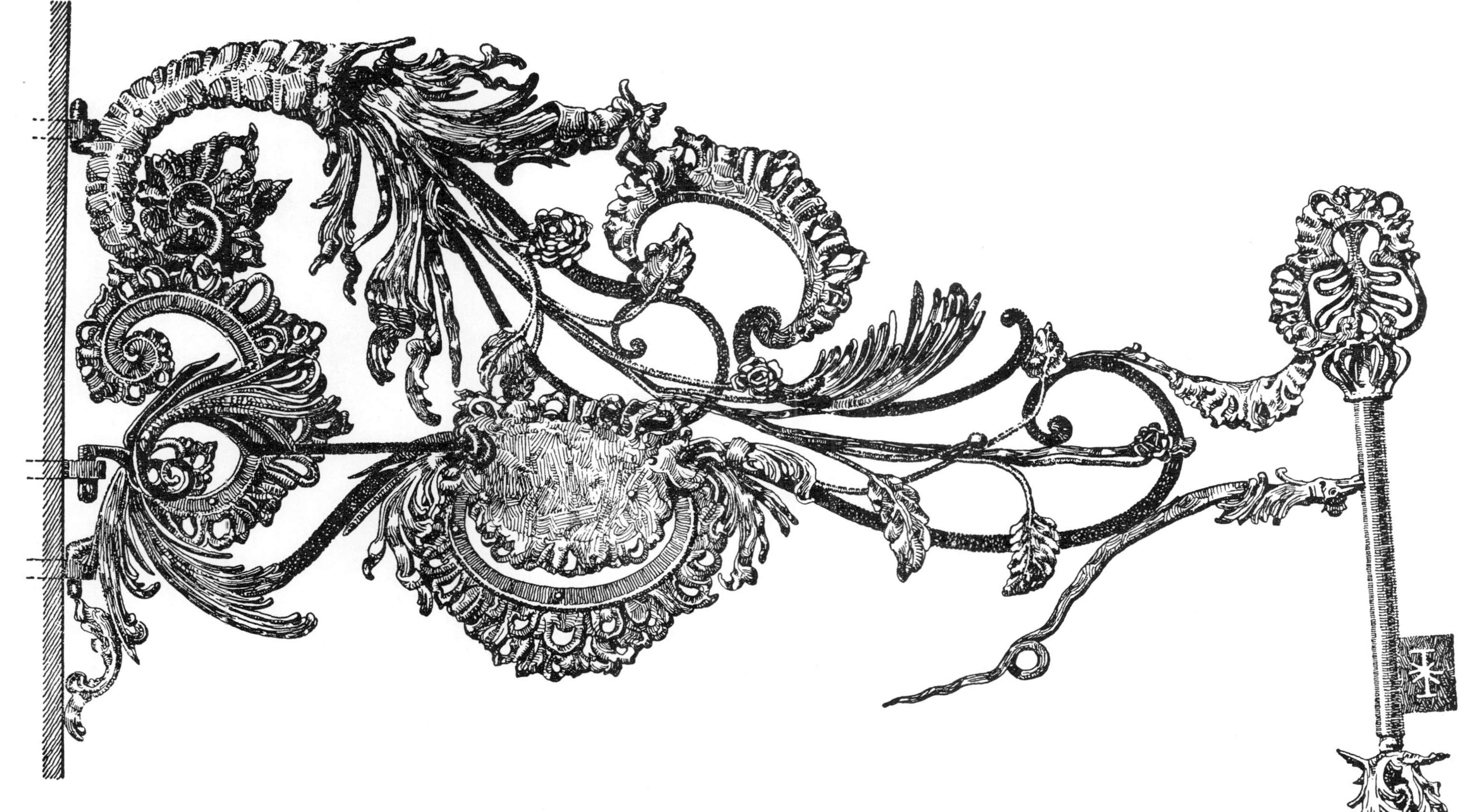

Locksmith's Sign, Musée Carnavalet, Paris

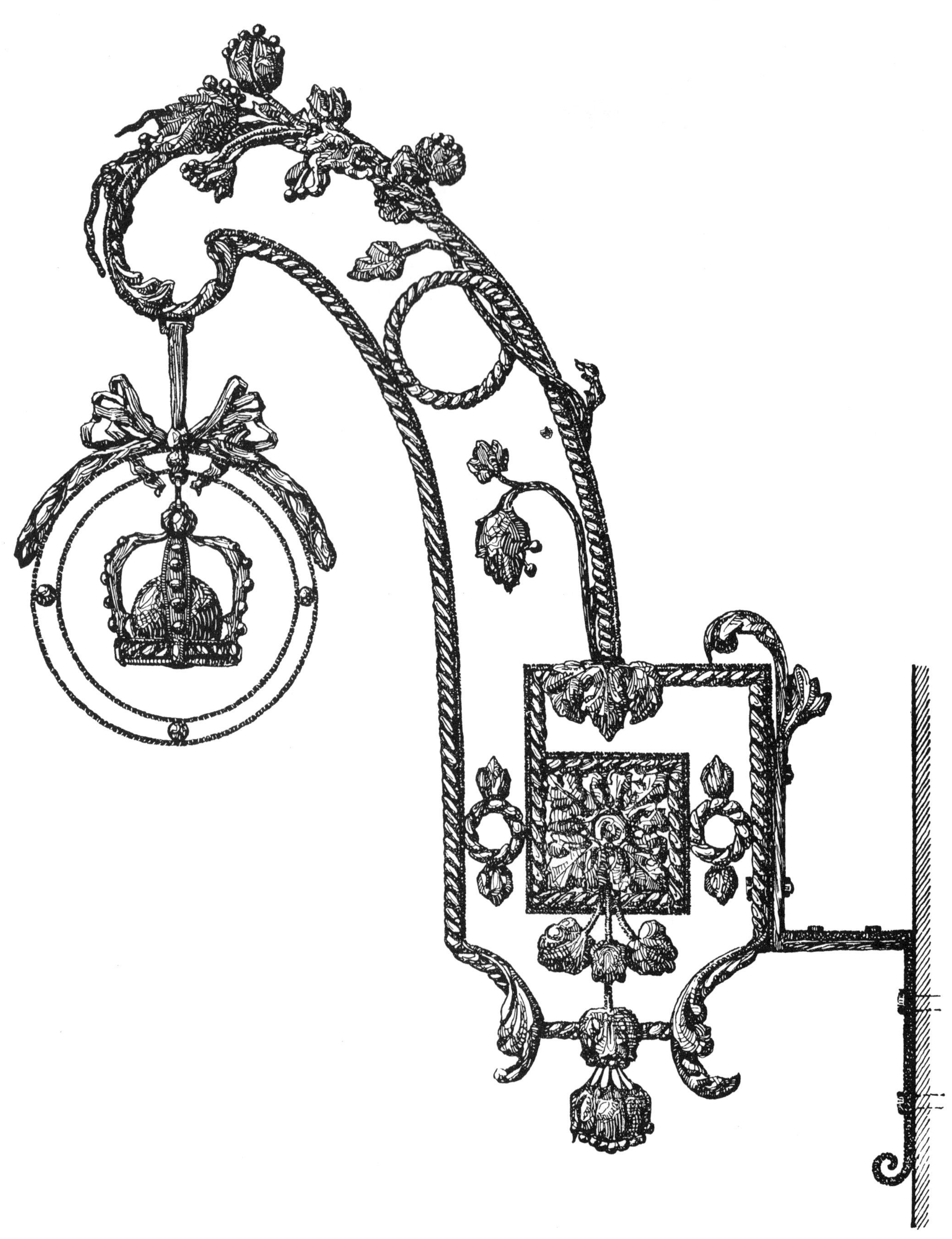

Inn Sign, Musée Lesecq des Tournelles, Rouen

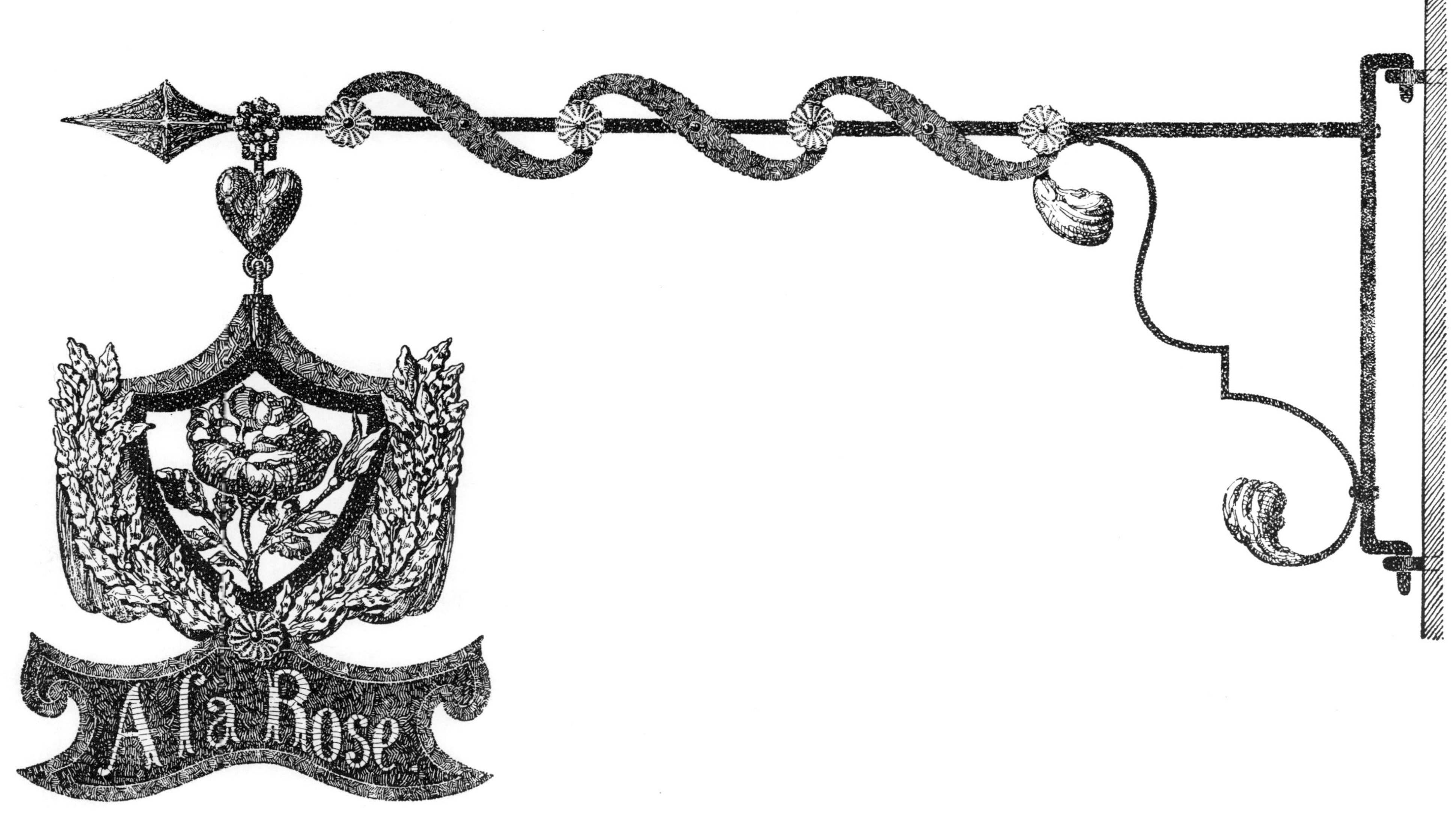

Sign, Musée Carnavalet, Paris

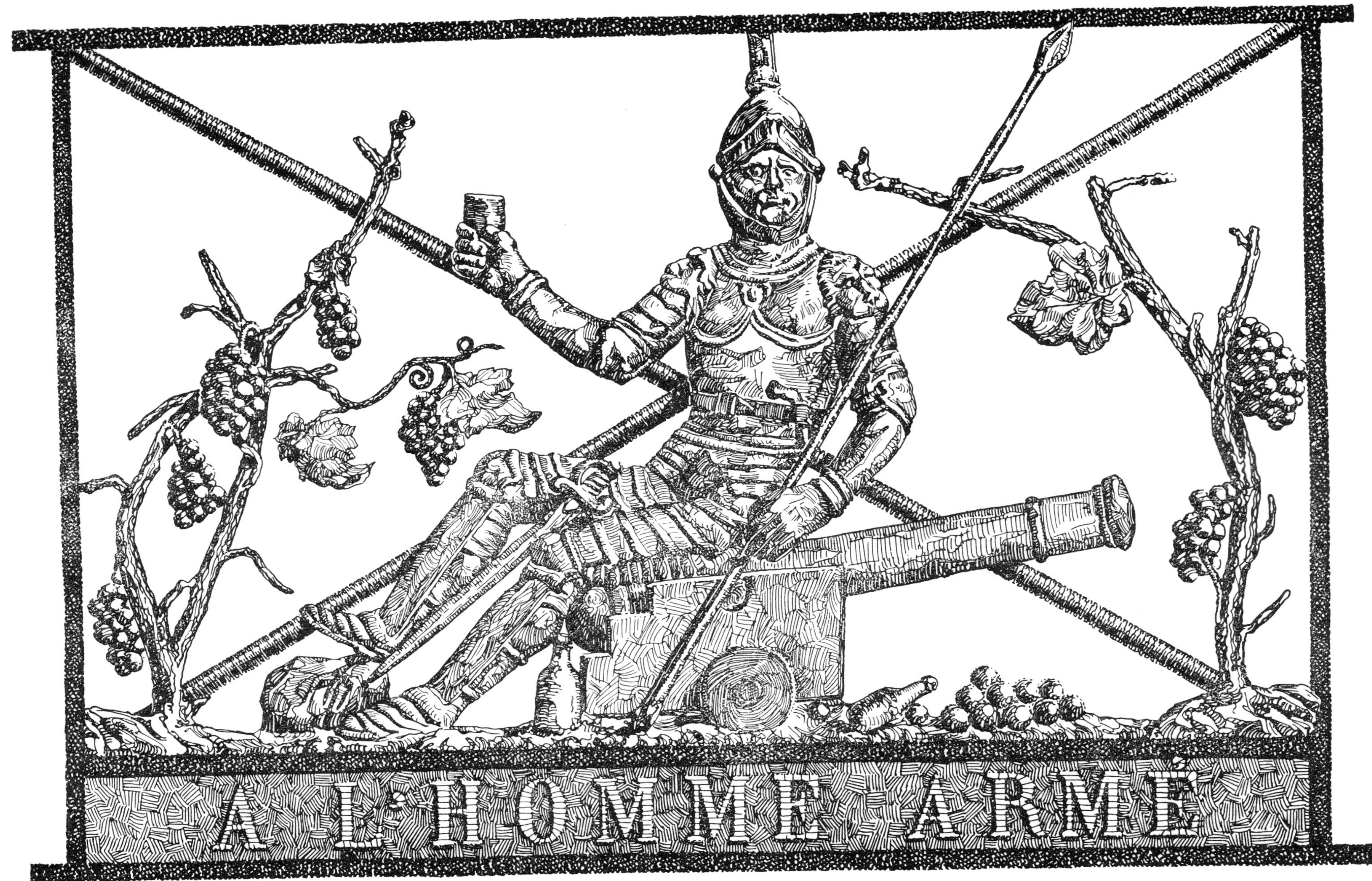

Cabaret Sign, Musée Lesecq des Tournelles, Rouen

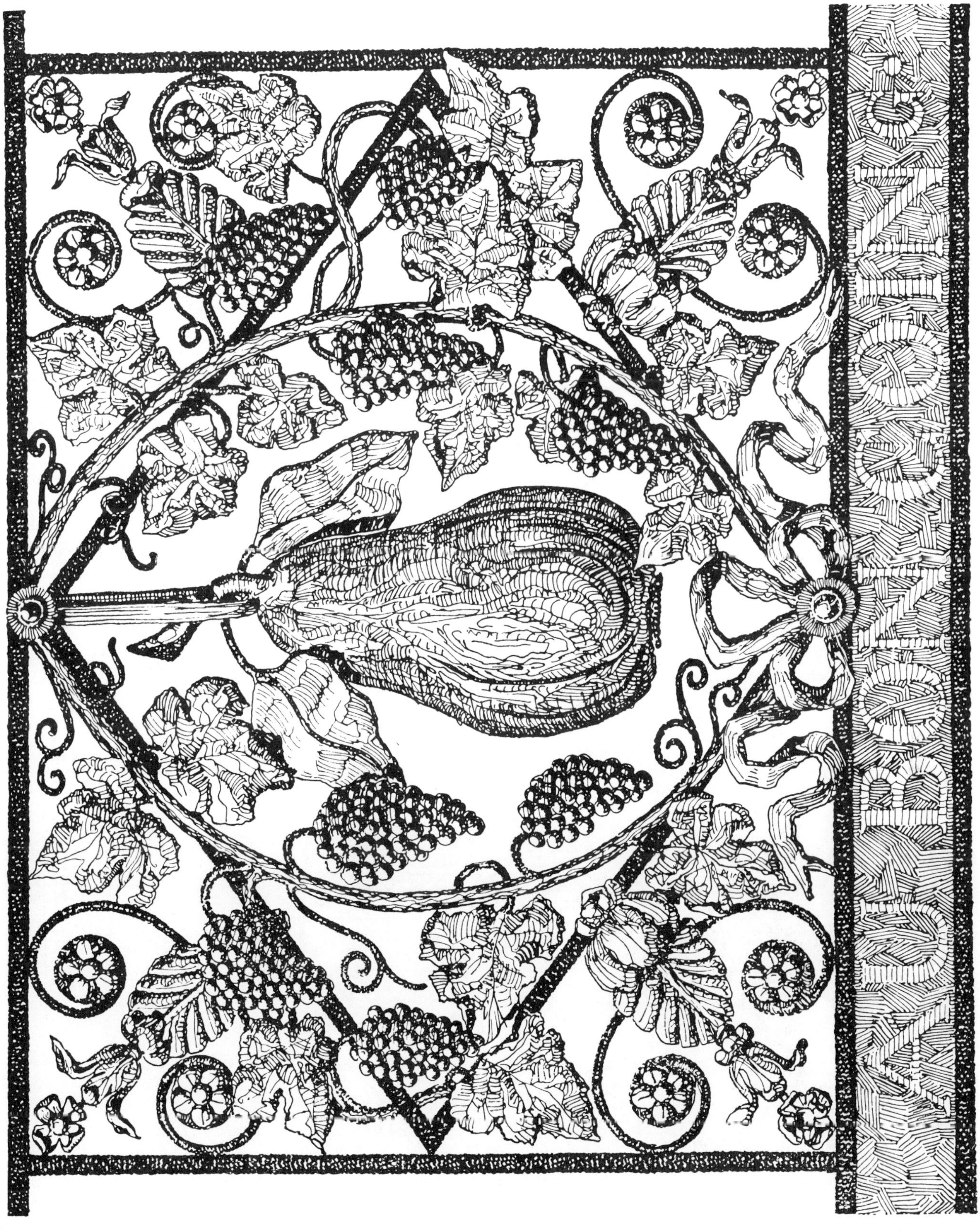

Wine Dealer's Sign, Rue St.-Denis, Paris

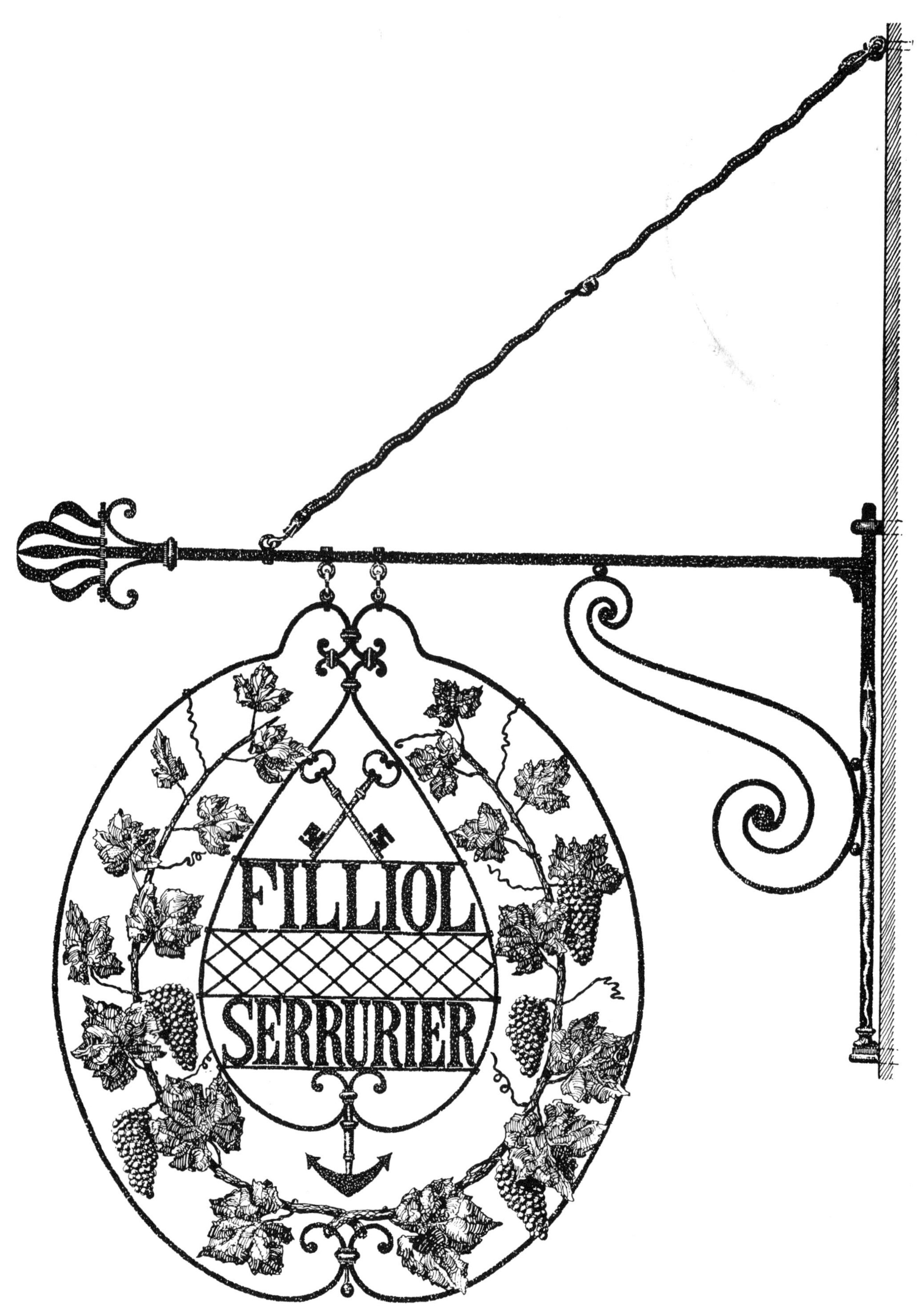

Locksmith's Sign, Musée Carnavalet, Paris

Cooper's Sign, Musée de Cluny, Paris

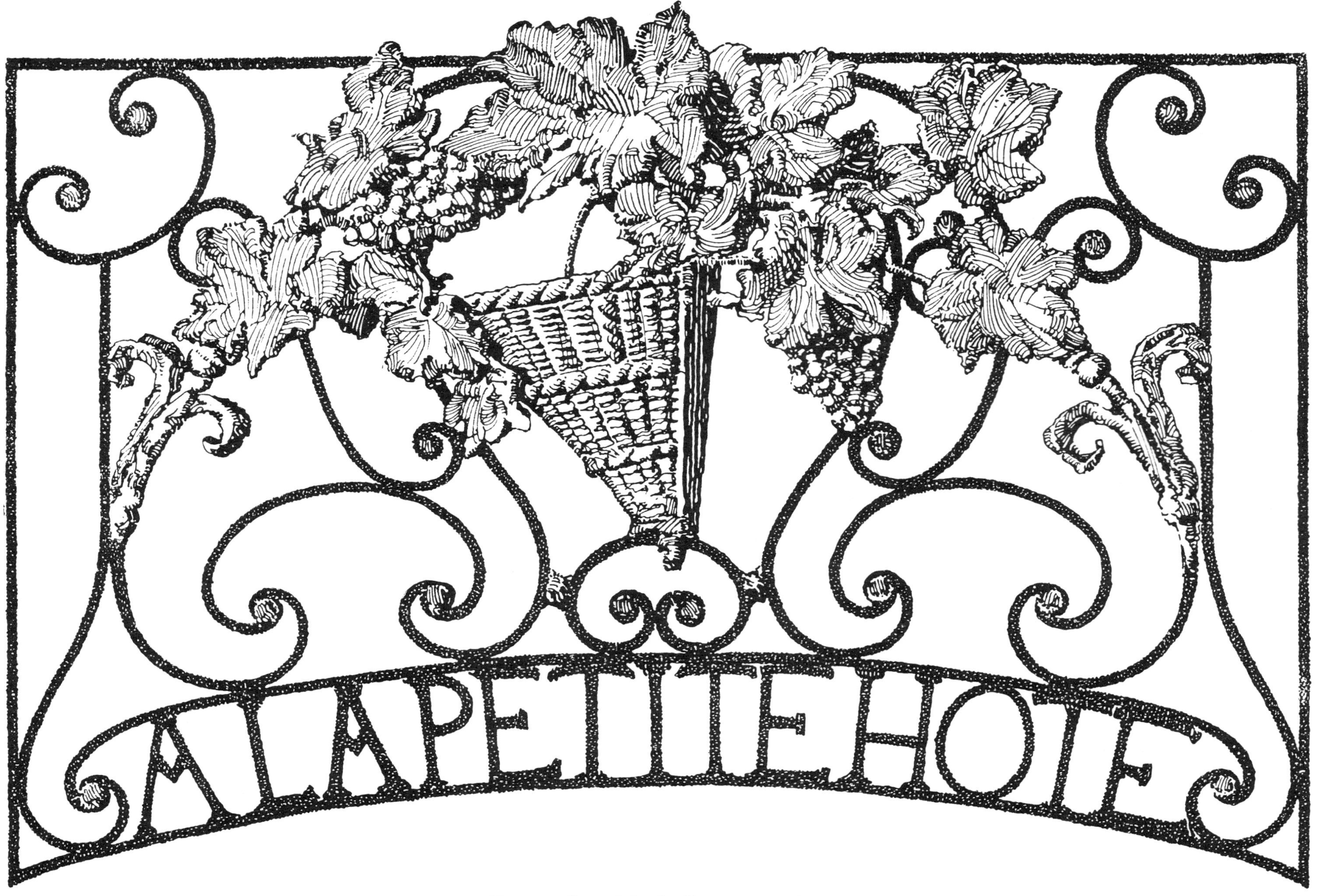

Cabaret Sign, Musée Carnavalet, Paris

Cabaret Sign, Rue de Condé, Paris

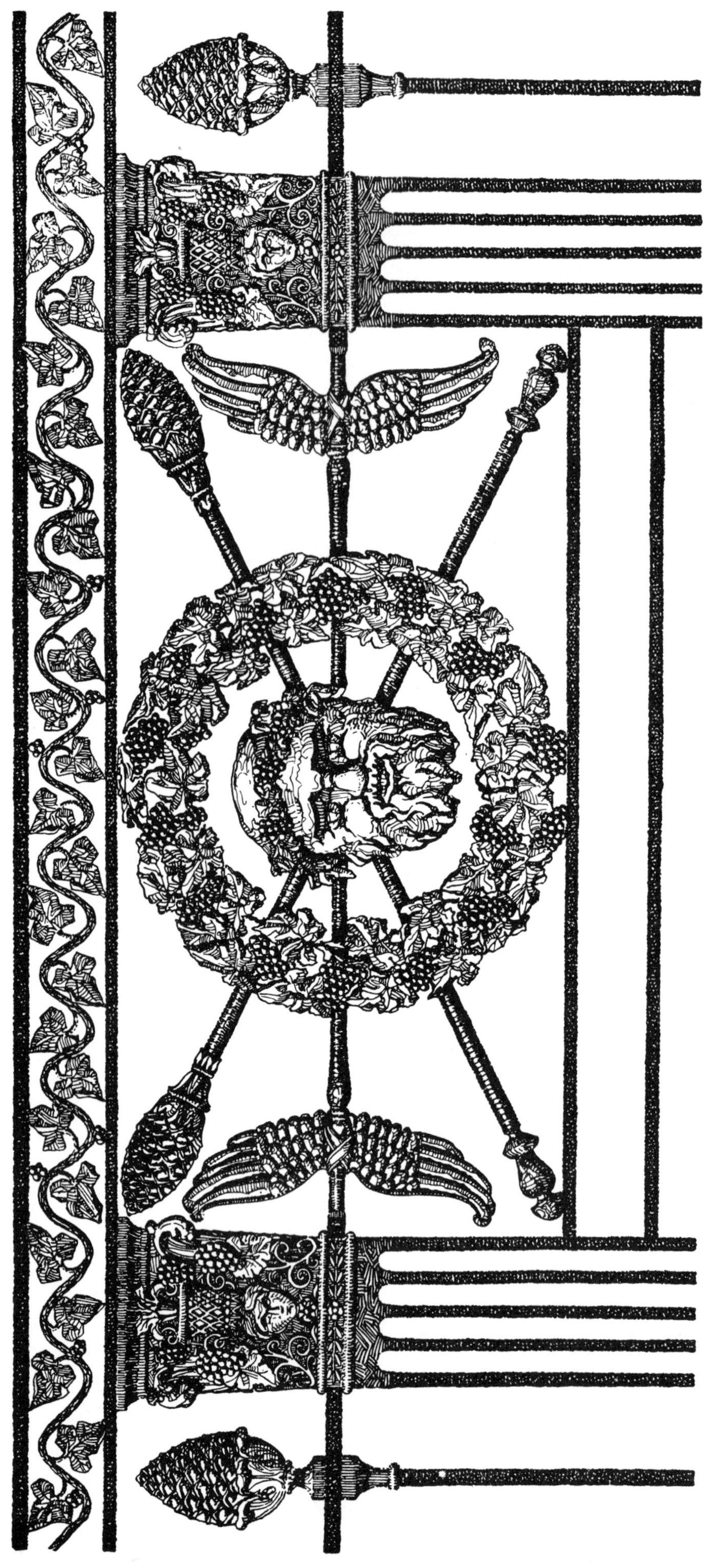

Wine Dealer's Sign, Paris

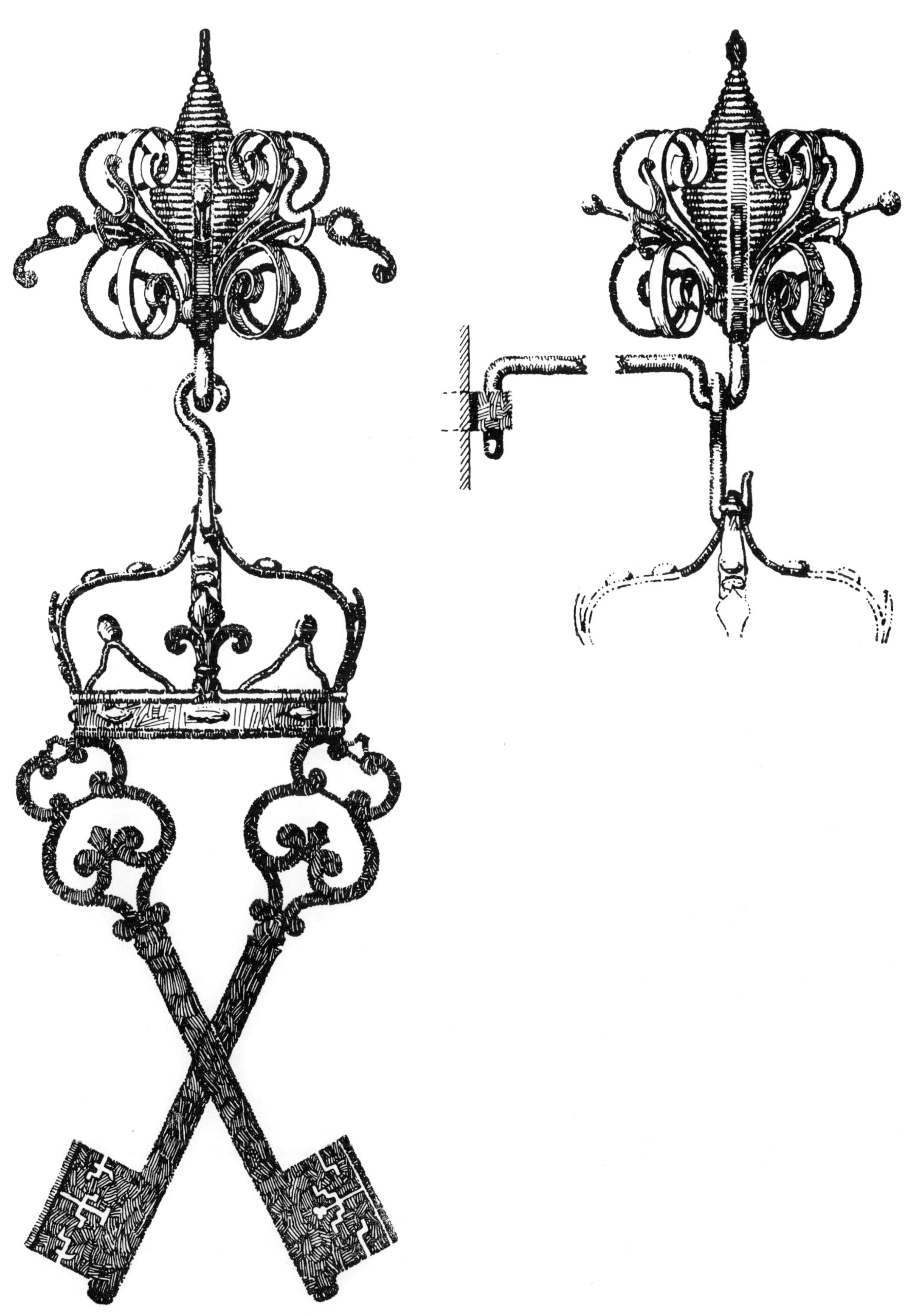

Locksmith's Sign, Musée Carnavalet, Paris

Cabaret Sign, 121 rue Montmartre, Paris

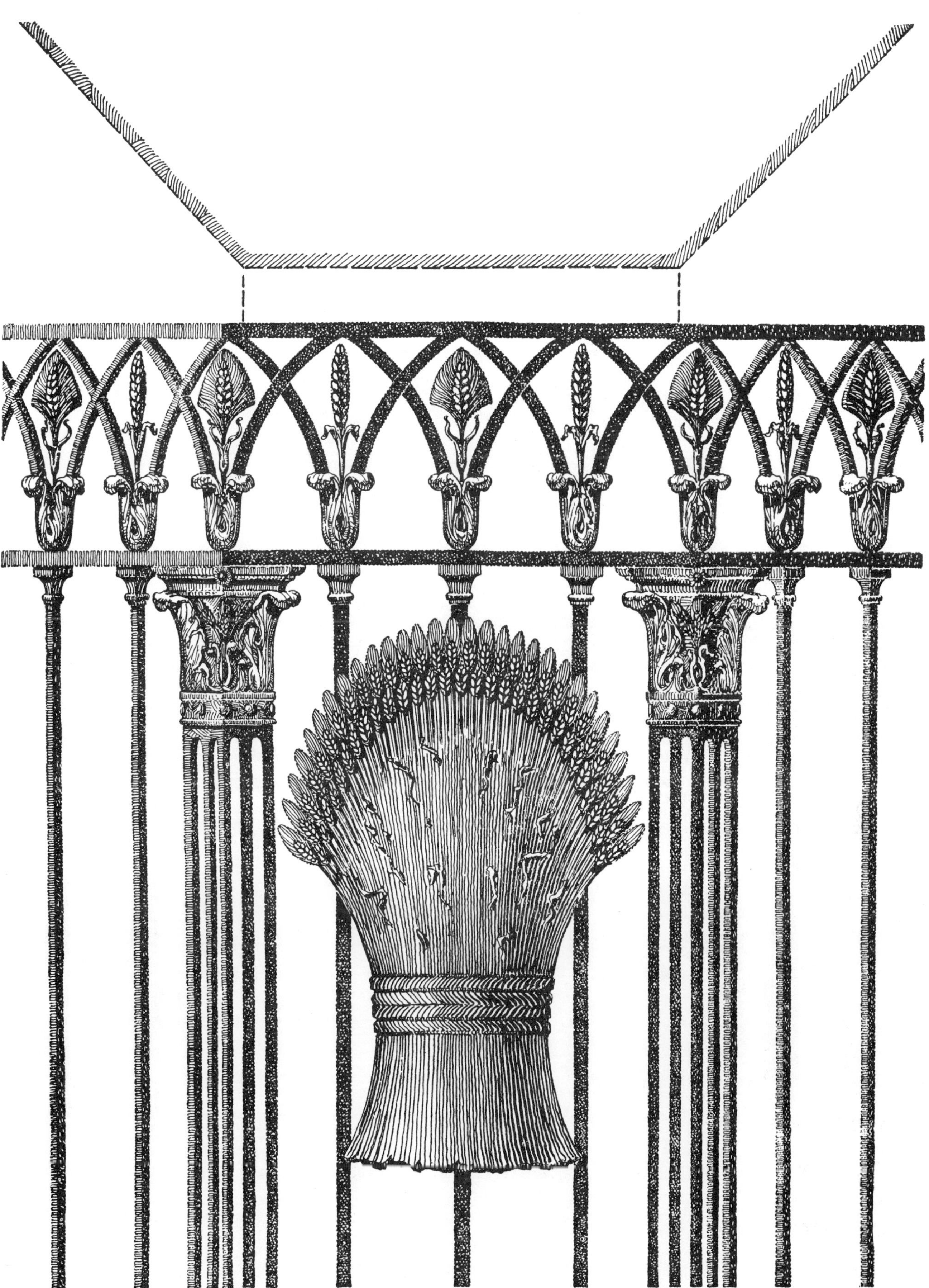

Baker's Sign, Paris

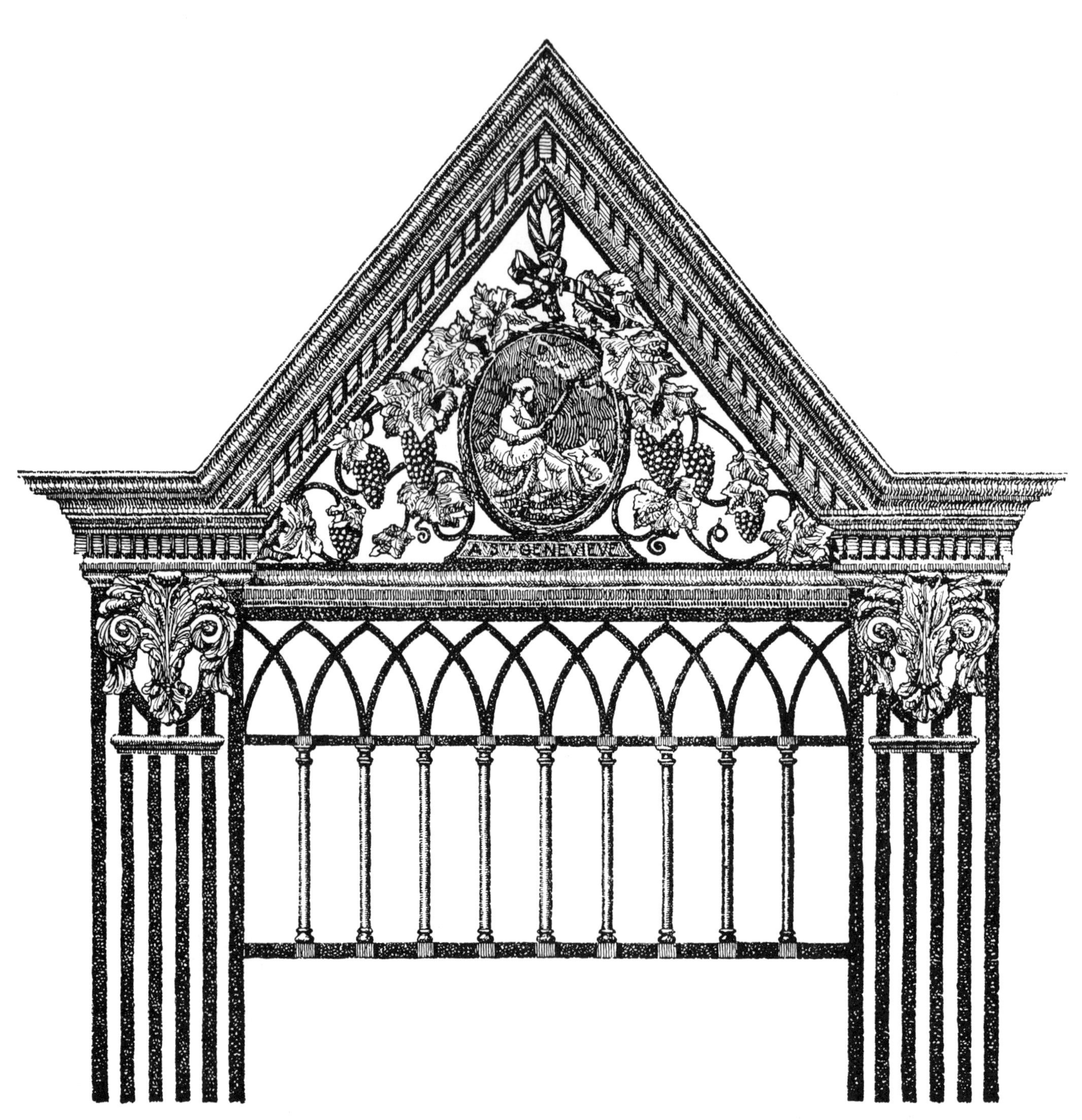

Cabaret Sign, Paris

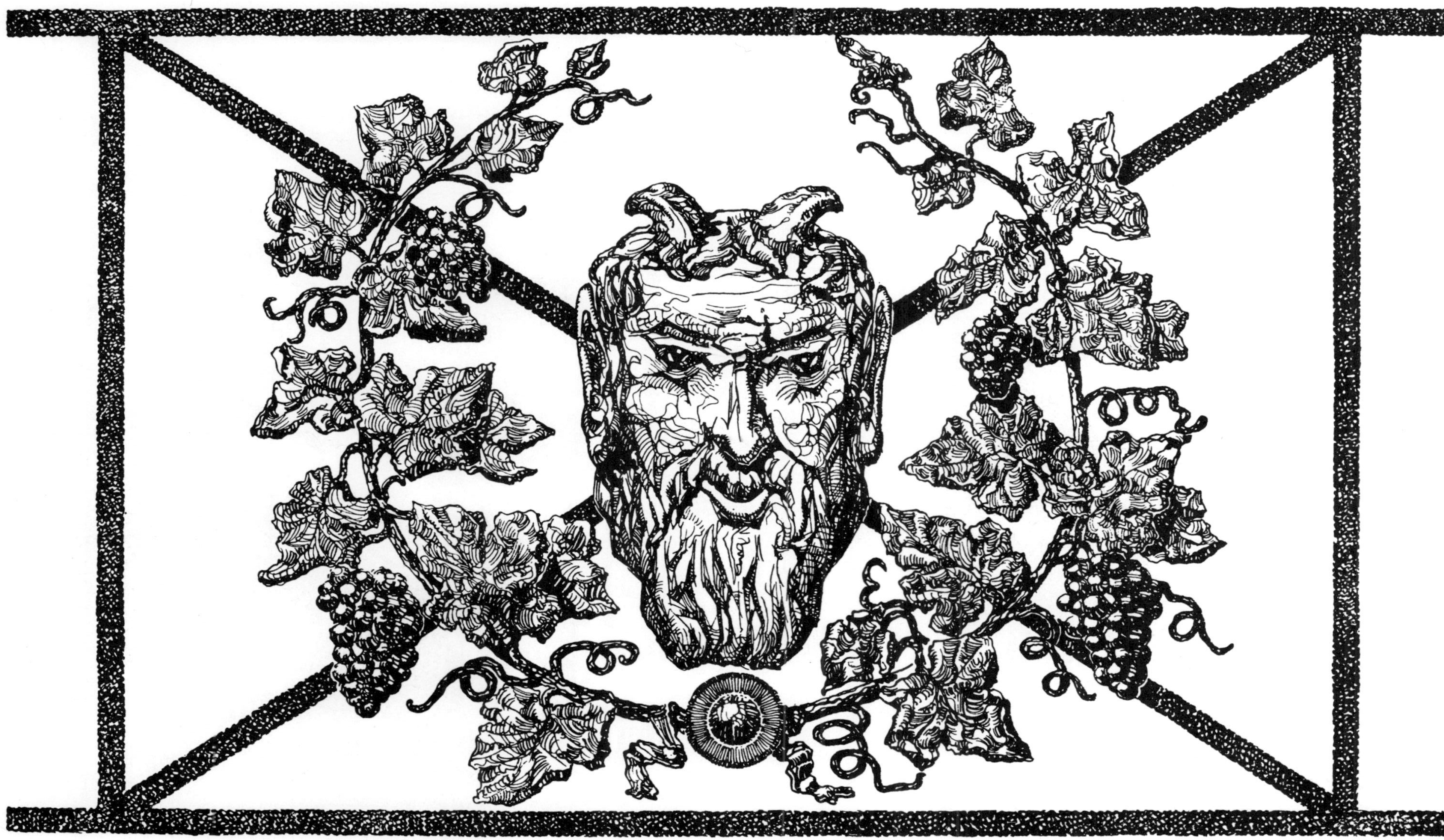

Cabaret Sign, Paris

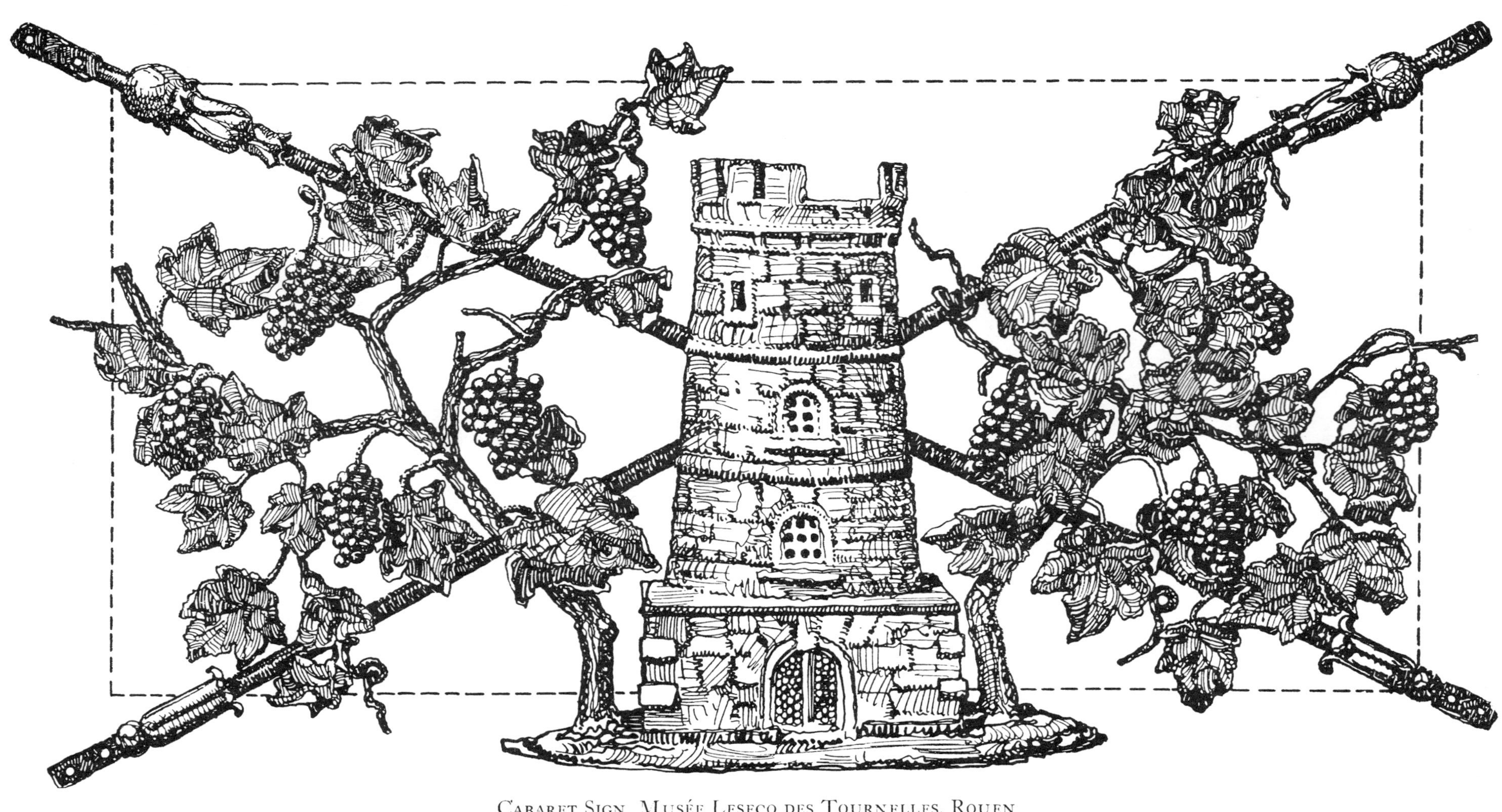

Cabaret Sign, Musée Lesecq des Tournelles, Rouen

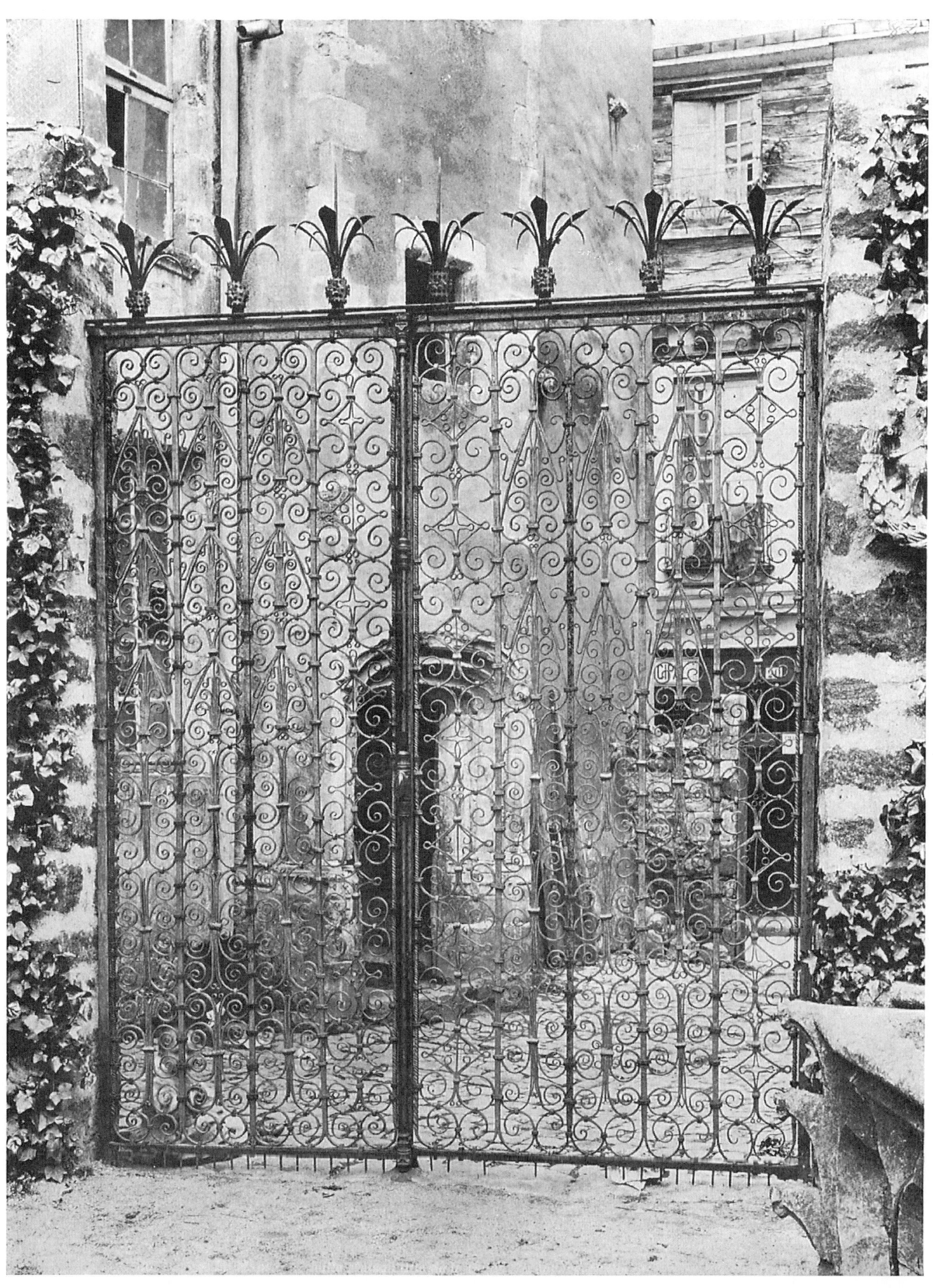

Gates, Le Mans

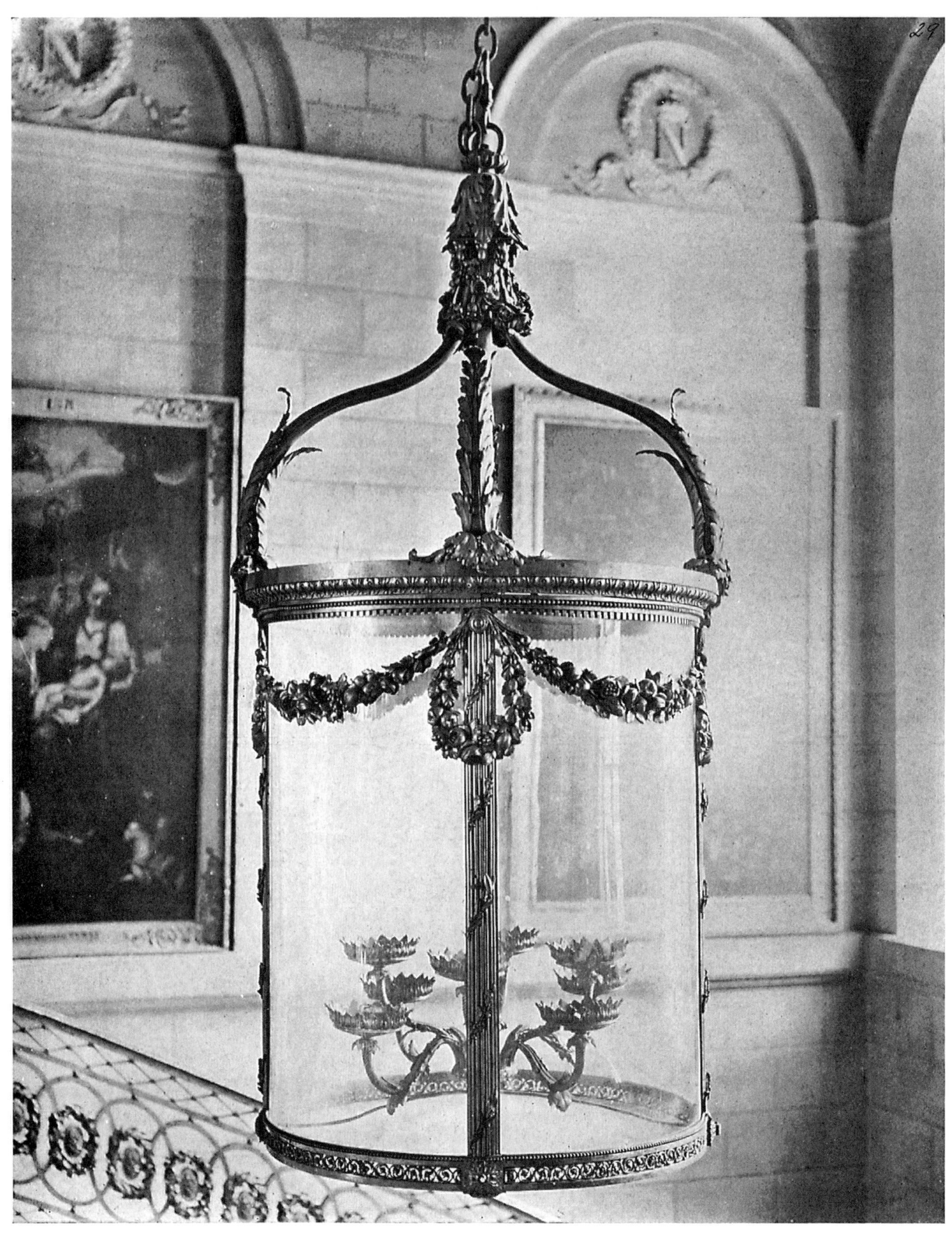

Lamp, Compiegne, Louis XVI

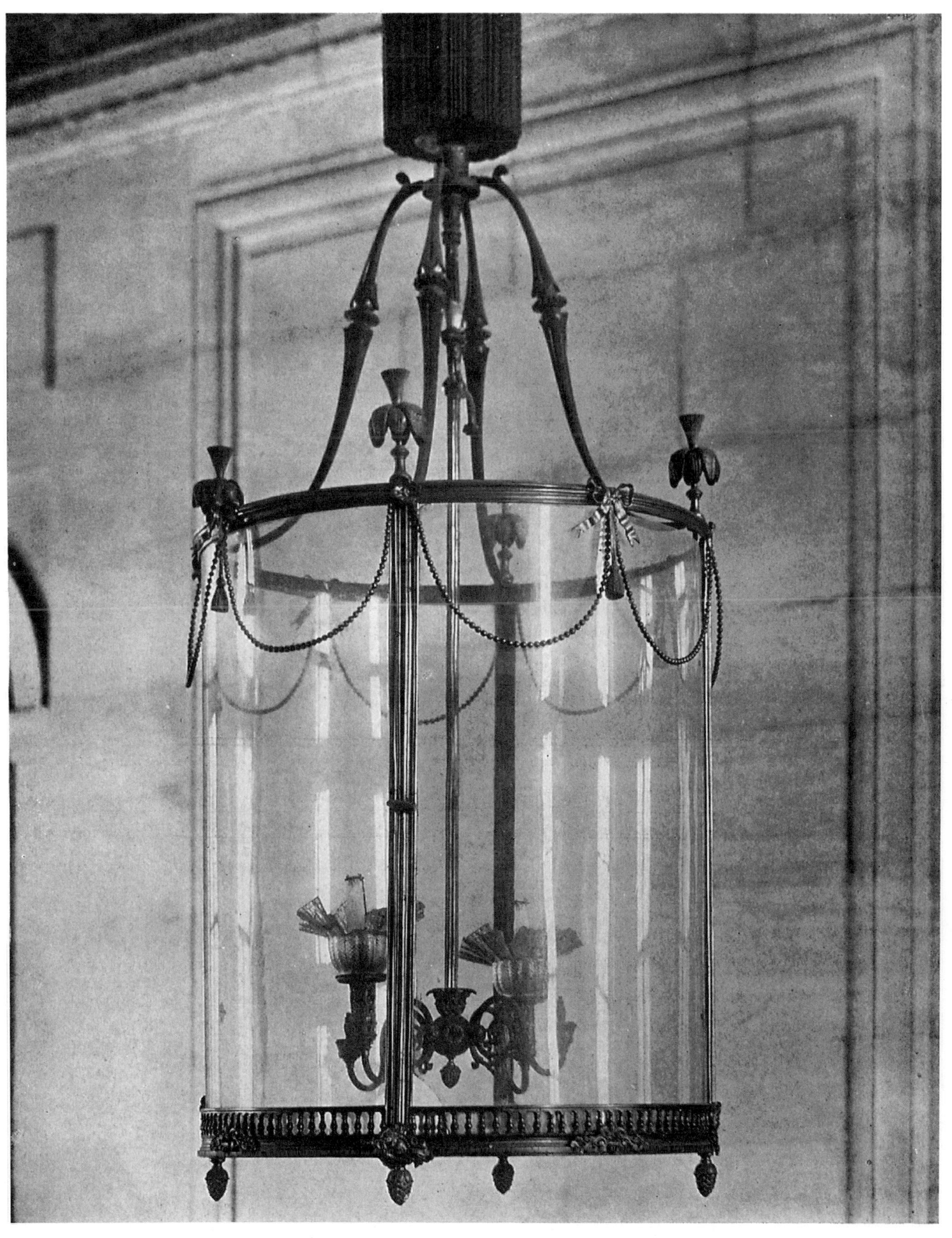

Lamp, Ecole Superieure de Guerre, Paris, Louis XVI

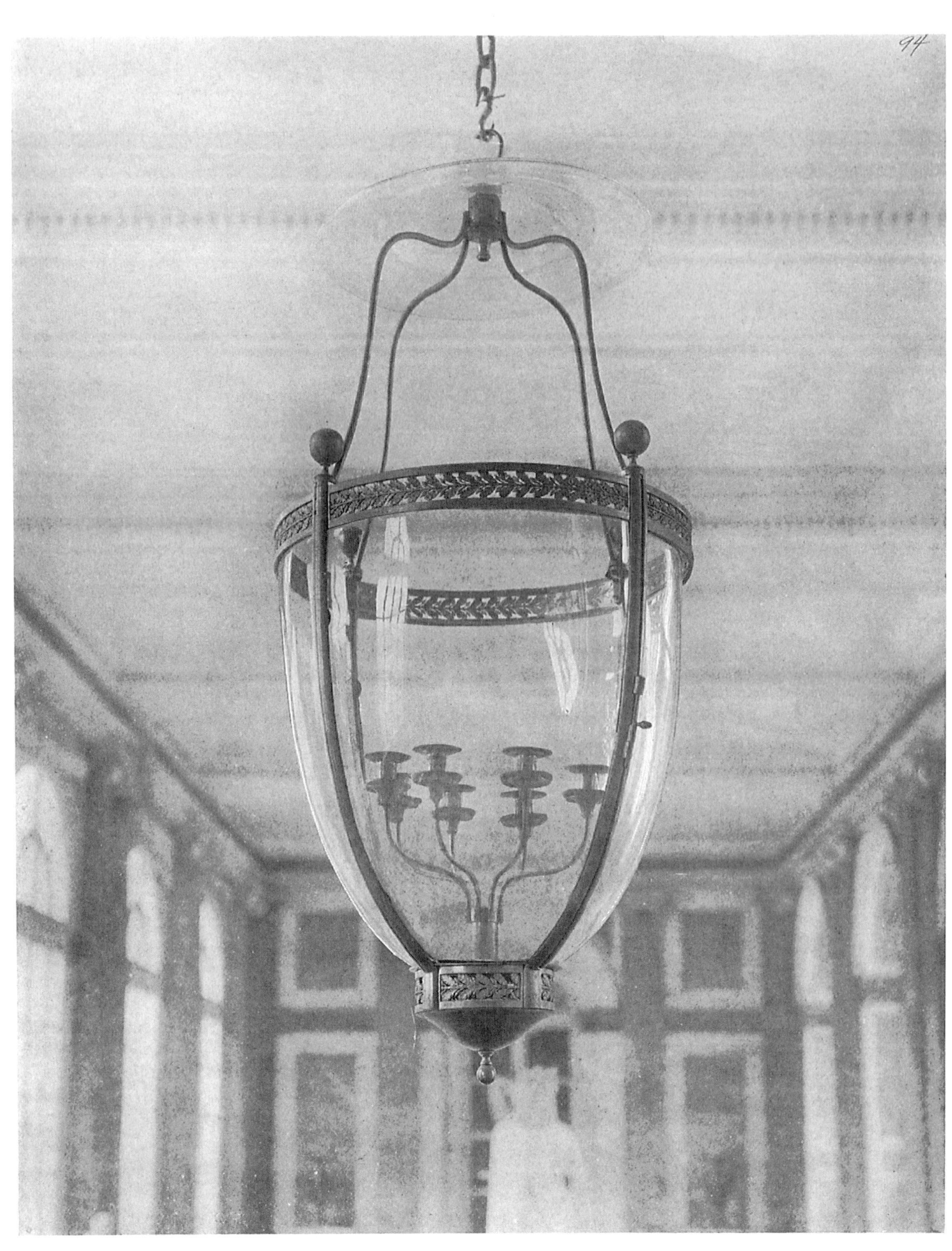

Lamp, Grand-Trianon, Paris-Empire

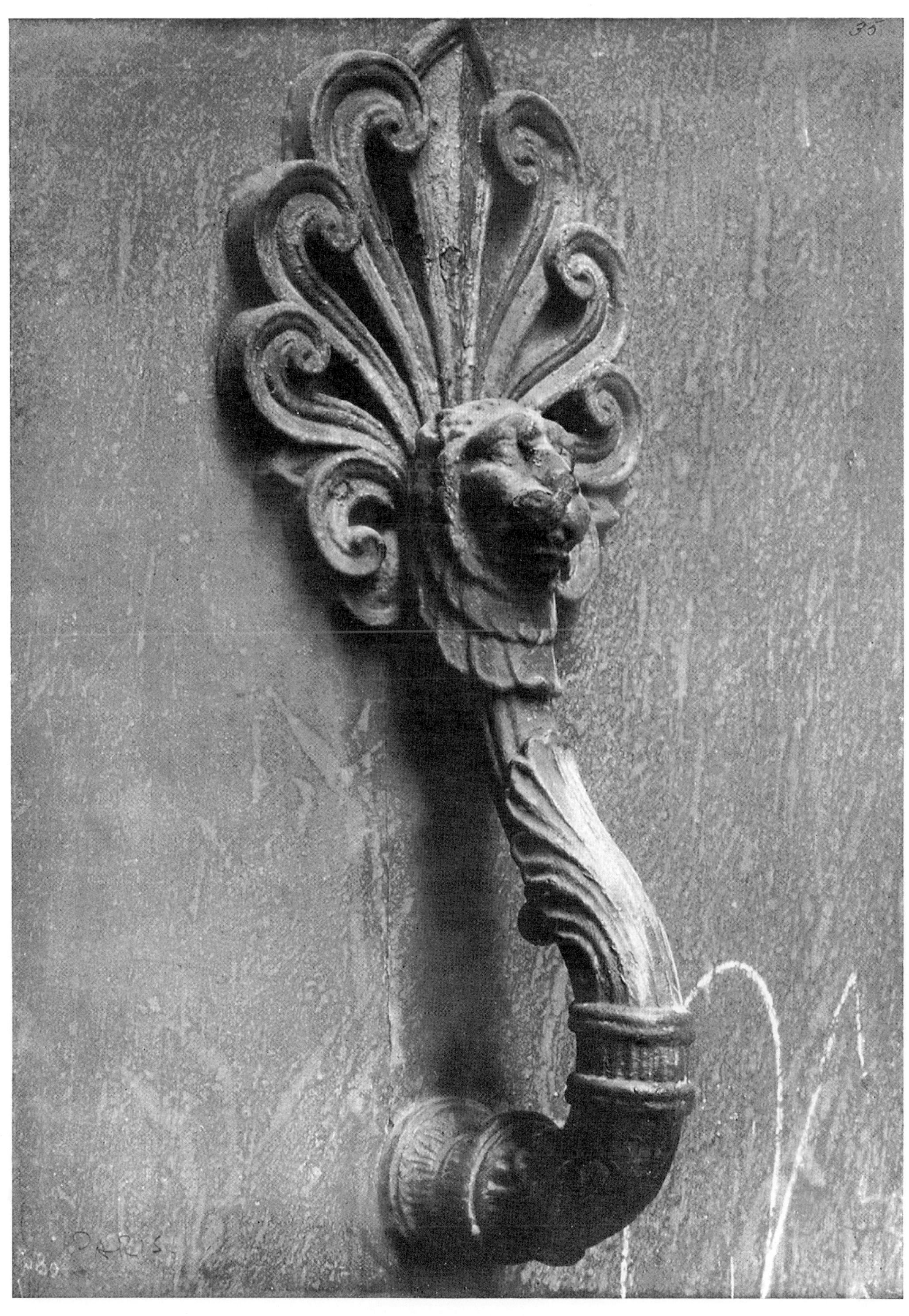

Knocker, Paris

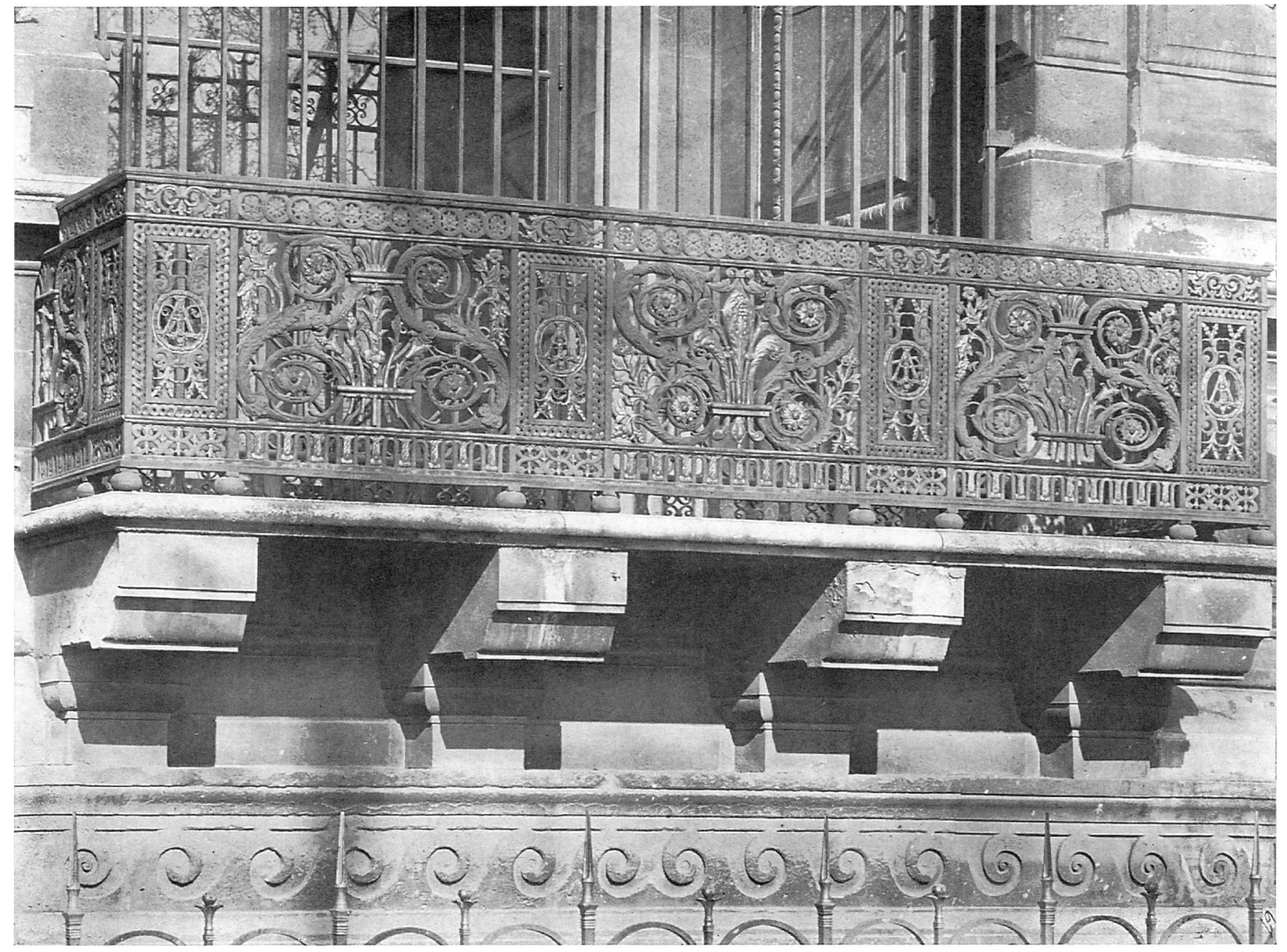

Balcony, Musée du Louvre-Paris, Louis XIV

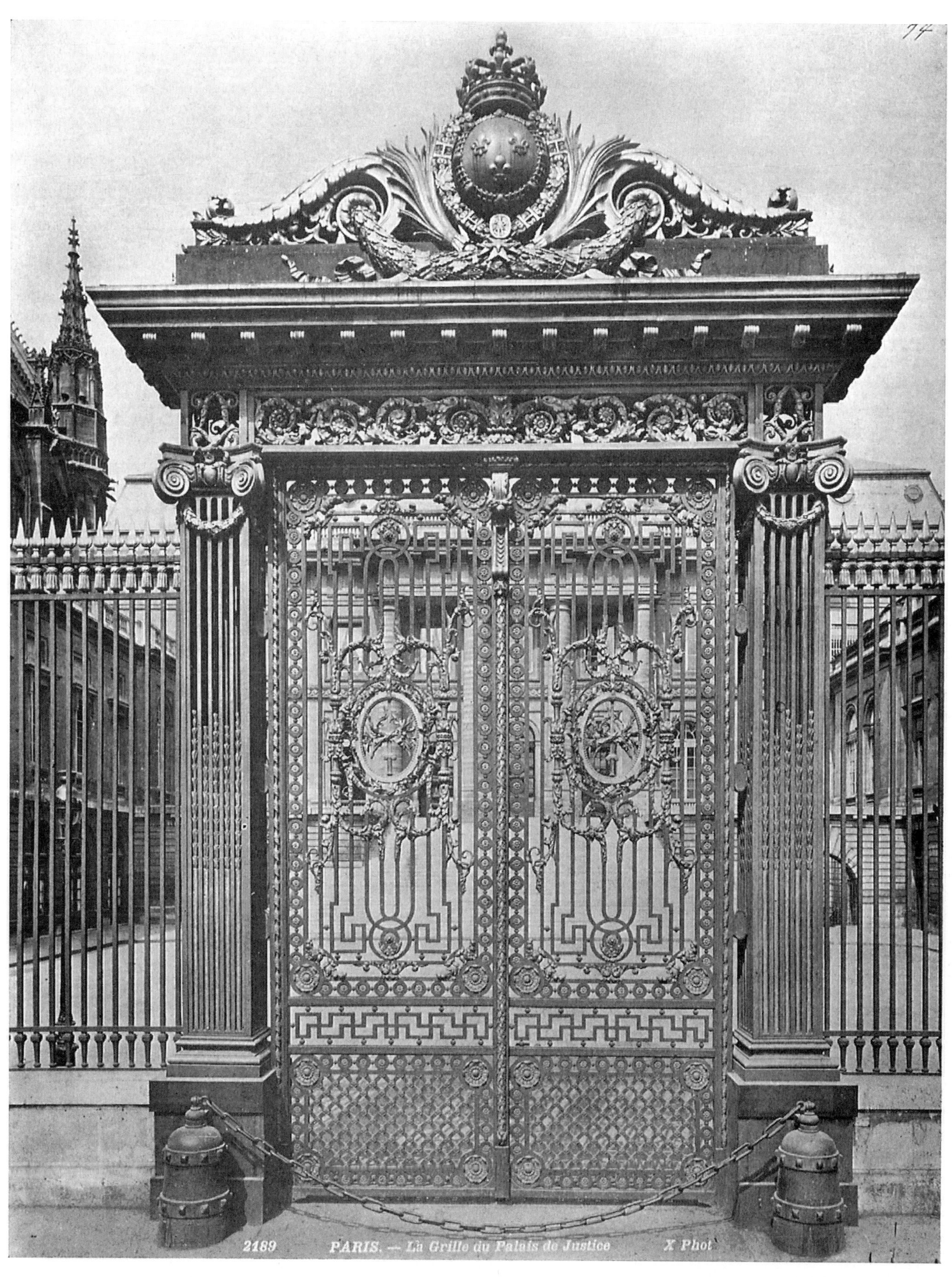

Gates, Palais de Justice, Paris

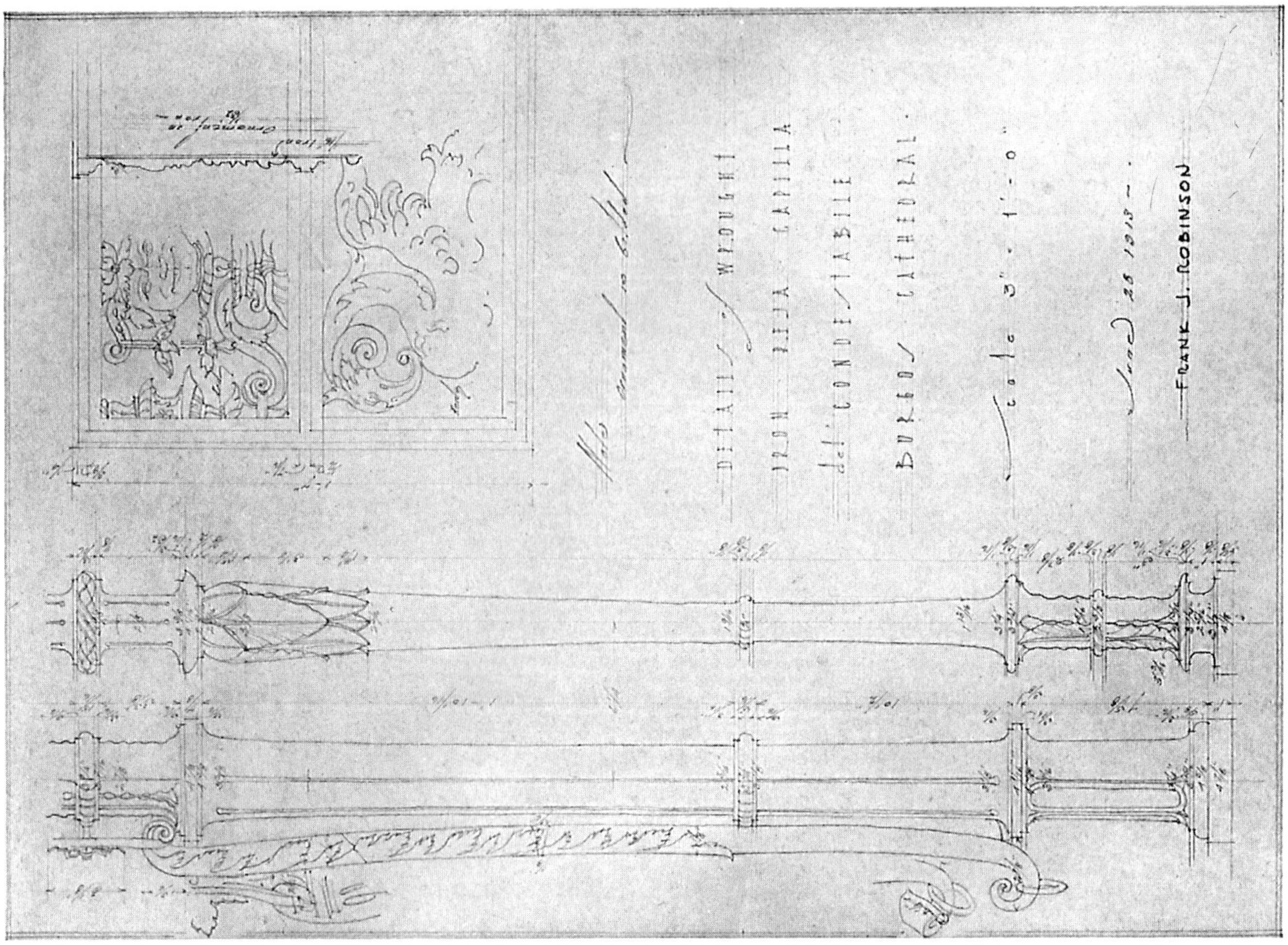

SECTION AT A

SECTION C

SECTION D

ELEVATION

Scale 1½" = 1'-0"

CATHEDRAL of TOLEDO

DEL DESCENSION D N SEÑORA

May 11 1913

FRANK J. ROBINSON

Note ornament is gilded

DETAILS of WROUGHT IRON REJA CAPILLA del CONDESTABLE BURGOS CATHEDRAL

Scale 3" = 1'-0"

June 25 1913

FRANK J. ROBINSON

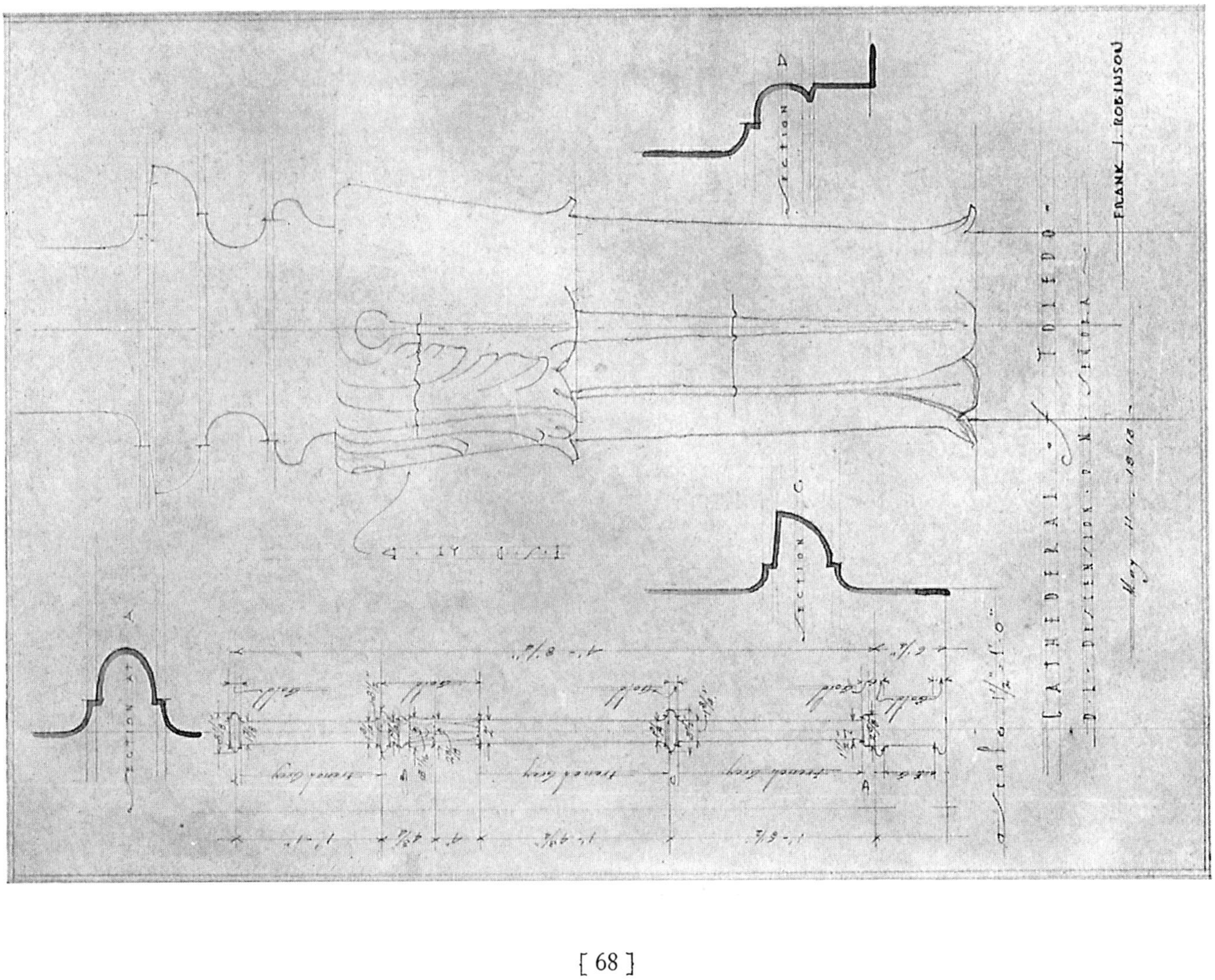

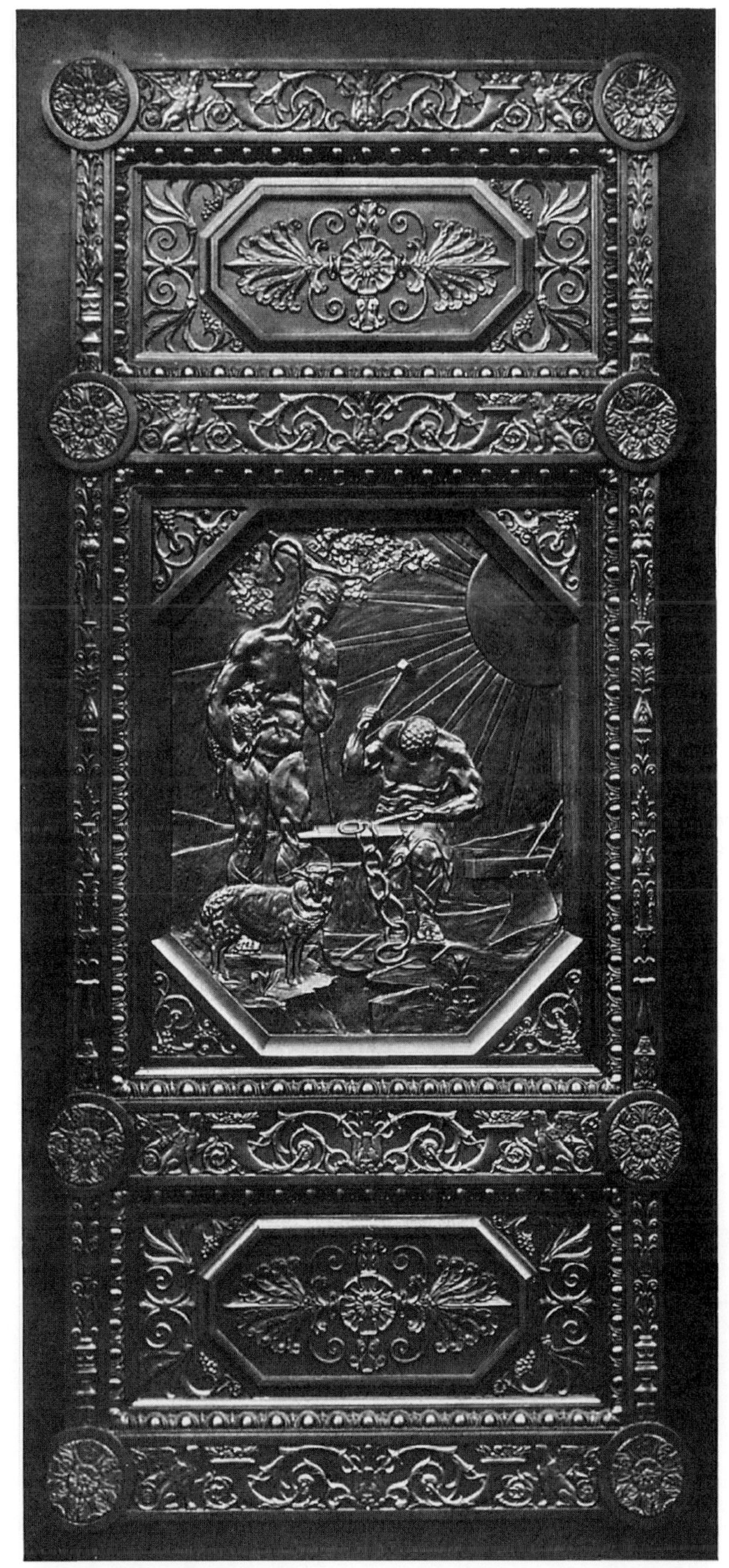

Courtesy of Metalcraft Magazine — Rendigs, Panzer & Martin, *Architects*

Detail of Panel Symbolizing "Interdependence"
The Liberal Savings & Loan Co., Cincinnati, Ohio.

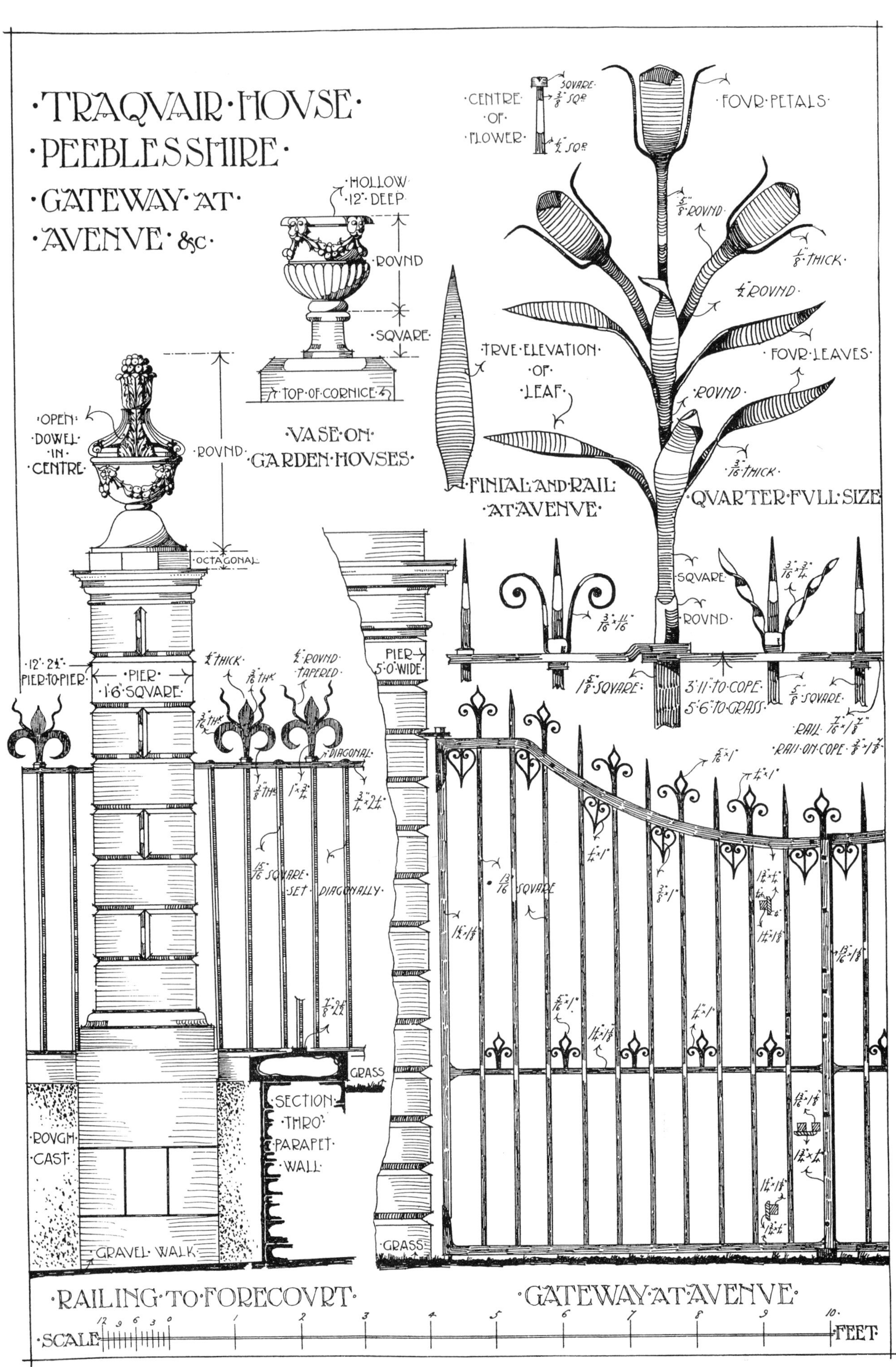
·TRAQVAIR·HOVSE·
·PEEBLESSHIRE·
·GATEWAY·AT·
·AVENVE·&c·
·HOLLOW·
·12"·DEEP·
·ROVND·
·SQVARE·
·TOP·OF·CORNICE·
·VASE·ON·
·GARDEN·HOVSES·
·CENTRE·
·OF·
·FLOWER·
·FOVR·PETALS·
·TRVE·ELEVATION·
·OF·
·LEAF·
·FOVR·LEAVES·
·FINIAL·AND·RAIL·
·AT·AVENVE·
·QVARTER·FVLL·SIZE·
·OPEN·
·DOWEL·
·IN·
·CENTRE·
·OCTAGONAL·
·12'·2¼"·
PIER·TO·PIER·
·PIER·
·1'6"·SQVARE·
·PIER·
·5'·0"·WIDE·
·SQVARE·
·ROVND·
3'·11"·TO·COPE·
5'·6"·TO·GRASS·
·DIAGONAL·
SQVARE·
·SET·
DIAGONALLY·
·GRASS·
·SECTION·
·THRO'·
·PARAPET·
·WALL·
·ROVGH·
·CAST·
·GRAVEL·WALK·
·GRASS·
·RAILING·TO·FORECOVRT·
·GATEWAY·AT·AVENVE·
·SCALE·
·FEET·

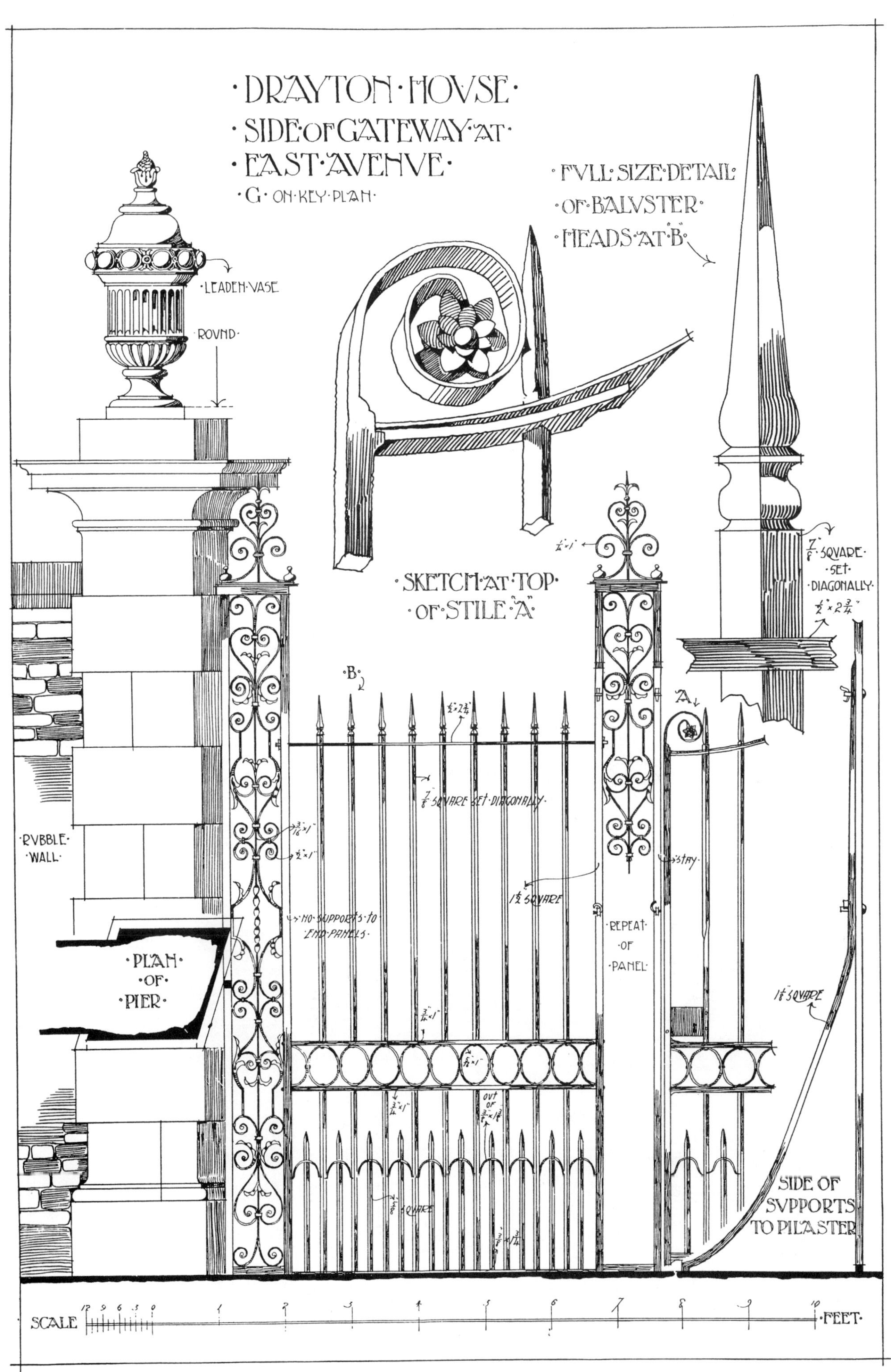
·DRAYTON·HOUSE·
·SIDE·OF·GATEWAY·AT·
·EAST·AVENUE·
·G·ON·KEY·PLAN·
·FULL·SIZE·DETAIL·
·OF·BALUSTER·
·HEADS·AT·B·
·LEADEN·VASE
·ROUND·
·SKETCH·AT·TOP·
·OF·STILE·"A"·
·RUBBLE·
·WALL·
·PLAN·
·OF·
·PIER·
·REPEAT·
·OF·
·PANEL·
·NO·SUPPORTS·TO·
·END·PANELS·
$\frac{7}{8}$ SQUARE SET DIAGONALLY
$1\frac{1}{2}$ SQUARE
$1\frac{1}{8}$ SQUARE
STAY
·SET·
·DIAGONALLY·
SIDE OF
SUPPORTS
TO PILASTER
SCALE
·FEET·

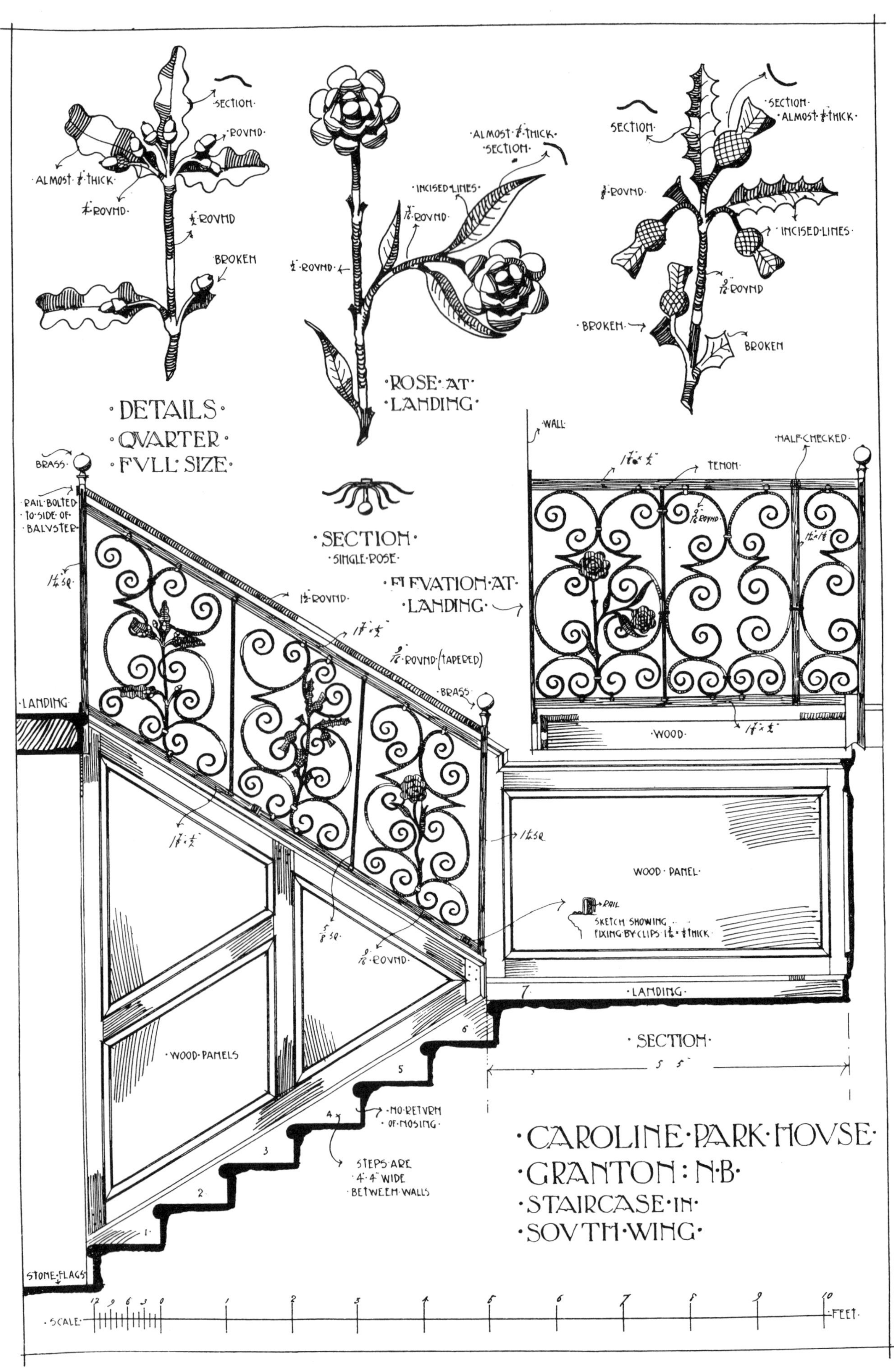
·DETAILS·
·QUARTER·
·FULL SIZE·
·ROSE·AT·
·LANDING·
·SECTION·
SINGLE·ROSE·
·ELEVATION·AT·
·LANDING·
·SECTION·
·WOOD·PANELS
WOOD·PANEL·
·LANDING·
·CAROLINE·PARK·HOUSE·
·GRANTON: N·B·
·STAIRCASE·IN·
·SOUTH·WING·
·SCALE·
·FEET·

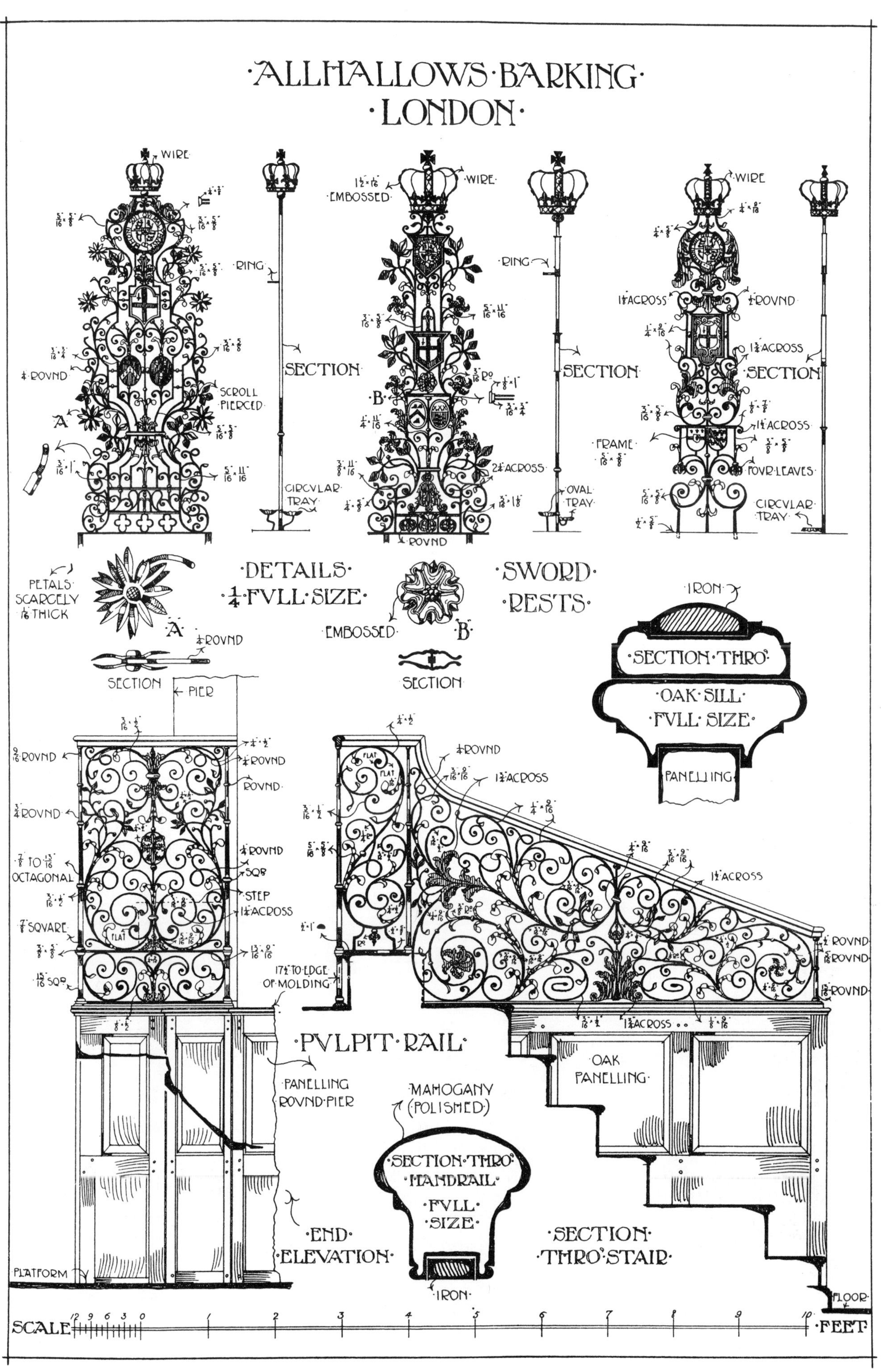
·ALLHALLOWS·BARKING·
·LONDON·
WIRE
EMBOSSED
RING
SECTION
SCROLL PIERCED
ROVND
CIRCVLAR TRAY
OVAL TRAY
ACROSS
FRAME
FOVR LEAVES
PETALS SCARCELY 1/16 THICK
·DETAILS·
·¼·FVLL·SIZE·
·SWORD·
·RESTS·
SECTION
PIER
IRON
·SECTION·THRO·
·OAK·SILL·
·FVLL·SIZE·
PANELLING
OCTAGONAL
SQVARE
STEP
FLAT
17¼ TO EDGE OF MOLDING
·PVLPIT·RAIL·
PANELLING ROVND PIER
MAHOGANY (POLISHED)
OAK PANELLING
·SECTION·THRO·
·HANDRAIL·
·FVLL·
·SIZE·
·END·
·ELEVATION·
·SECTION·
·THRO·STAIR·
PLATFORM
FLOOR
SCALE
FEET

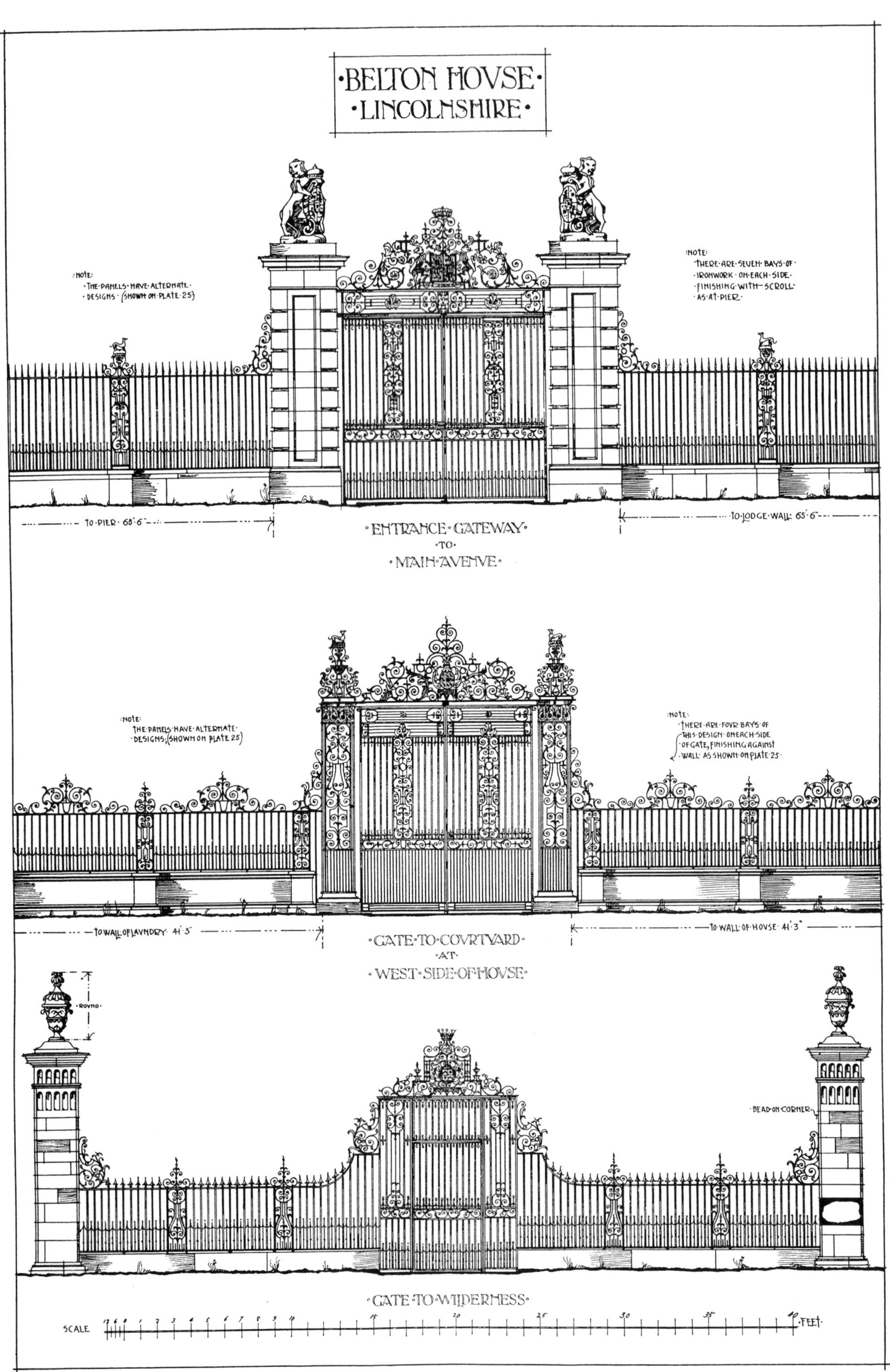
·BELTON HOVSE·
·LINCOLNSHIRE·
:NOTE:
·THE·PANELS·HAVE·ALTERNATE·
·DESIGNS·(SHOWN ON·PLATE·25)
:NOTE:
THERE·ARE·SEVEN·BAYS·OF·
·IRONWORK·ON·EACH·SIDE·
·FINISHING·WITH SCROLL·
·AS·AT·PIER·
TO·PIER·65'·6"
TO·LODGE·WALL·65'·6"
·ENTRANCE·GATEWAY·
·TO·
·MAIN·AVENVE·
:NOTE:
THE·PANELS·HAVE·ALTERNATE·
·DESIGNS;(SHOWN ON PLATE 25)
:NOTE:
·THERE·ARE·FOVR·BAYS·OF
THIS·DESIGN·ON EACH·SIDE
·OF GATE, FINISHING AGAINST
·WALL·AS SHOWN·ON PLATE·25·
TO WALL OF LAVNDRY 41'·3"
TO·WALL·OF·HOVSE·41'·3"
·GATE·TO·COVRTYARD·
·AT·
·WEST·SIDE·OF·HOVSE·
·ROVND·
BEAD·ON·CORNER
·GATE·TO·WILDERNESS·
SCALE 12 6 0 1 2 3 4 5 6 7 8 9 10 15 20 25 30 35 40 FEET

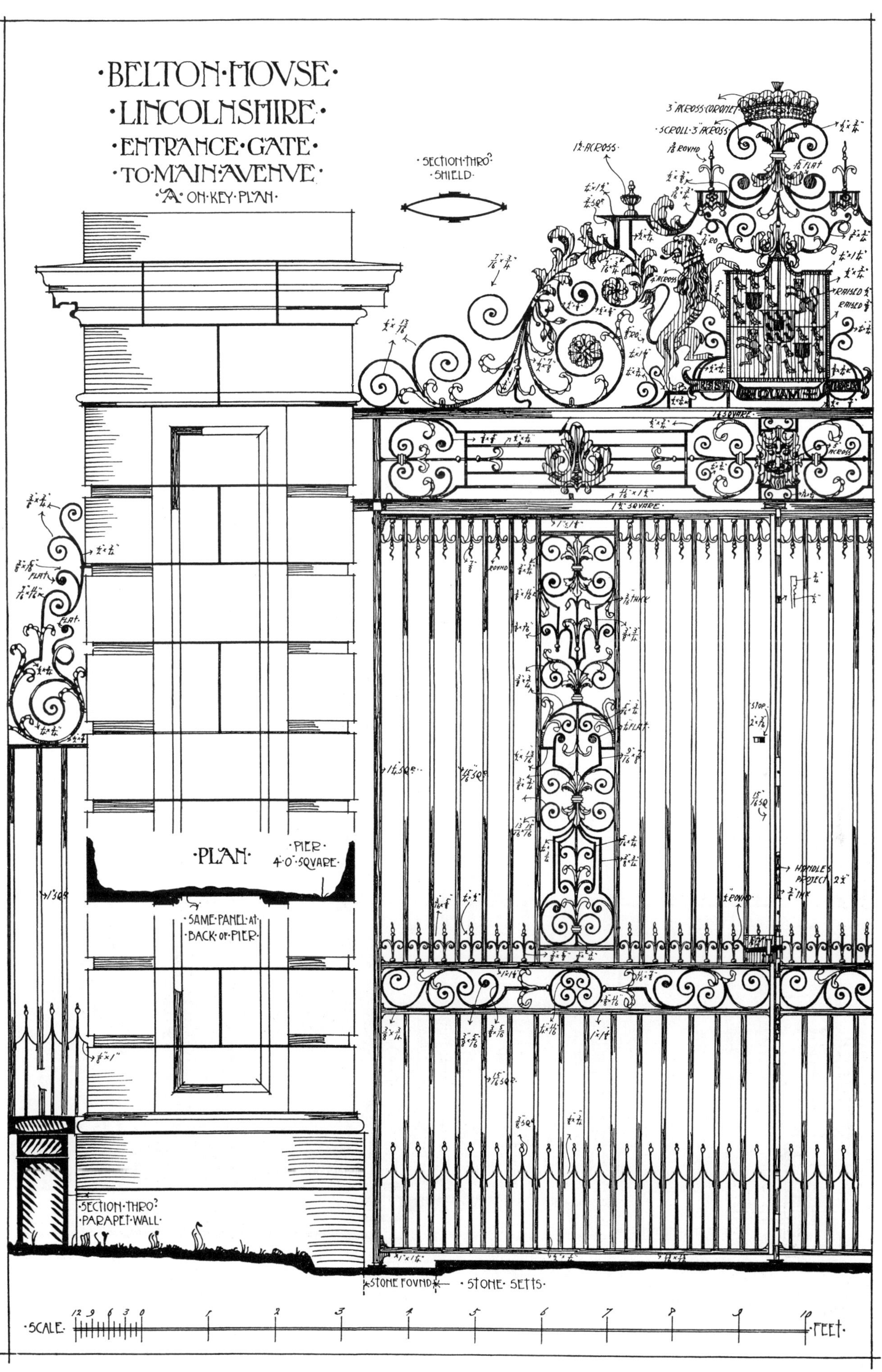
·BELTON·HOUSE·
·LINCOLNSHIRE·
·ENTRANCE·GATE·
·TO·MAIN·AVENUE·
·"A" ON·KEY·PLAN·
·SECTION·THRO? SHIELD·
3" ACROSS CORONET
·SCROLL·3" ACROSS·
·PLAN·
·PIER· 4'·0" SQUARE·
·SAME·PANEL·AT· BACK·OF·PIER·
HANDLES PROJECT 2½"
·SECTION·THRO? ·PARAPET·WALL·
·STONE FOUND·
·STONE· SETTS·
·SCALE·
·FEET·

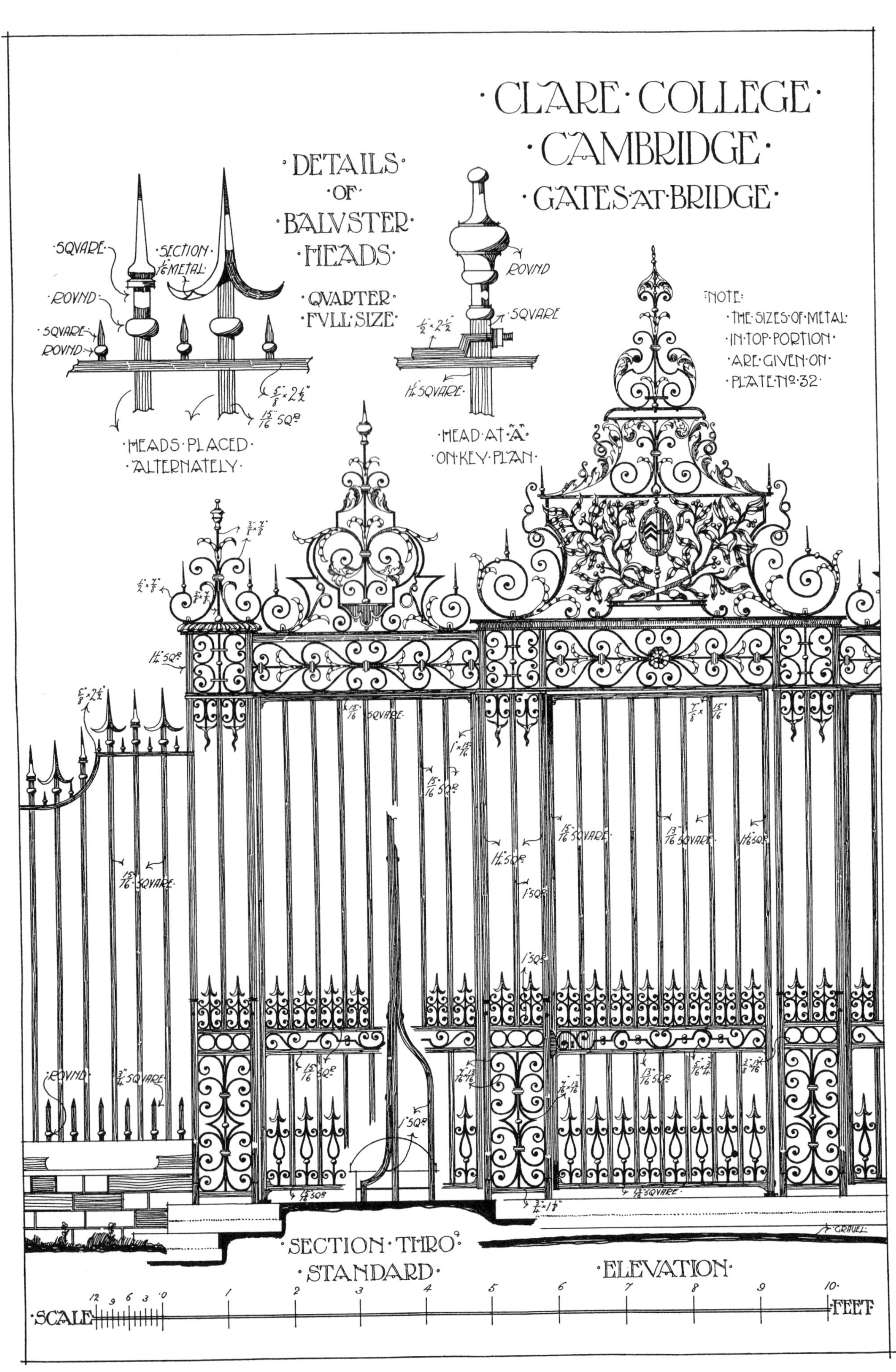
·CLARE·COLLEGE·
·CAMBRIDGE·
·GATES·AT·BRIDGE·
·DETAILS·
·OF·
·BALVSTER·
·HEADS·
·QVARTER·
·FVLL·SIZE·
·NOTE:
·THE·SIZES·OF·METAL·
·IN·TOP·PORTION·
·ARE·GIVEN·ON·
·PLATE·No·32·
·HEADS·PLACED·
·ALTERNATELY·
·HEAD·AT·"A"·
·ON·KEY·PLAN·
·SECTION·THRO·
·STANDARD·
·ELEVATION·
·SCALE·
·FEET·

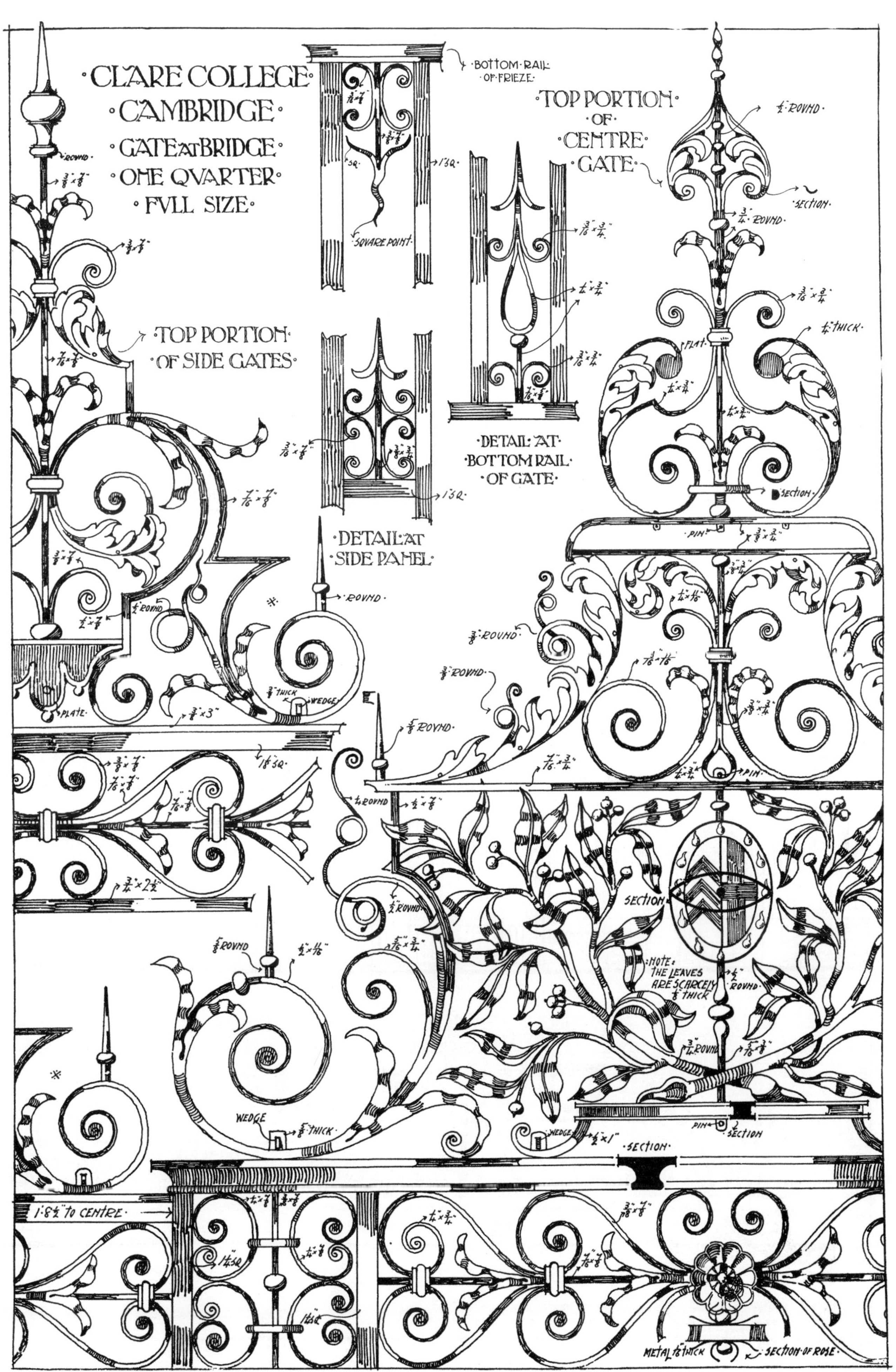
CLARE COLLEGE
CAMBRIDGE
GATE AT BRIDGE
ONE QUARTER
FULL SIZE
TOP PORTION OF SIDE GATES
BOTTOM RAIL OF FRIEZE
SQUARE POINT
DETAIL AT SIDE PANEL
DETAIL AT BOTTOM RAIL OF GATE
TOP PORTION OF CENTRE GATE
SECTION
FLAT
THICK
ROUND
PLATE
WEDGE
PIN
NOTE: THE LEAVES ARE SCARCELY 1/8" THICK
1'·8¼" TO CENTRE
METAL 1/16" THICK
SECTION OF ROSE

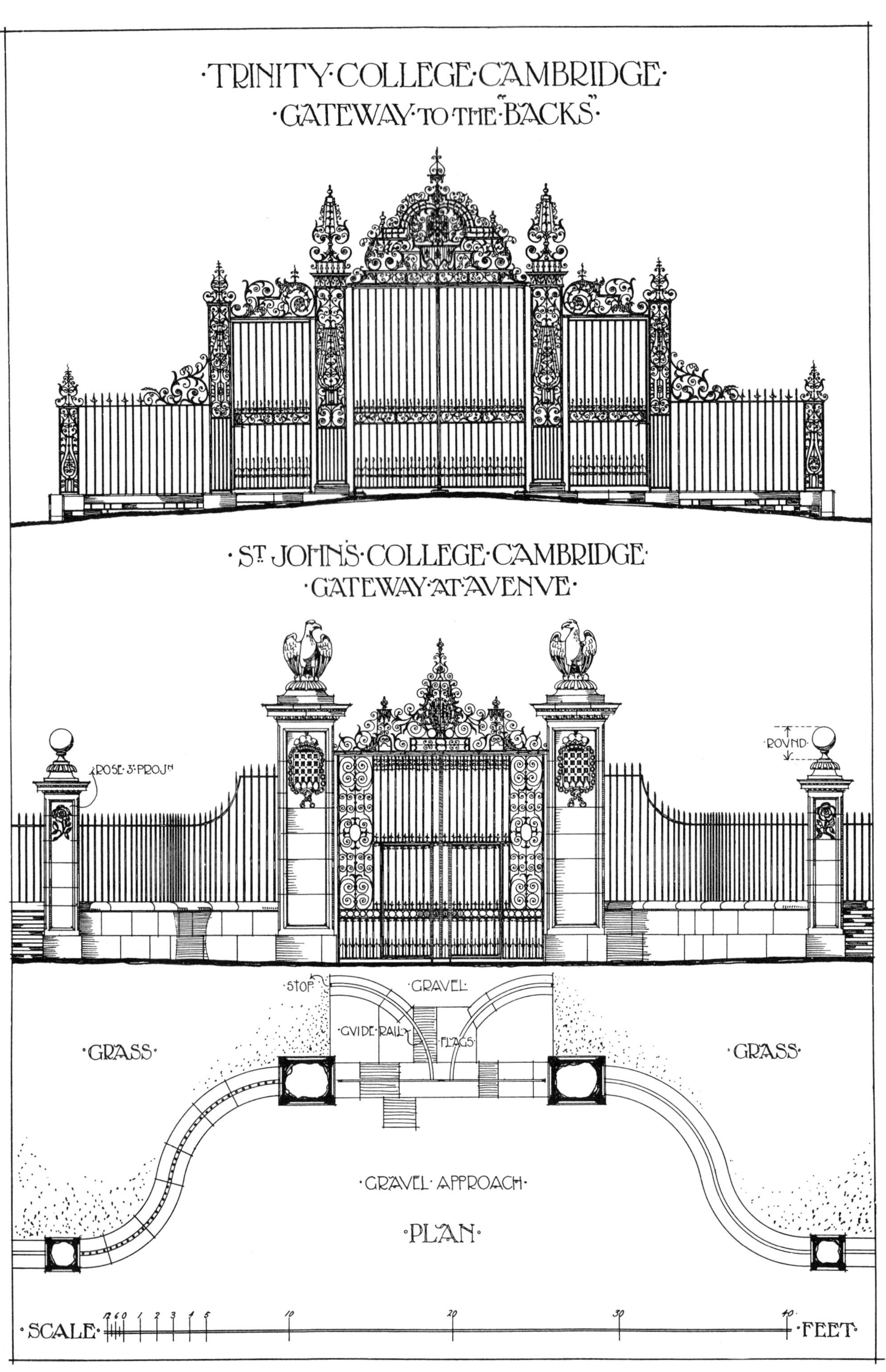
·TRINITY·COLLEGE·CAMBRIDGE·
·GATEWAY·TO·THE·"BACKS"·
·ST JOHN'S·COLLEGE·CAMBRIDGE·
·GATEWAY·AT·AVENVE·
ROSE 3" PROJn
·ROVND·
·STOP·
·GRAVEL·
·GVIDE·RAIL·
·FLAGS·
·GRASS·
·GRASS·
·GRAVEL·APPROACH·
·PLAN·
·SCALE·
12 6 0 1 2 3 4 5 10 20 30 40
·FEET·

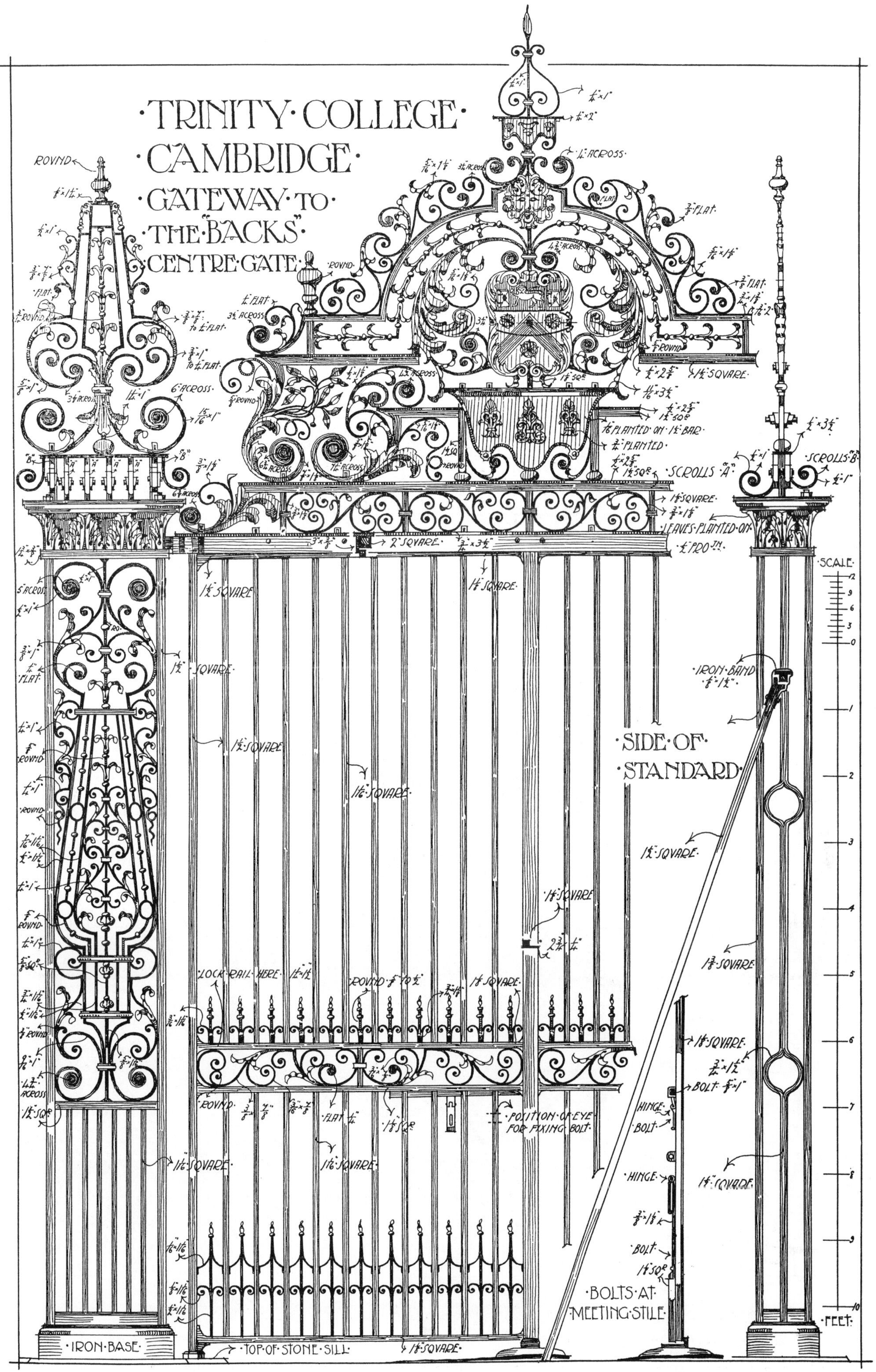
·TRINITY·COLLEGE·
·CAMBRIDGE·
·GATEWAY·TO·
·THE·"BACKS"·
·CENTRE·GATE·
·SIDE·OF·
·STANDARD·
·SCALE·
·FEET·
·IRON·BASE·
·TOP·OF·STONE·SILL·
·BOLTS·AT·
·MEETING·STILE·
·LOCK·RAIL·HERE·
·POSITION·OF·EYE·
FOR·FIXING·BOLT·
·IRON·BAND·
·SCROLLS·"A"·
·SCROLLS·"B"·
·LEAVES·PLANTED·ON·
·HINGE·
·BOLT·

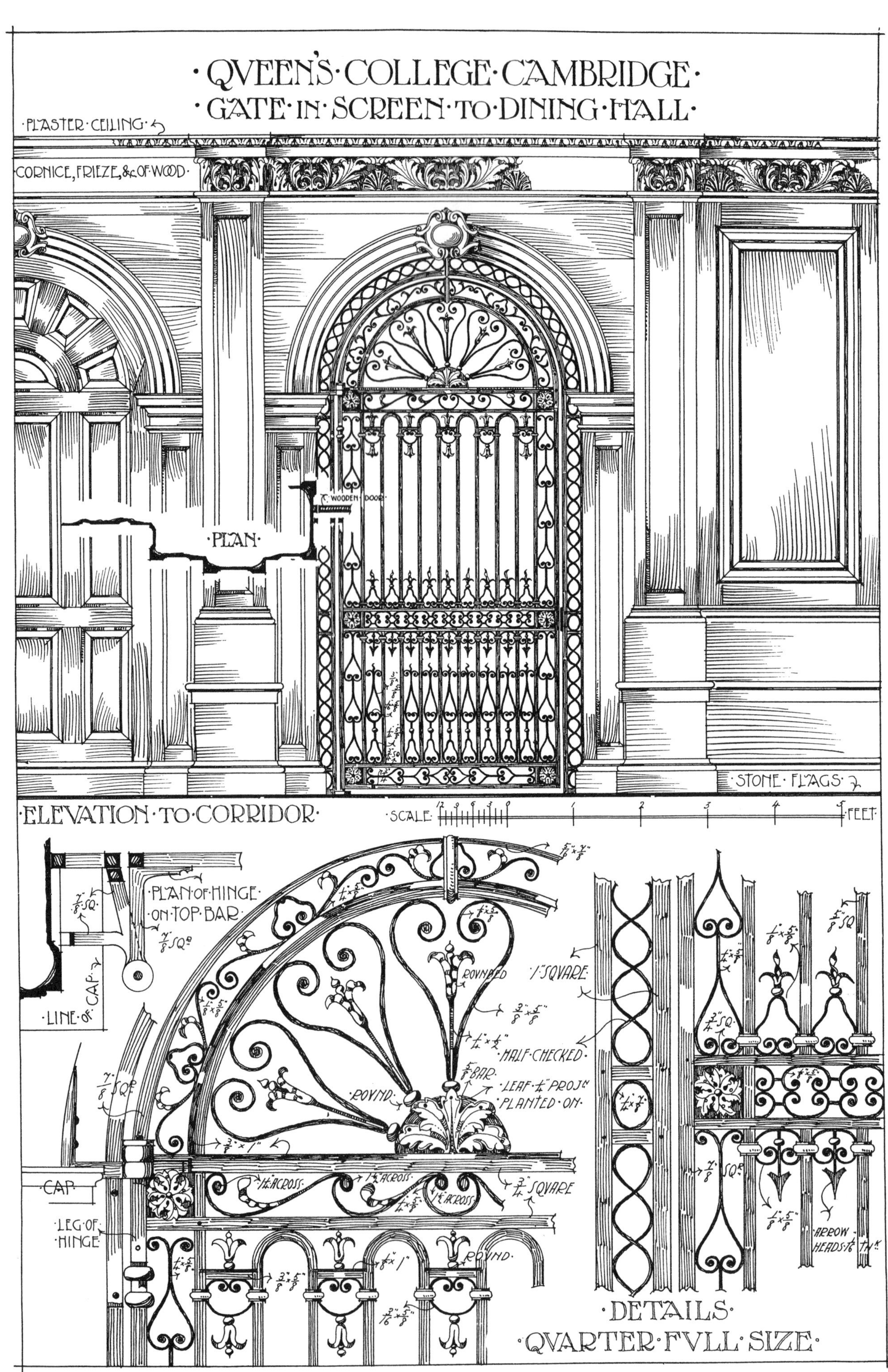
·QVEEN'S·COLLEGE·CAMBRIDGE·
·GATE·IN·SCREEN·TO·DINING·HALL·
·PLASTER·CEILING·
CORNICE, FRIEZE, &c OF WOOD
·PLAN·
WOODEN DOOR
·STONE·FLAGS·
·ELEVATION·TO·CORRIDOR·
·SCALE·
FEET
·PLAN·OF·HINGE·ON·TOP·BAR·
·LINE·OF·CAP·
·CAP·
·LEG·OF·HINGE·
ROVNDED
1" SQVARE
HALF·CHECKED
·LEAF·PROJN·PLANTED·ON·
ROVND
ACROSS
SQVARE
ROVND
ARROW HEADS
·DETAILS·
·QVARTER·FVLL·SIZE·

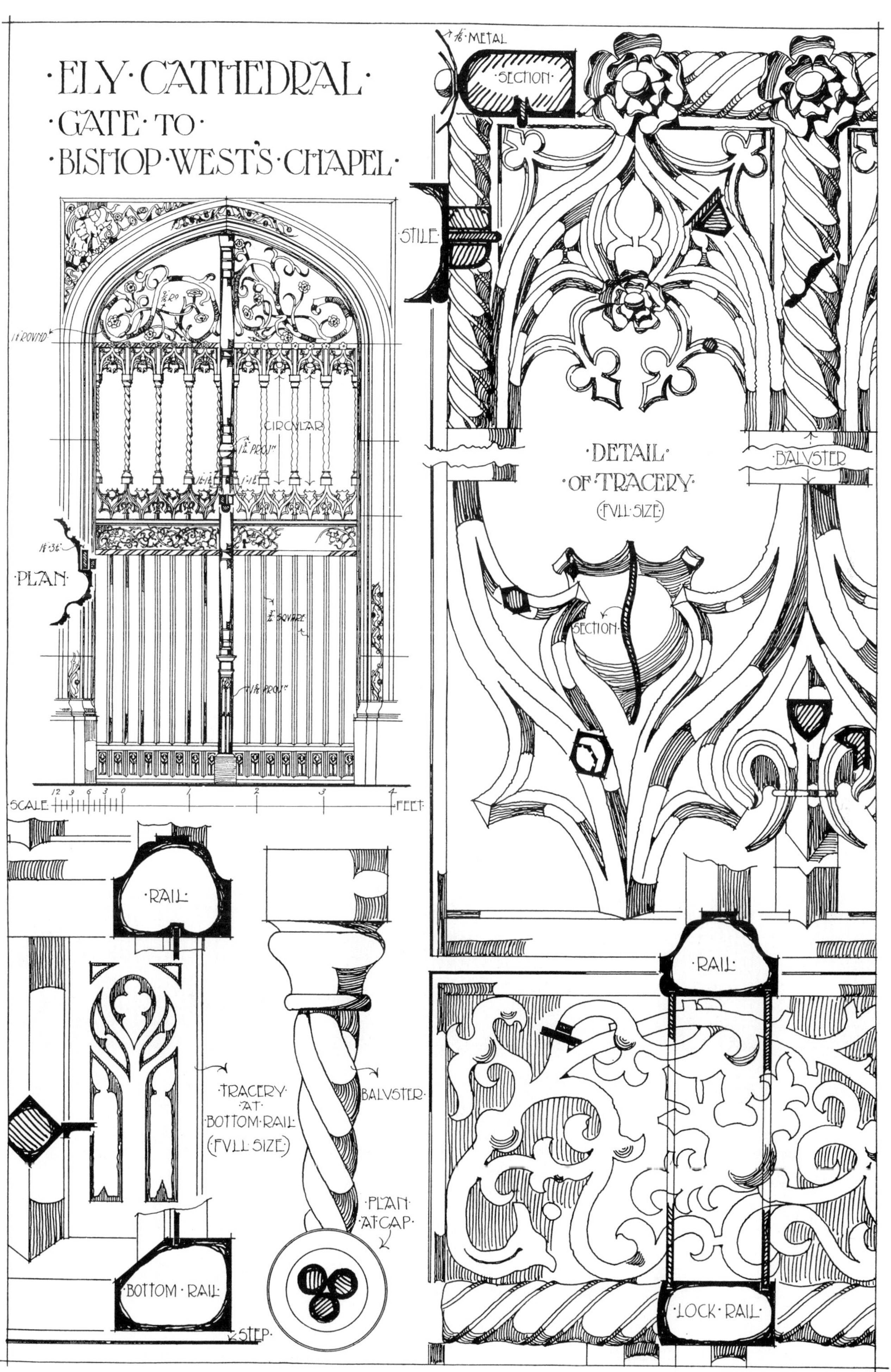
·ELY·CATHEDRAL·
·GATE·TO·
·BISHOP·WEST'S·CHAPEL·
1/8·METAL
·SECTION·
·STILE·
CIRCULAR
·PLAN·
SCALE
FEET
·DETAIL·
·OF·TRACERY·
(FULL·SIZE)
·BALUSTER·
·SECTION·
·RAIL·
·TRACERY·
·AT·
·BOTTOM·RAIL·
(FULL·SIZE)
BALUSTER·
·PLAN·
·AT·CAP·
·BOTTOM·RAIL·
STEP
·RAIL·
·LOCK·RAIL·

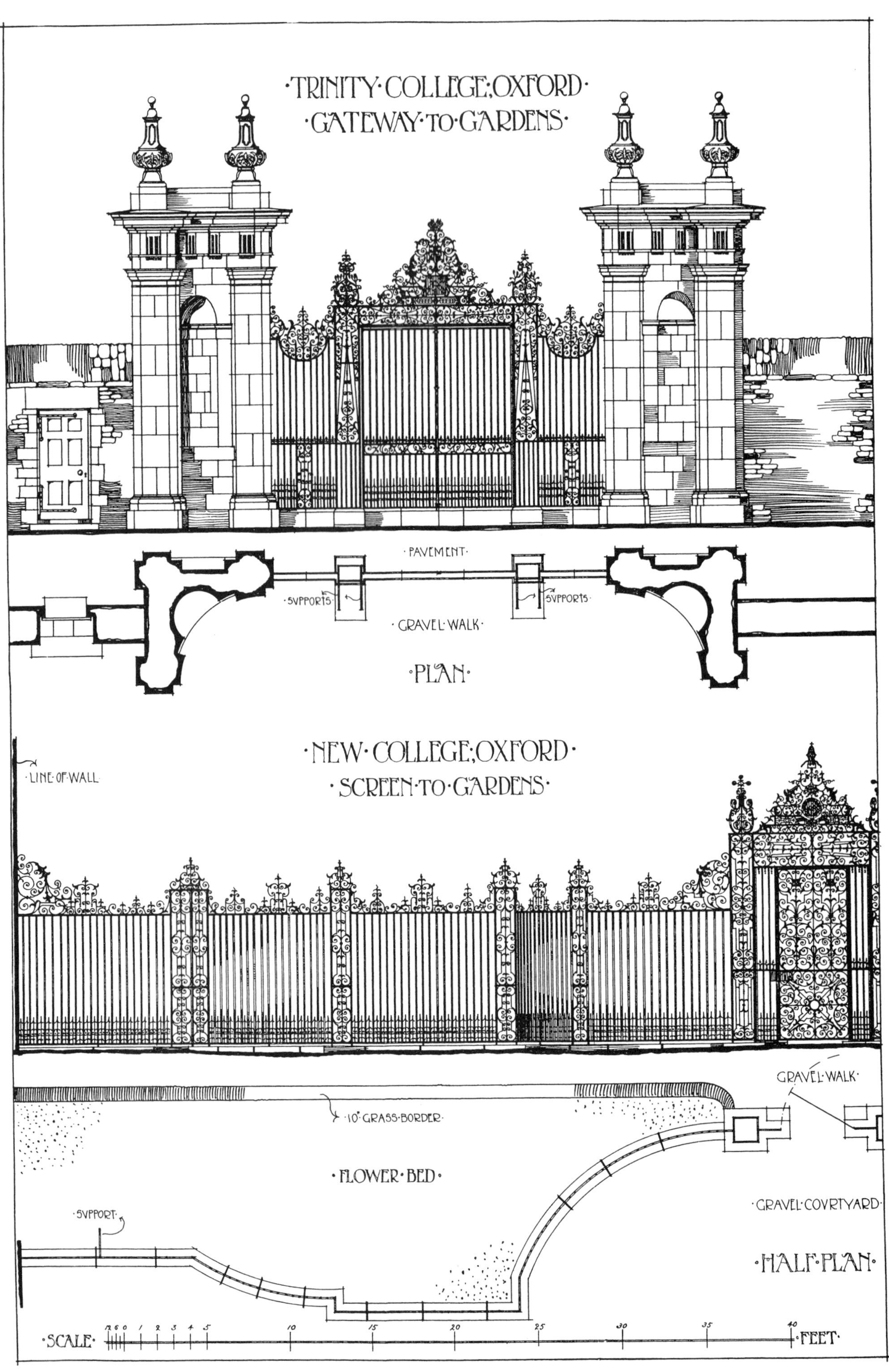
·TRINITY·COLLEGE;OXFORD·
·GATEWAY·TO·GARDENS·
·PAVEMENT·
·SUPPORTS·
·SUPPORTS·
·GRAVEL·WALK·
·PLAN·
·NEW·COLLEGE;OXFORD·
·SCREEN·TO·GARDENS·
·LINE·OF·WALL
·10'·GRASS·BORDER·
·GRAVEL·WALK·
·FLOWER·BED·
·SUPPORT·
·GRAVEL·COURTYARD·
·HALF·PLAN·
·SCALE·
12 6 0 1 2 3 4 5 10 15 20 25 30 35 40
·FEET·

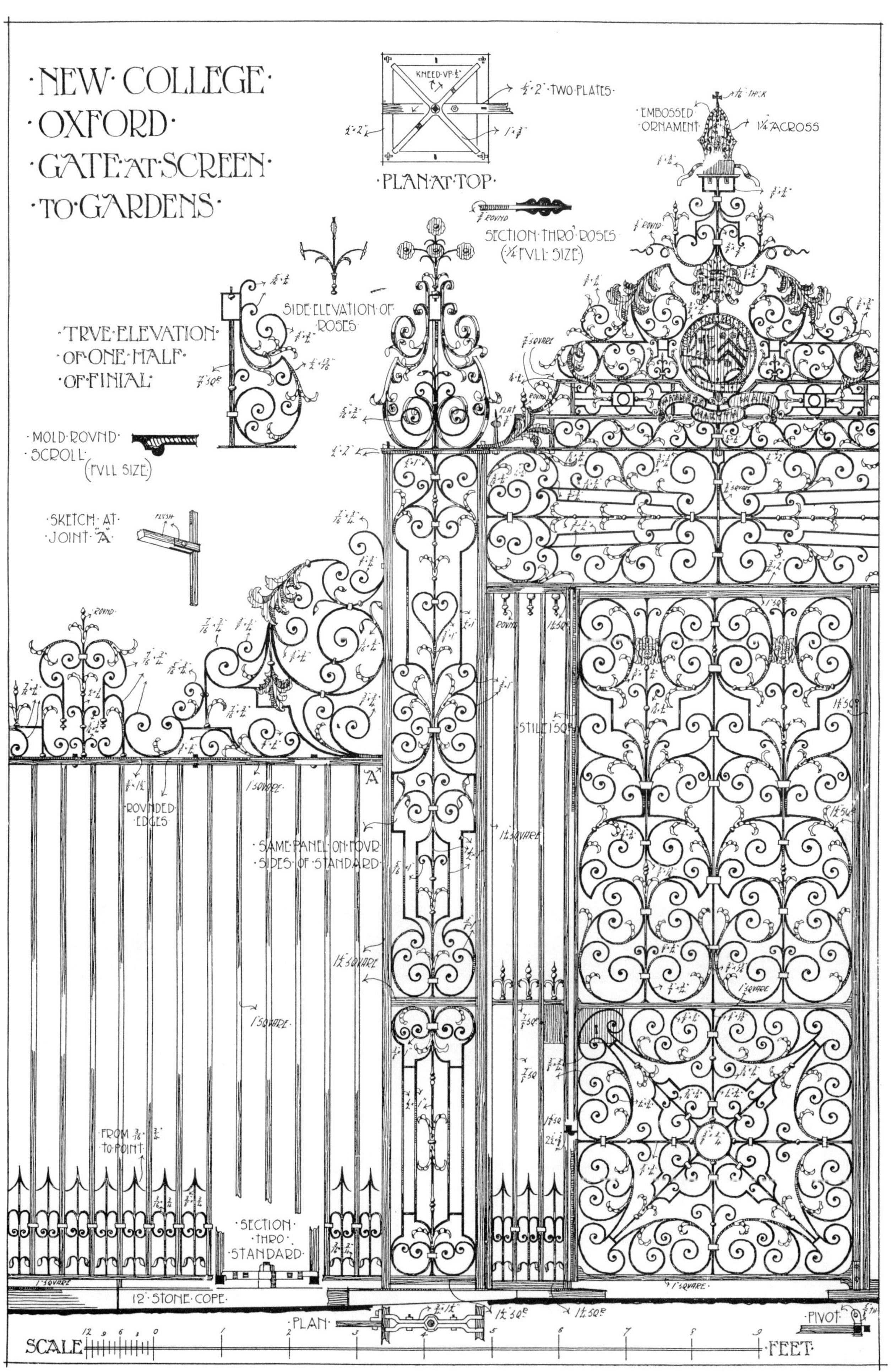

·NEW·COLLEGE·
·OXFORD·
·GATE·AT·SCREEN·
·TO·GARDENS·
·PLAN·AT·TOP·
TWO·PLATES
·EMBOSSED·
·ORNAMENT·
1¼" ACROSS
SECTION·THRO·ROSES
(¼ FVLL·SIZE)
SIDE·ELEVATION·OF·
·ROSES·
·TRVE·ELEVATION·
·OF·ONE·HALF·
·OF·FINIAL·
·MOLD·ROVND·
·SCROLL·
(FVLL·SIZE)
·SKETCH·AT·
·JOINT·"A"·
·ROVNDED·
EDGES·
·SAME·PANEL·ON·FOVR·
·SIDES·OF·STANDARD·
·STILE·1½ SQ·
·FROM
·TO·POINT·
·SECTION·
·THRO·
·STANDARD·
12" STONE·COPE·
·PLAN·
·PIVOT·
SCALE
·FEET·

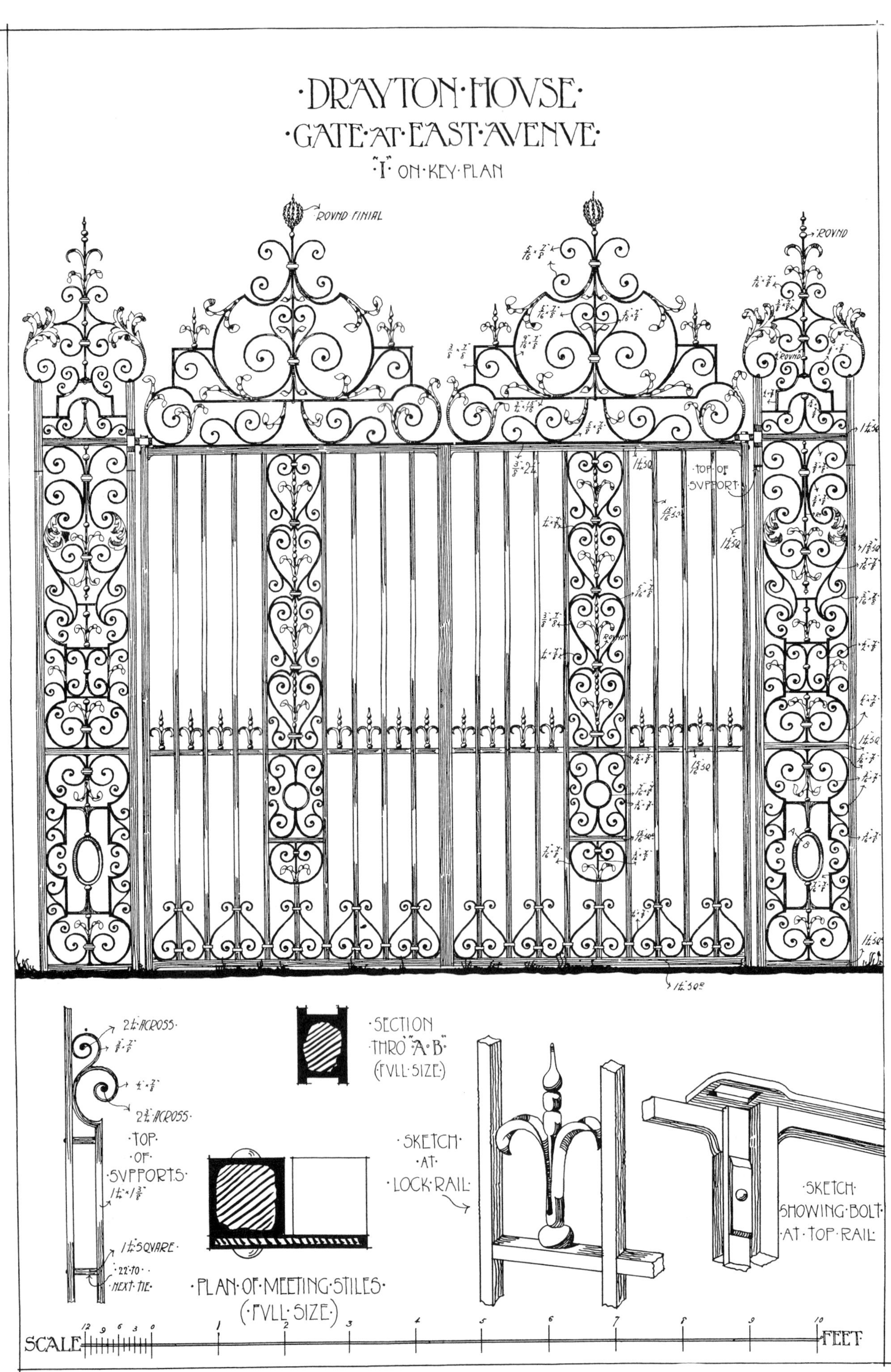

·DRAYTON·HOUSE·
·GATE·AT·EAST·AVENUE·
"I" ON·KEY·PLAN
ROUND FINIAL
ROUND
TOP OF SUPPORT
2¼ ACROSS
2¼ ACROSS
·TOP·OF·SUPPORTS·
1¼ SQUARE
22 TO NEXT TIE
·SECTION THRO "A·B" (FULL·SIZE)
·PLAN·OF·MEETING·STILES· (·FULL·SIZE·)
·SKETCH·AT·LOCK·RAIL·
·SKETCH·SHOWING·BOLT·AT·TOP·RAIL·
SCALE
FEET

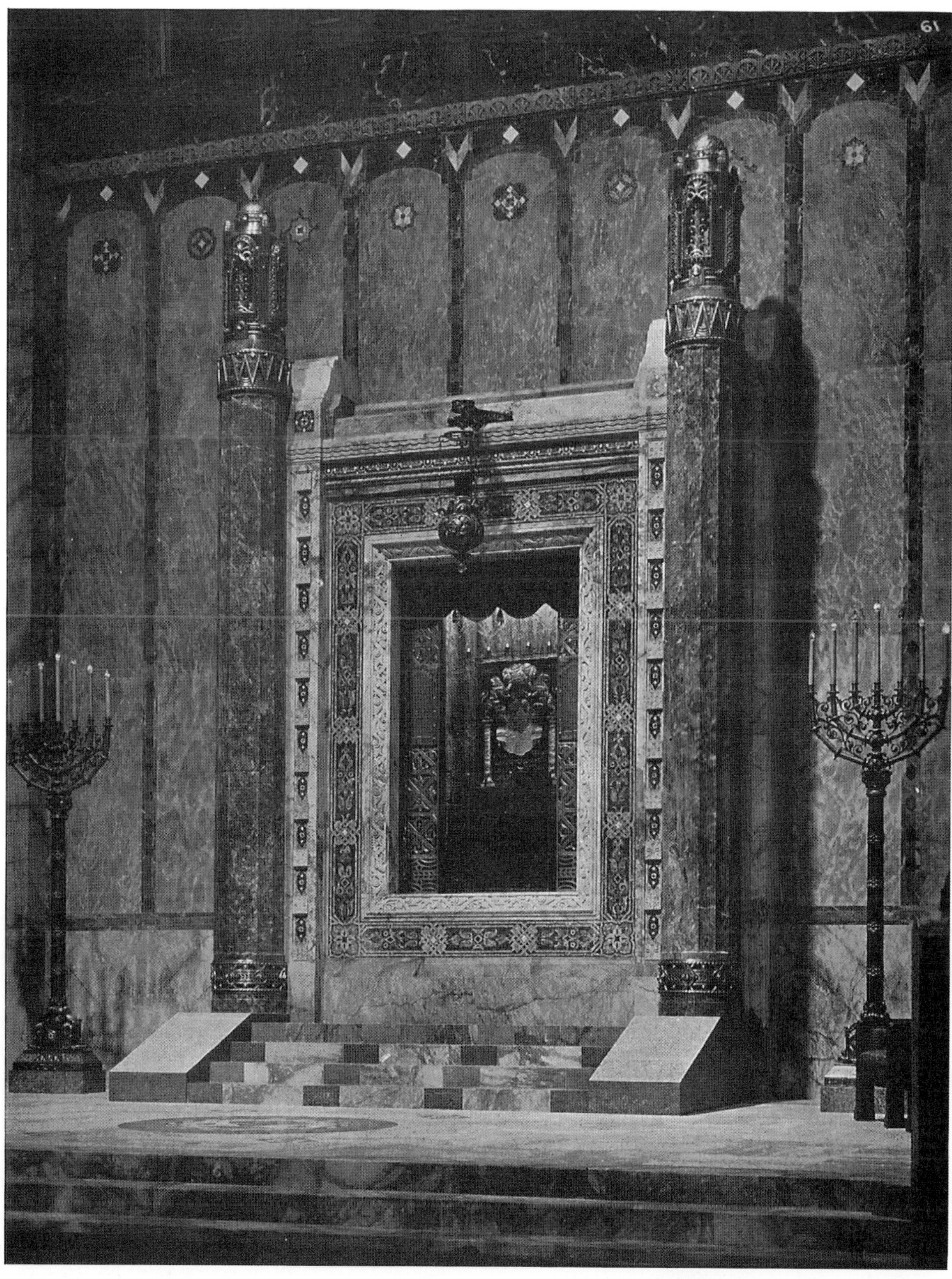

Courtesy The Metal Arts

R. D. Kohn, C. Butler & C. S. Stein, *Architects*
F. L. Mayers, O. H. Murray & H. Phillip, *Associate Architects*

The Ark of the Temple Emanu-el, New York City

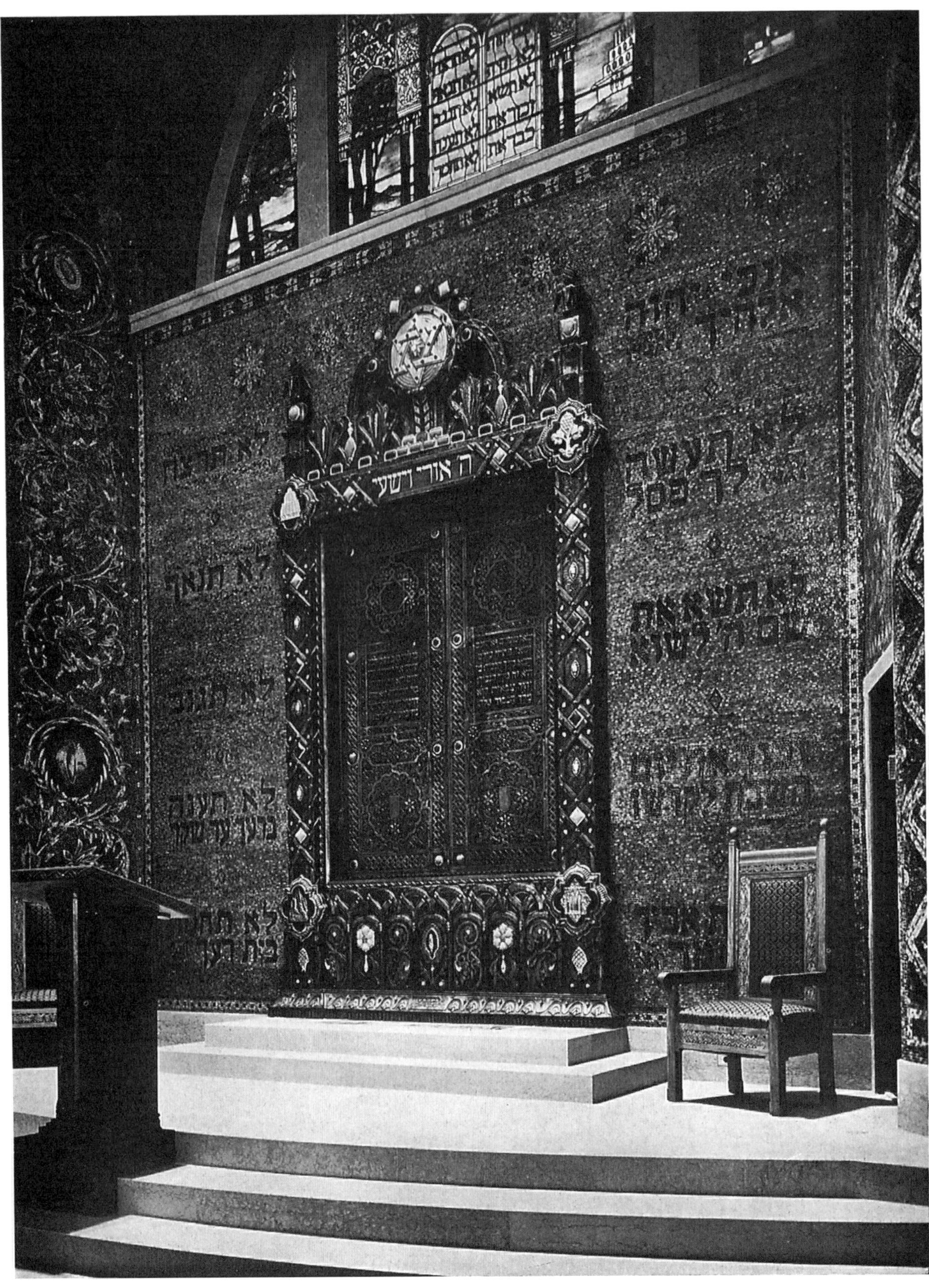

Courtesy The Metal Arts

R. D. Kohn, C. Butler & C. S. Stein, *Architects*
F. L. Mayers, O. H. Murray & H. Phillip, *Associate Architects*

The Ark of the Chapel, Temple Emanu-el, New York City

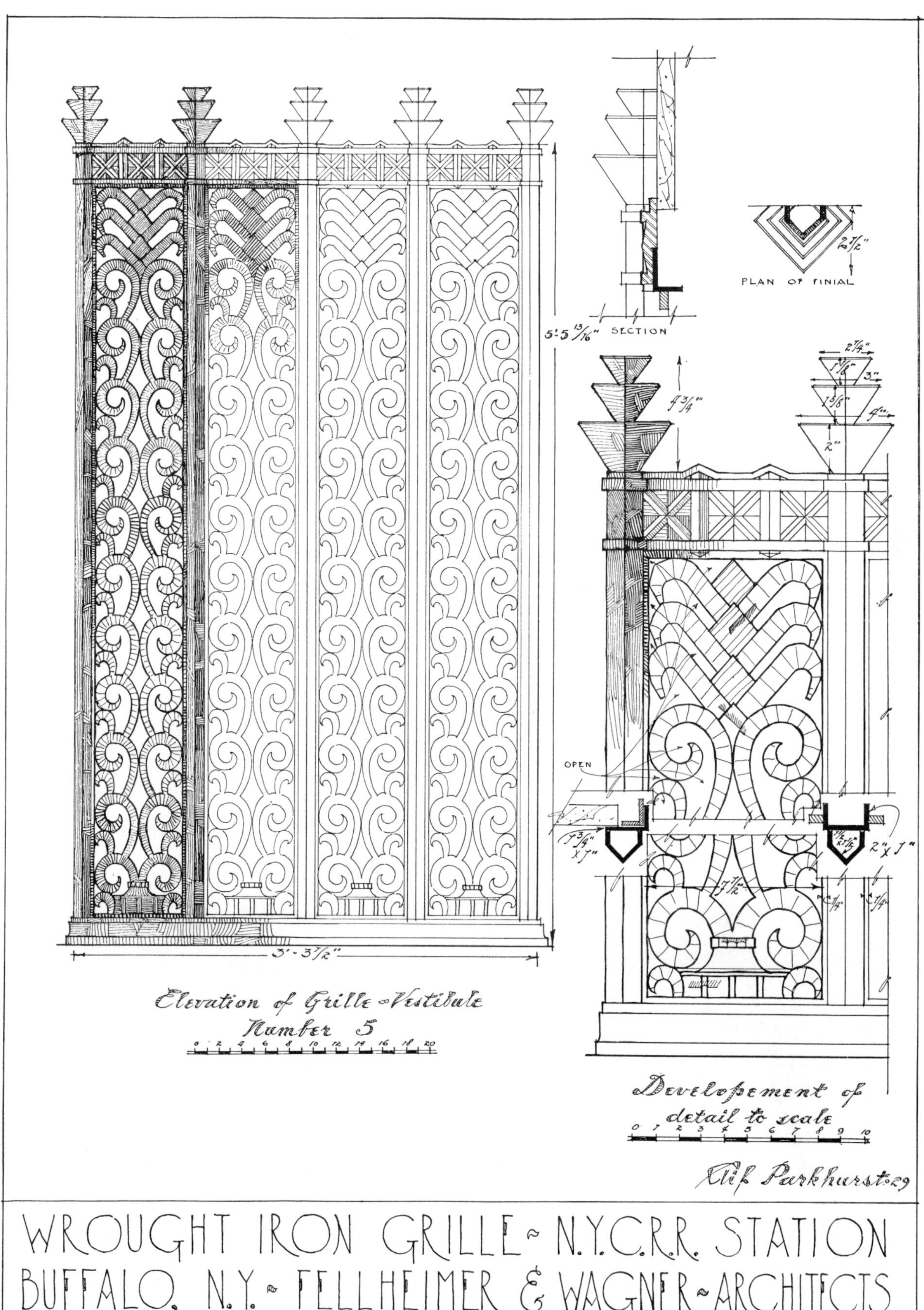

Courtesy of Metalcraft Magazine

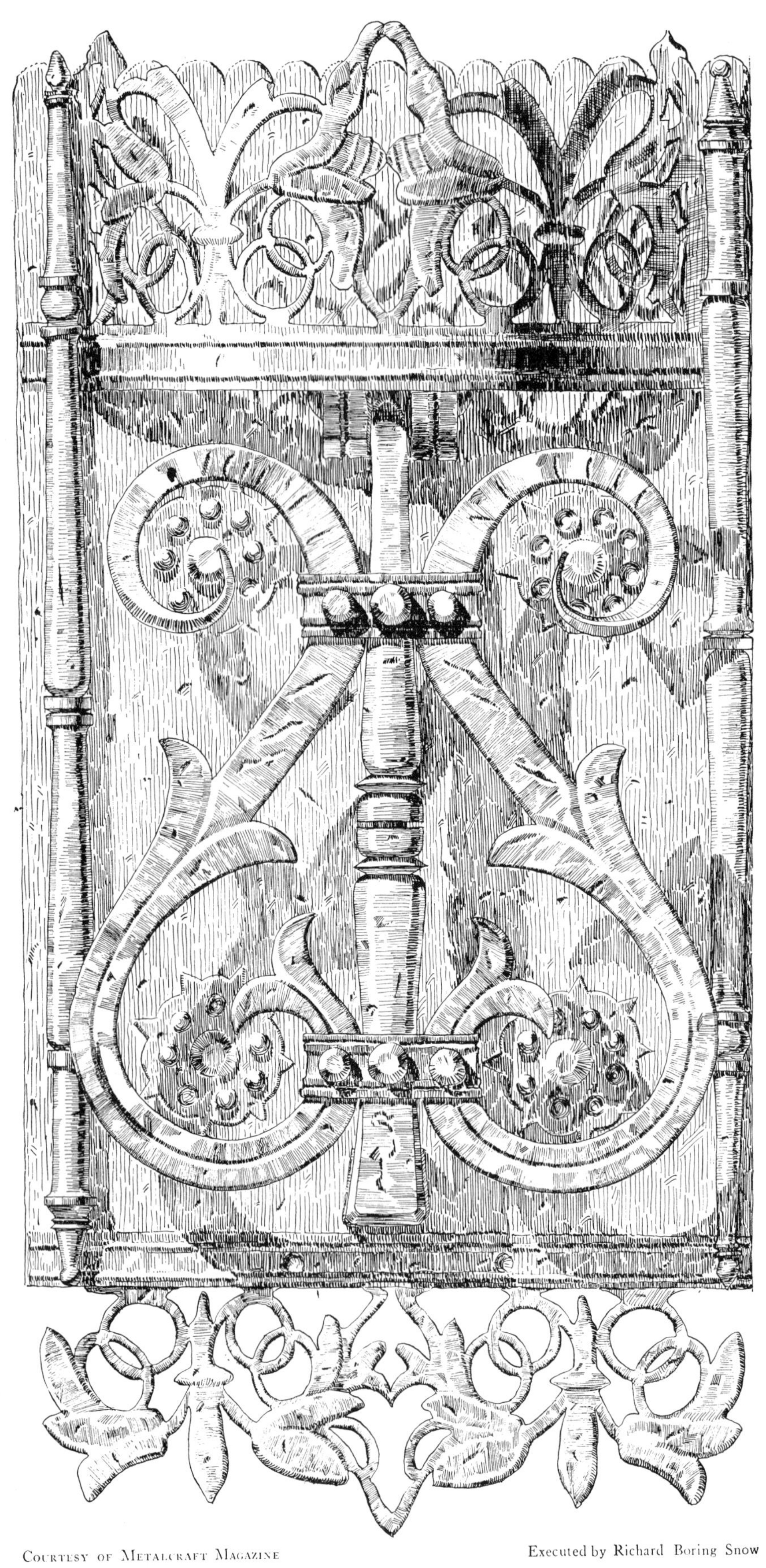

Courtesy of Metalcraft Magazine — Executed by Richard Boring Snow

Full Sized Drawing, Door Knocker, Spanish, XVII Century, Metropolitan Museum of Art

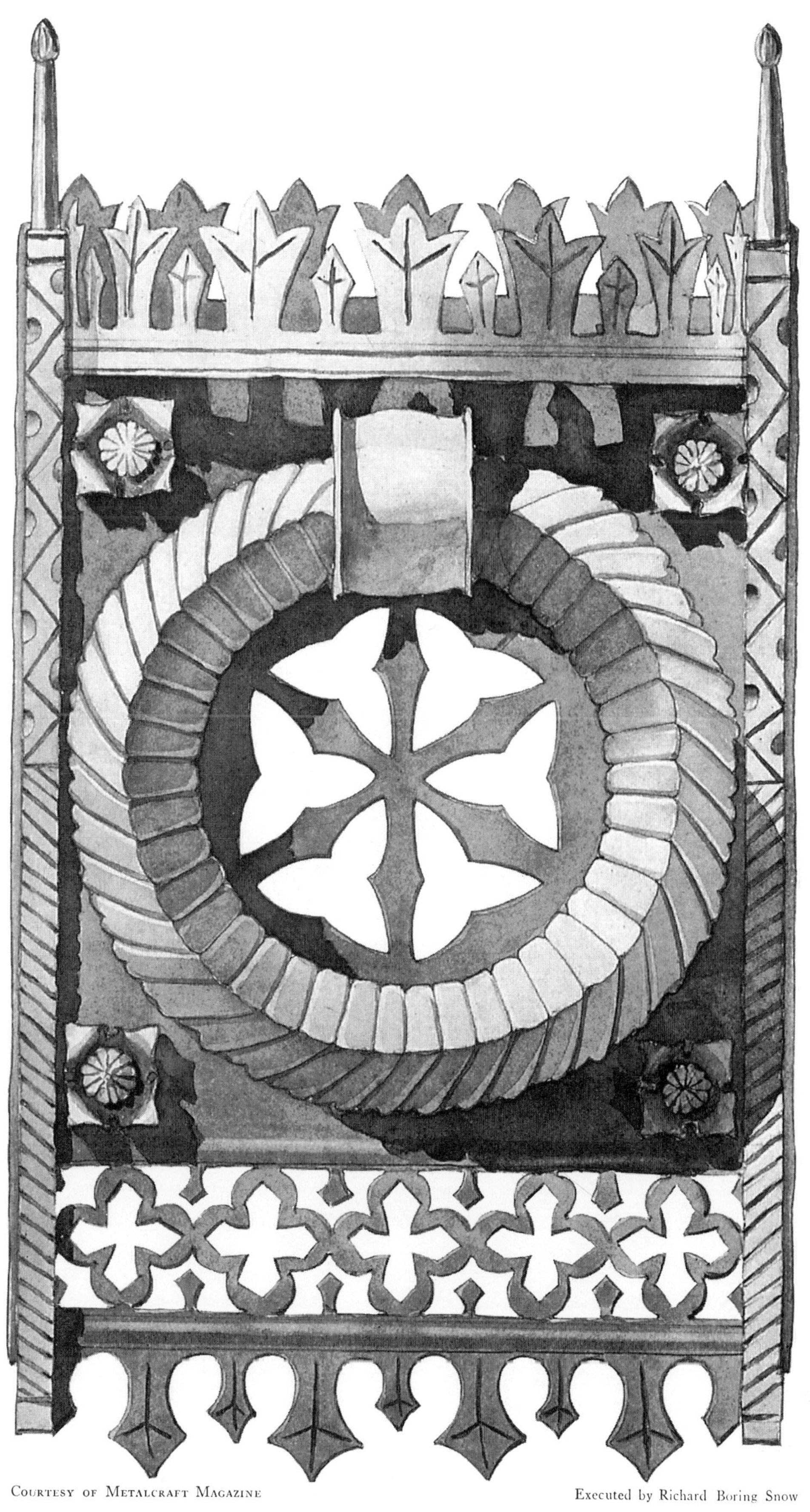

Courtesy of Metalcraft Magazine

Executed by Richard Boring Snow

Full Sized Drawing, Door Knocker, Mudejar Style, Spanish, 18th Century

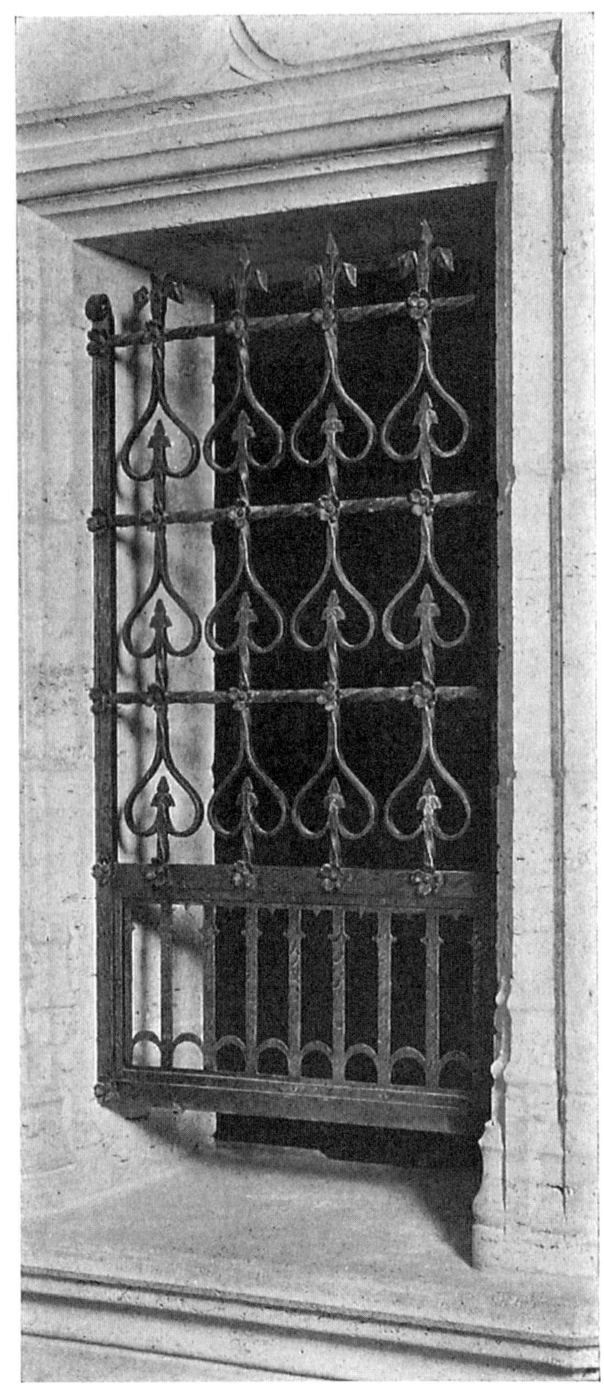

Courtesy of Metalcraft Magazine Raymond Hood, *Architect*

Grille of Wrought Iron, Scottish Rite Cathedral, Scranton, Pa.

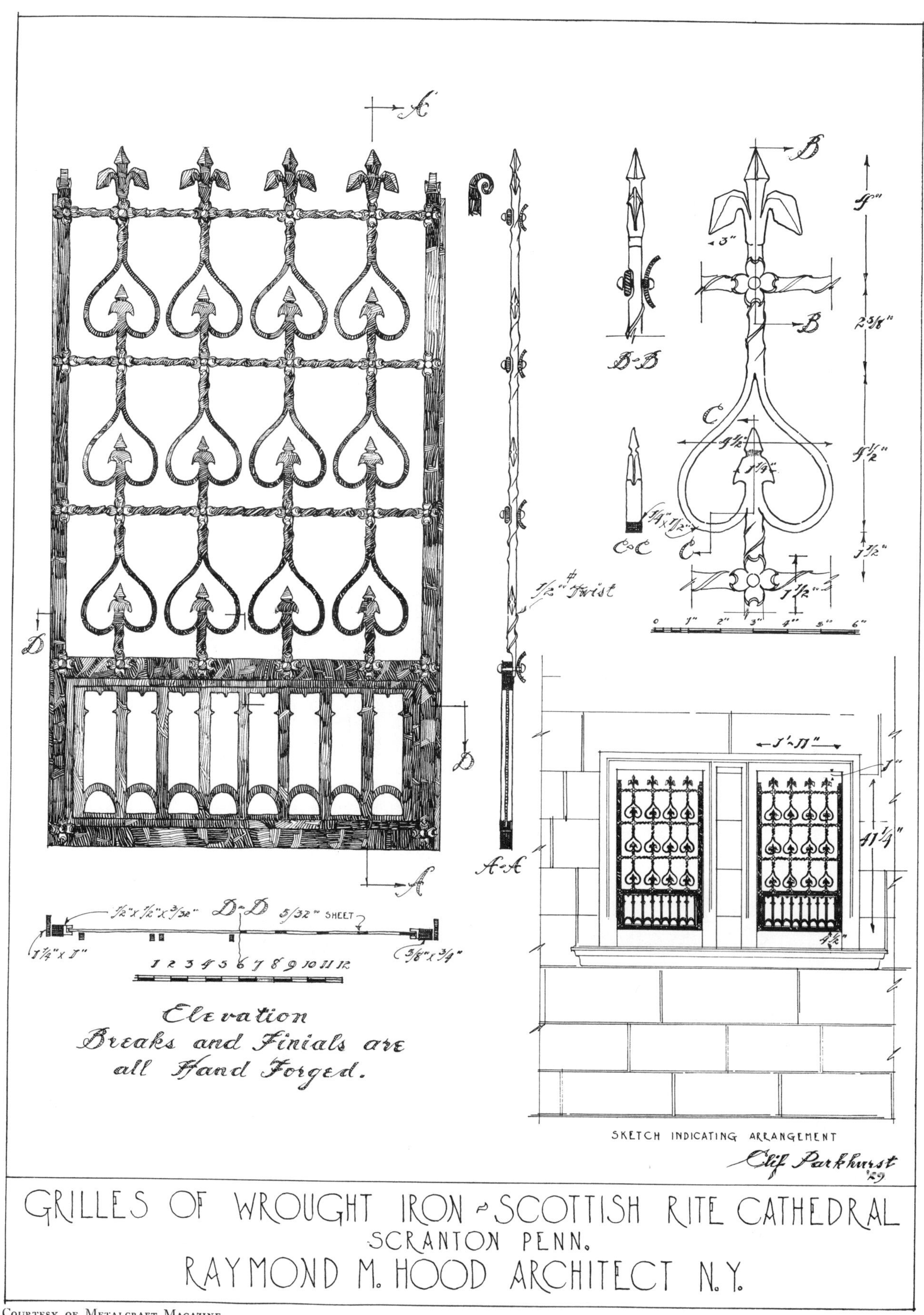

Courtesy of Metalcraft Magazine

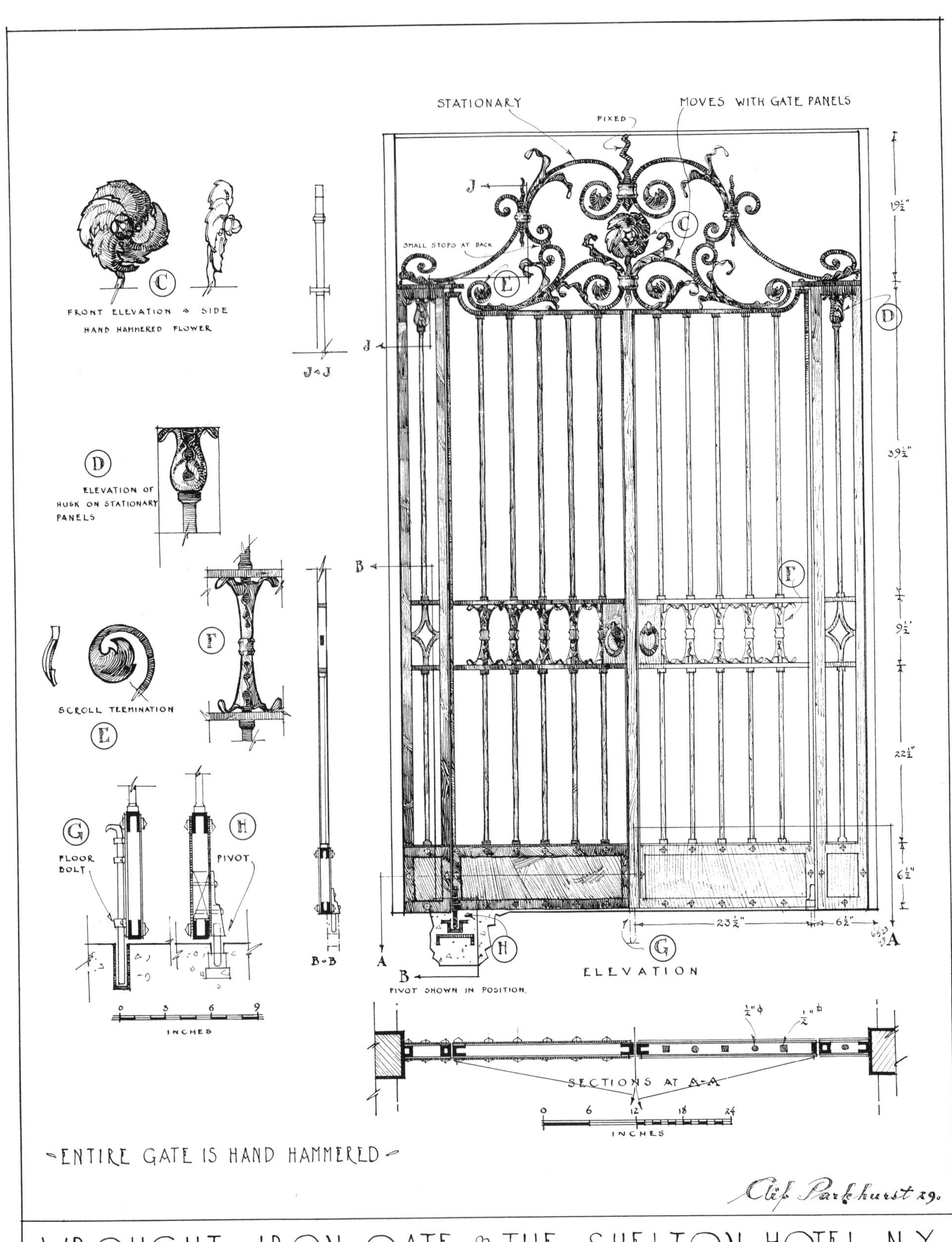

WROUGHT IRON GATE ~ THE SHELTON HOTEL N.Y.
ARTHUR LOOMIS HARMON ~ ARCHITECT.

Courtesy of Metalcraft Magazine

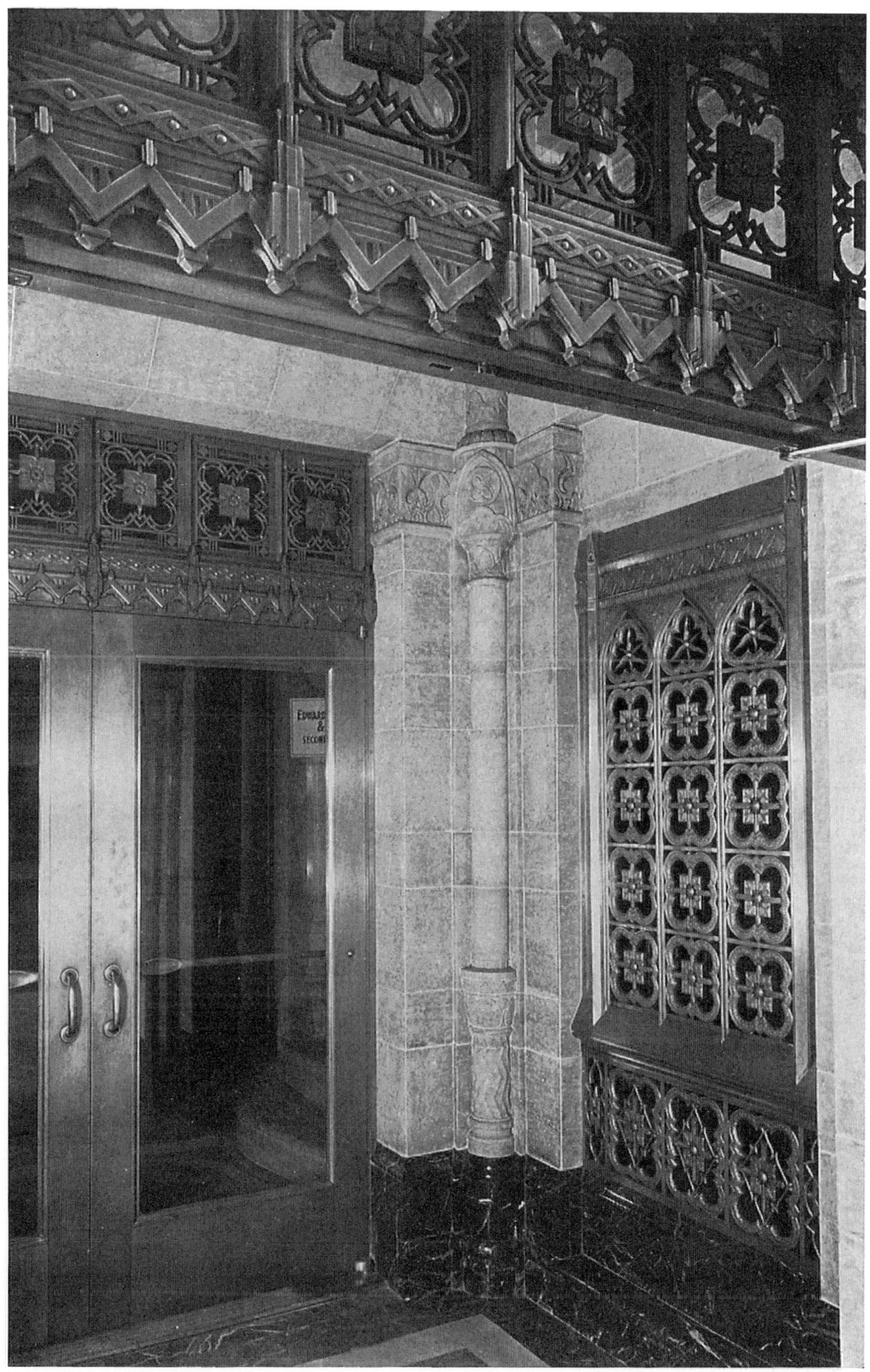

Courtesy of Metalcraft Magazine — H. Craig Severance, *Architect*

Bronze Grilles, 400 Madison Ave., New York City

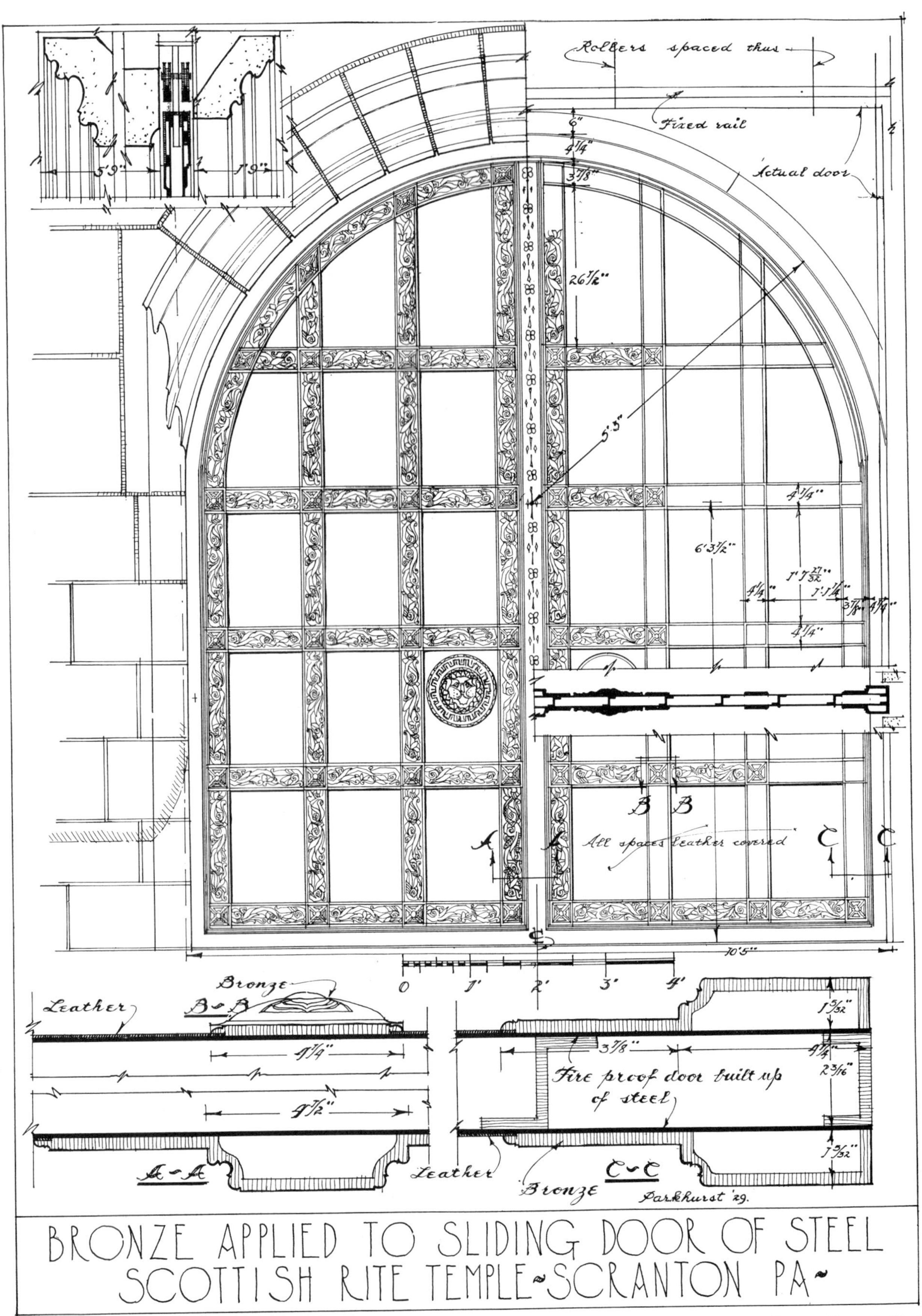

Courtesy of Metalcraft Magazine

Raymond Hood, *Architect*

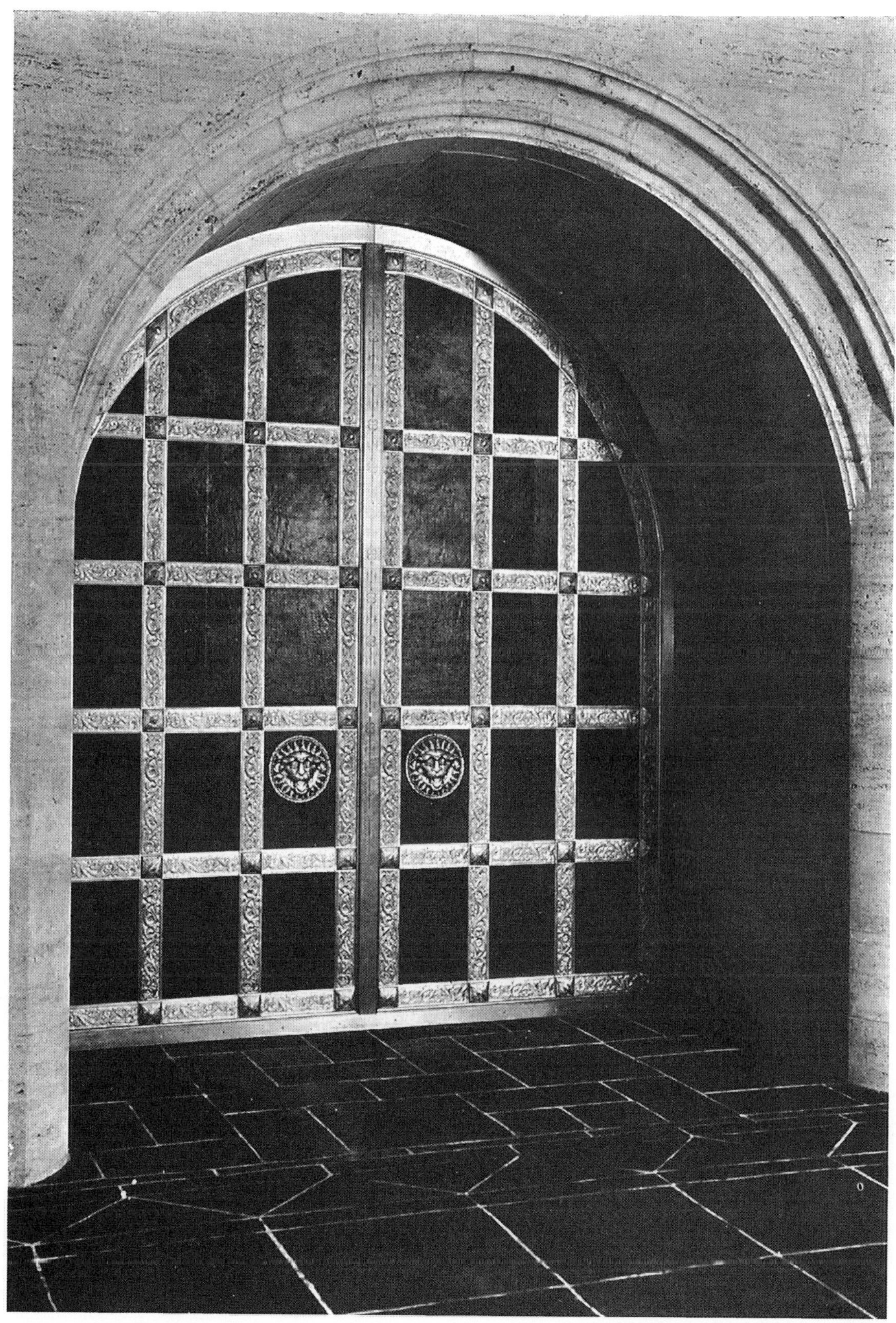

COURTESY OF METALCRAFT MAGAZINE RAYMOND HOOD, *Architect*

BRONZE DOORS, SCOTTISH RITE CATHEDRAL, SCRANTON, PA.

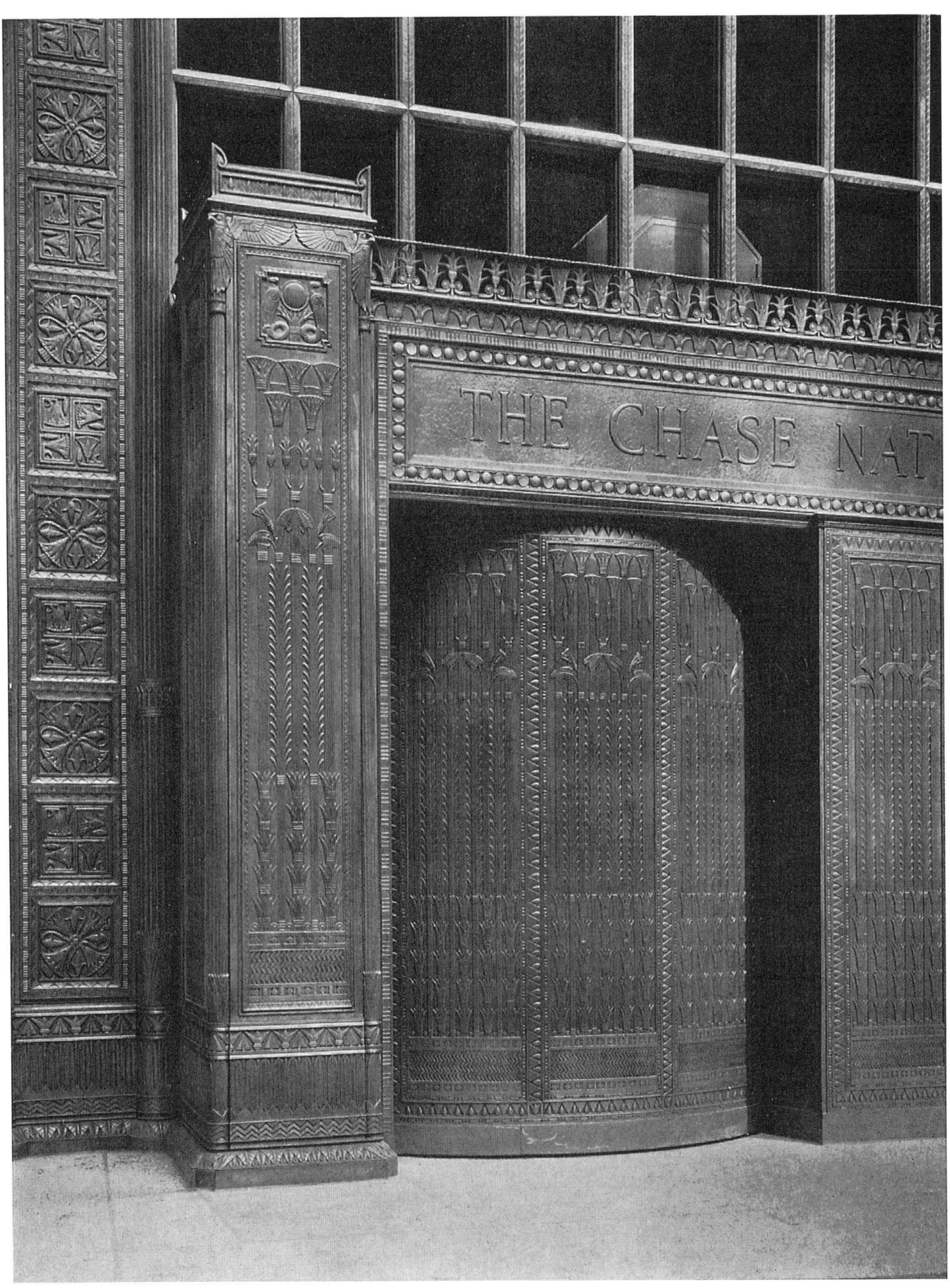

Courtesy The Metal Arts

Graham, Anderson, Probst & White, *Architects*

Detail of Entrance, Chase National Bank, New York

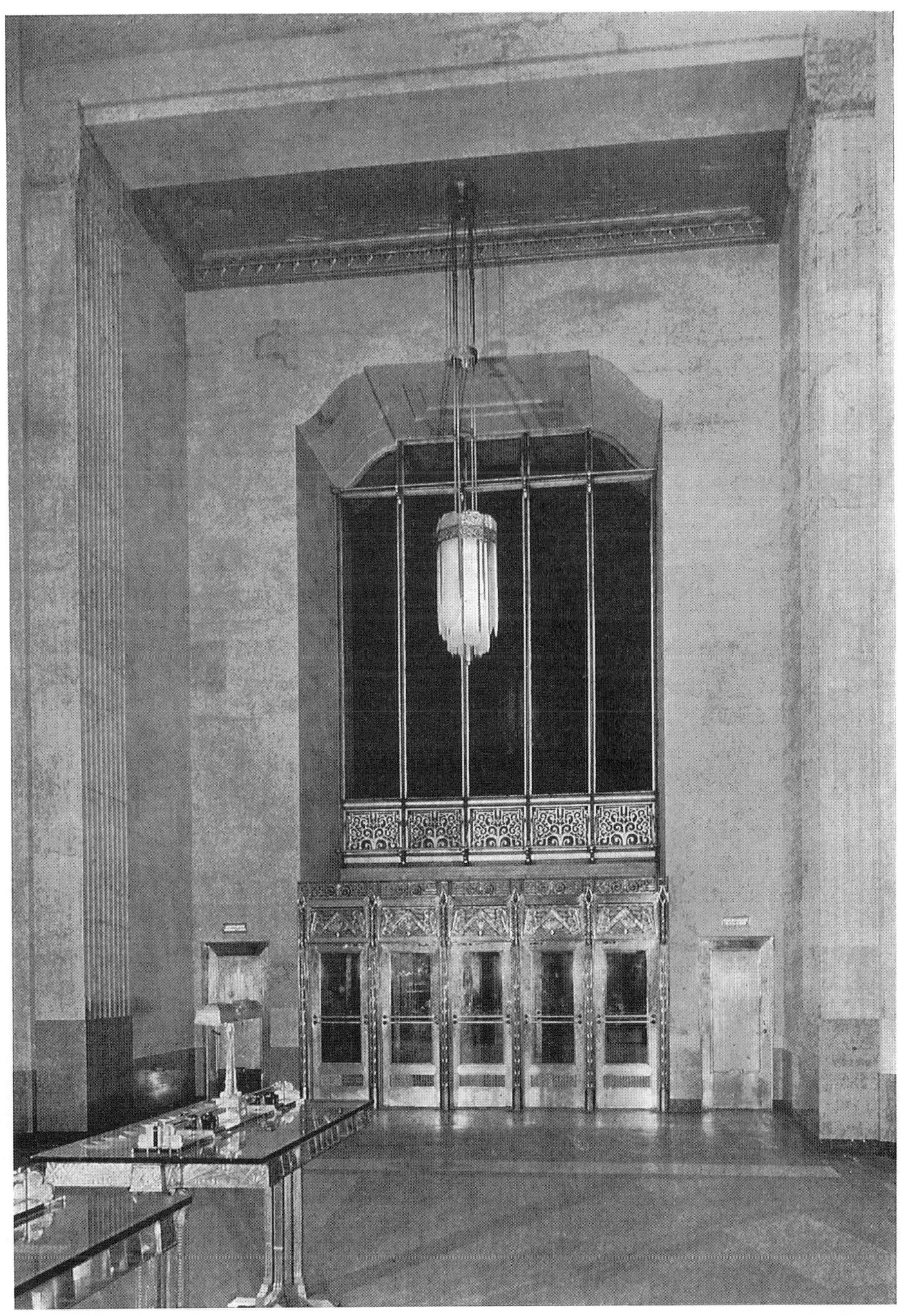

Courtesy of The Metal Arts

A. C. Finn, K. Franzheim & J. E. R. Carpenter, *Associated Architects*

Interior of Entrance, National Bank of Commerce, Houston, Texas

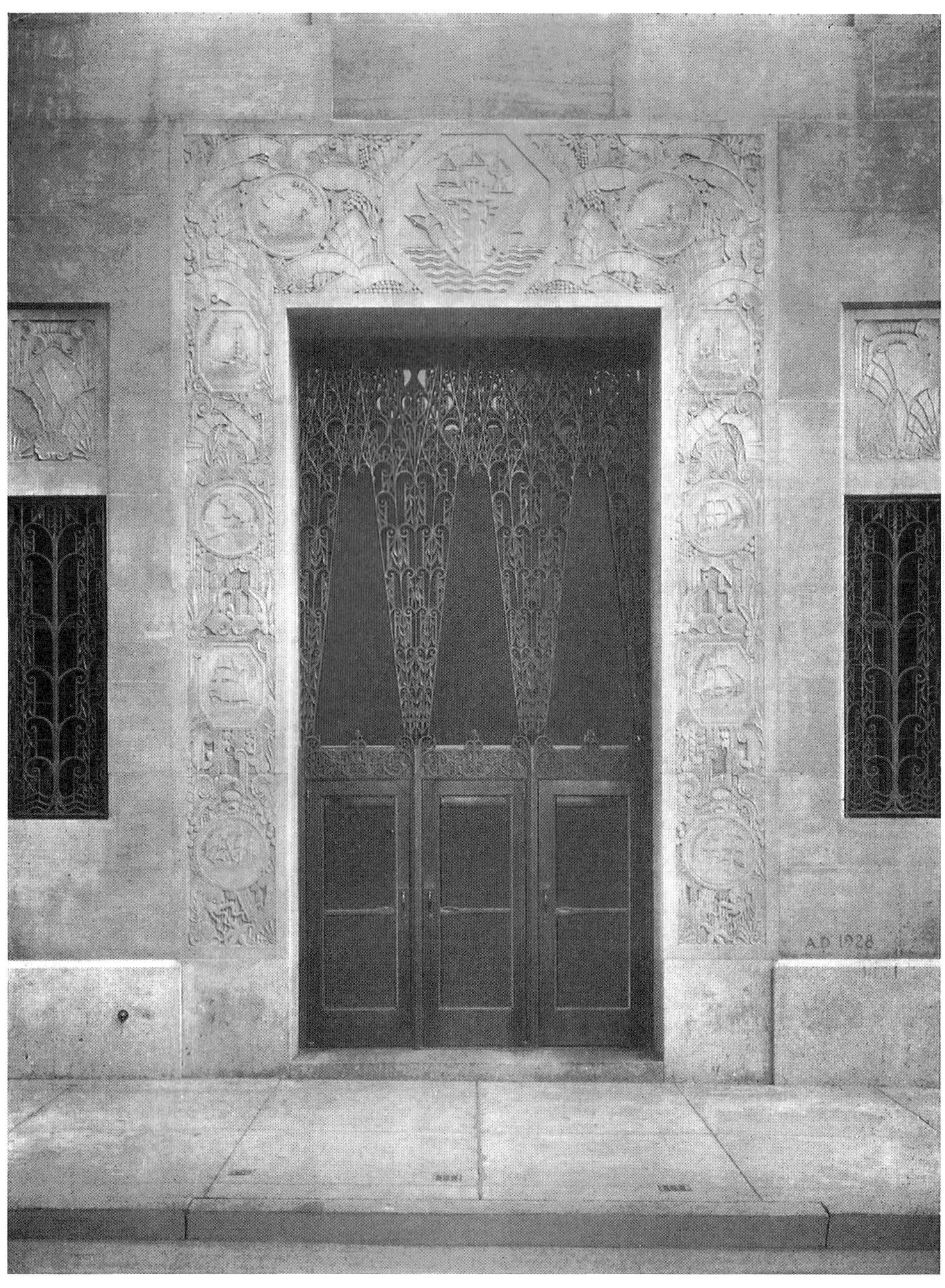

Courtesy The Metal Arts

Louis E. Jallade, *Architect*

Bronze Grilles at Entrance, Navy Y.M.C.A., Philadelphia, Pa.

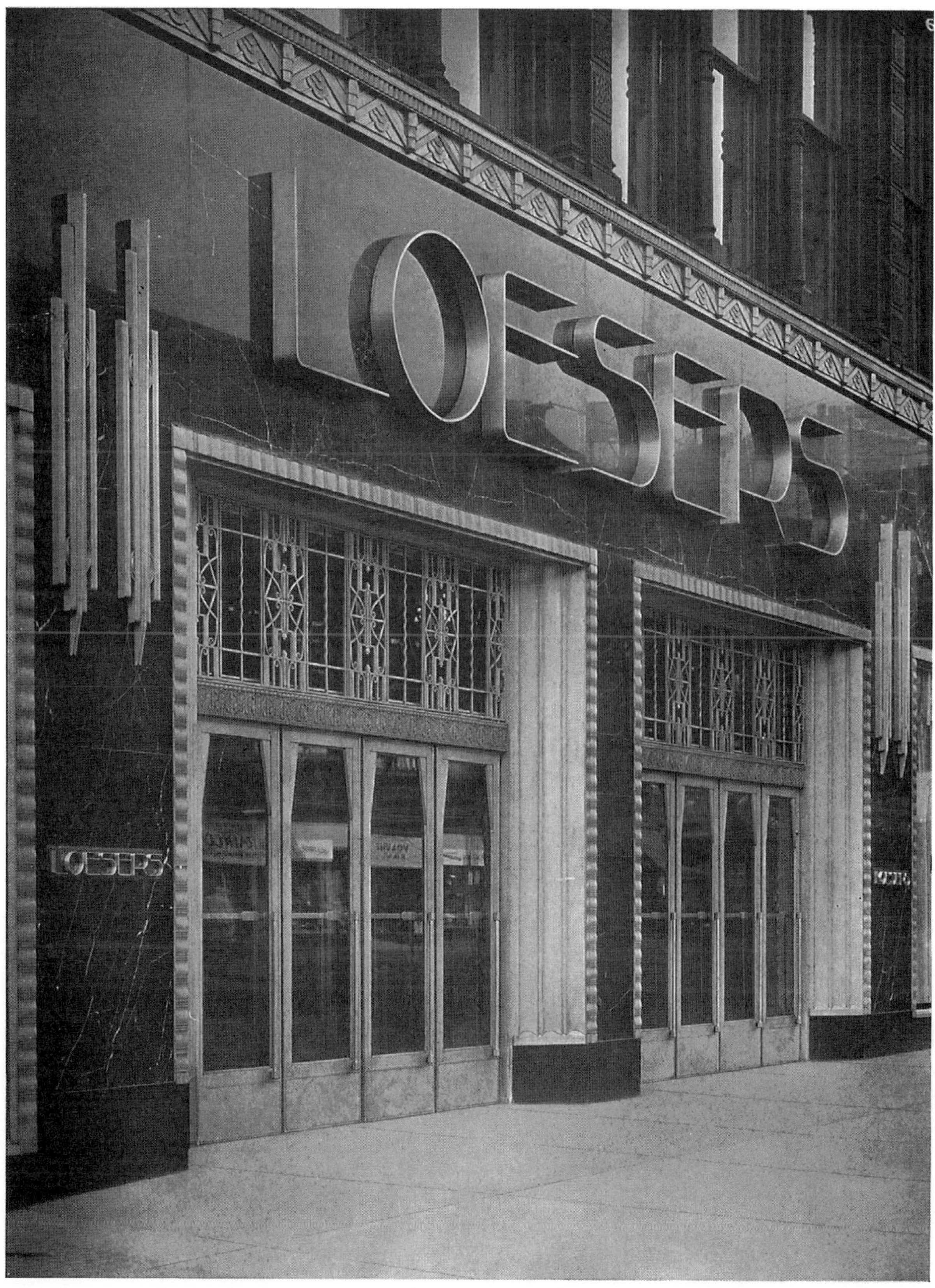

Courtesy The Metal Arts

Starrett & Van Vleck, *Architects*

Entrance, Frederick Loeser & Co. Store, Brooklyn, New York

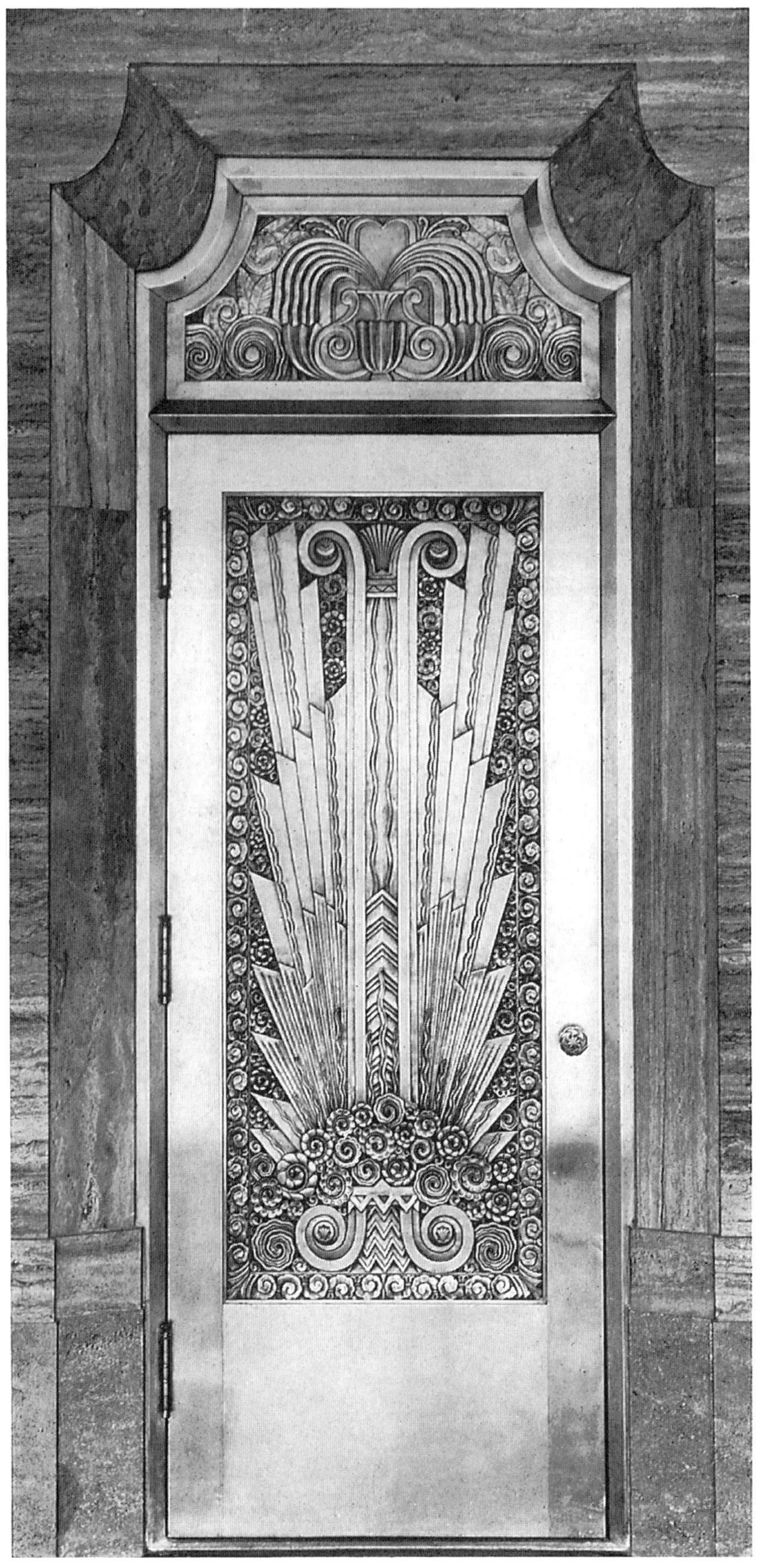

Courtesy of Metalcraft Magazine — Alfred C. Finn, *Architect*

Entrance Door, Gulf Building, Houston, Texas

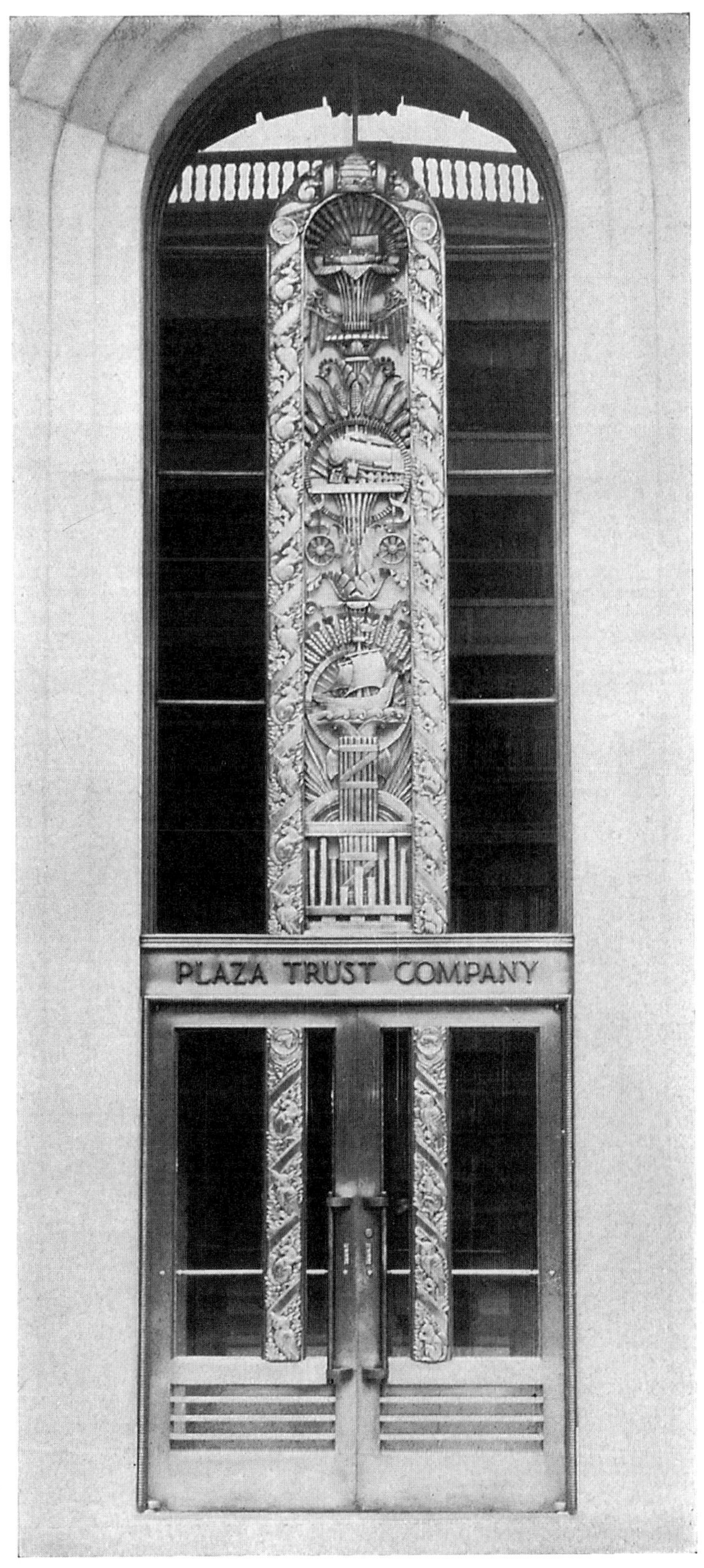

Courtesy of Metalcraft Magazine — Helmle, Corbett & Harrison, *Architects*

Main Entrance, Plaza Trust Co., New York City

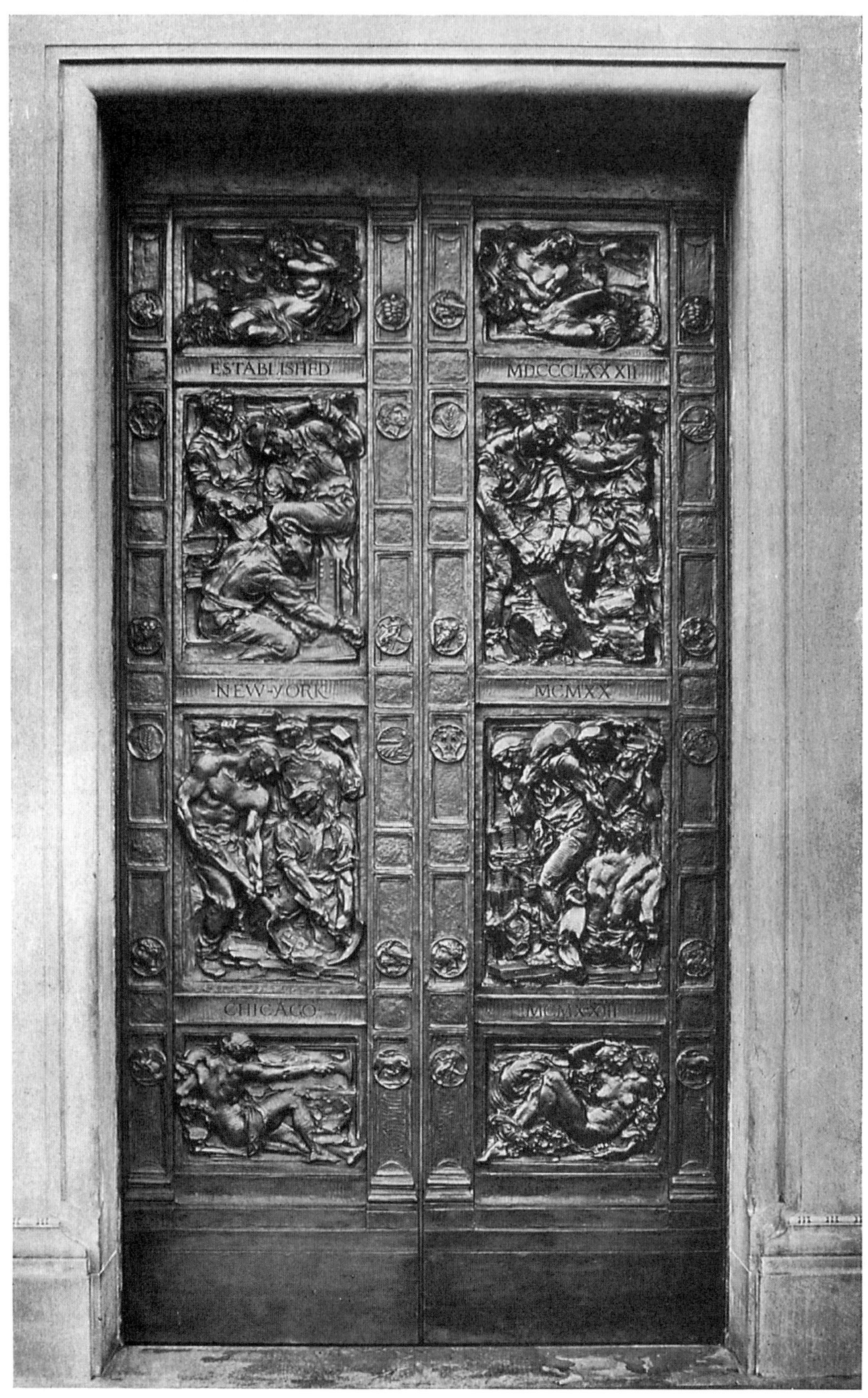

Courtesy of The Metal Arts

Graham, Anderson, Probst & White, *Architects*

Bronze Entrance Doors, S. W. Straus & Co. Bank, Chicago, Ill.

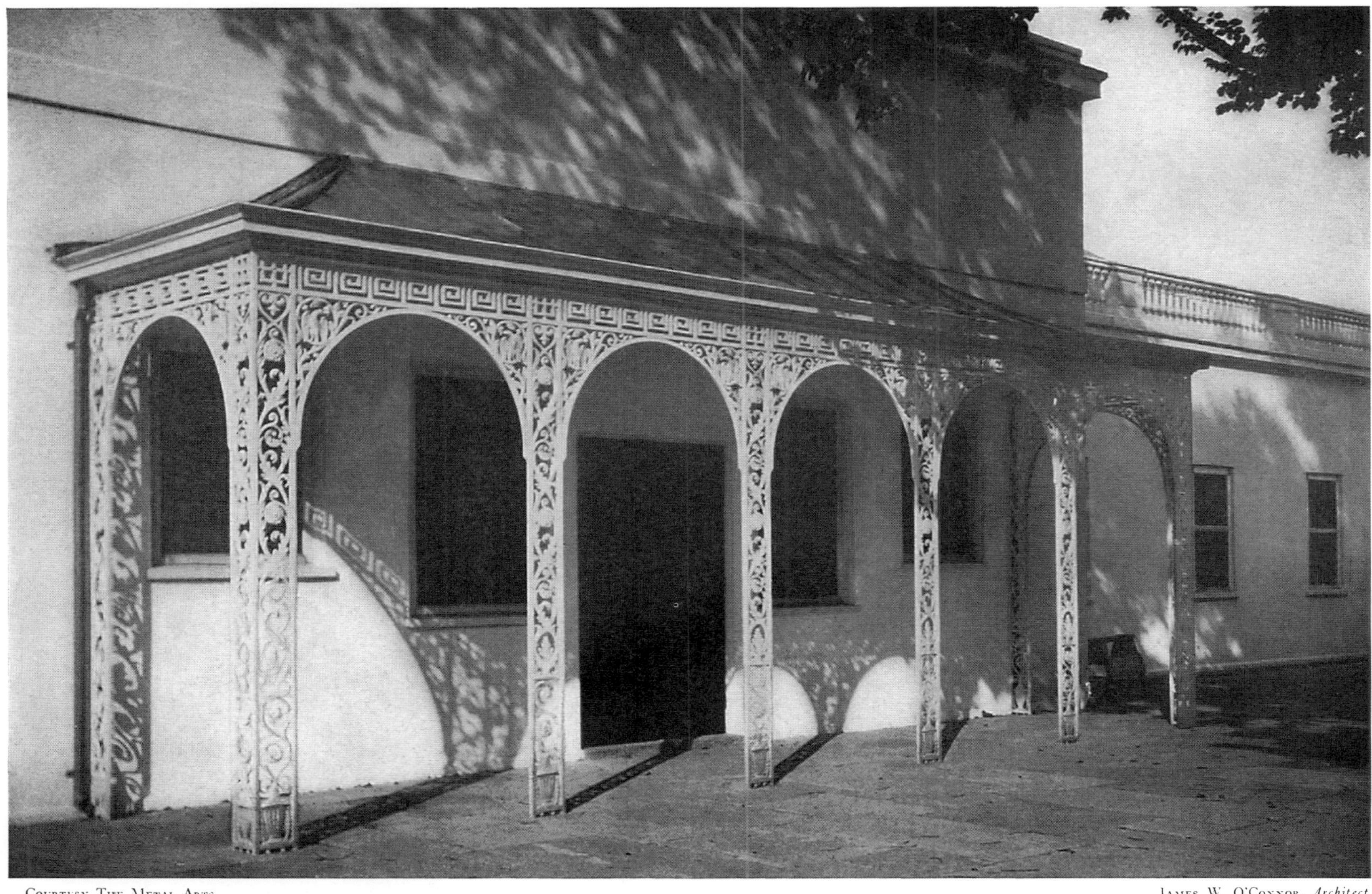

Courtesy The Metal Arts

James W. O'Connor, *Architect*

Porch of Ornamental Cast White Bronze, Residence of W. R. Grace, Esq., Old Westbury, Long Island, N. Y.

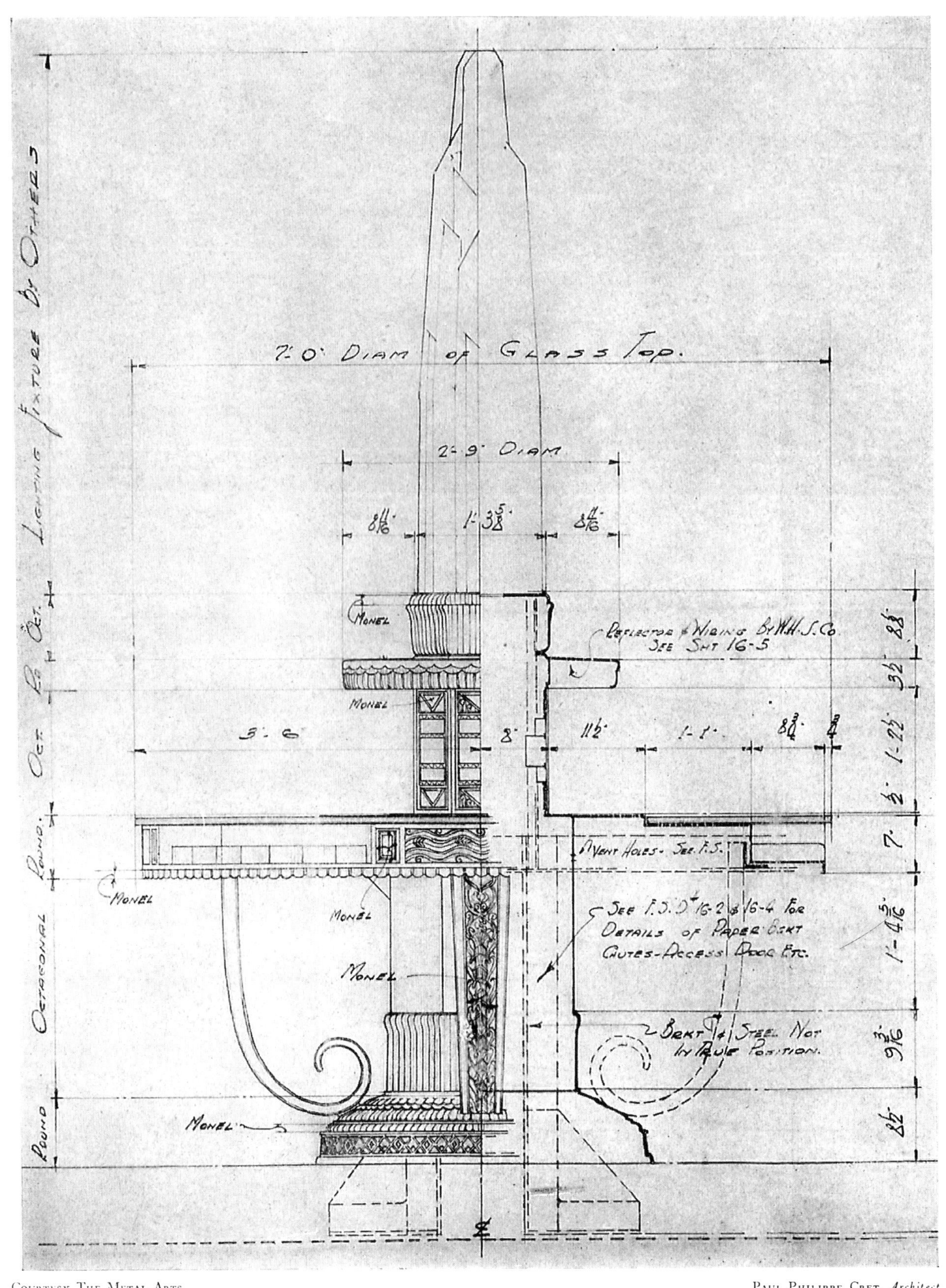

Courtesy The Metal Arts

Paul Philippe Cret, *Architect*

Working Drawing of Check Desk, Main Banking Room, Integrity Trust Co., Philadelphia, Pa.

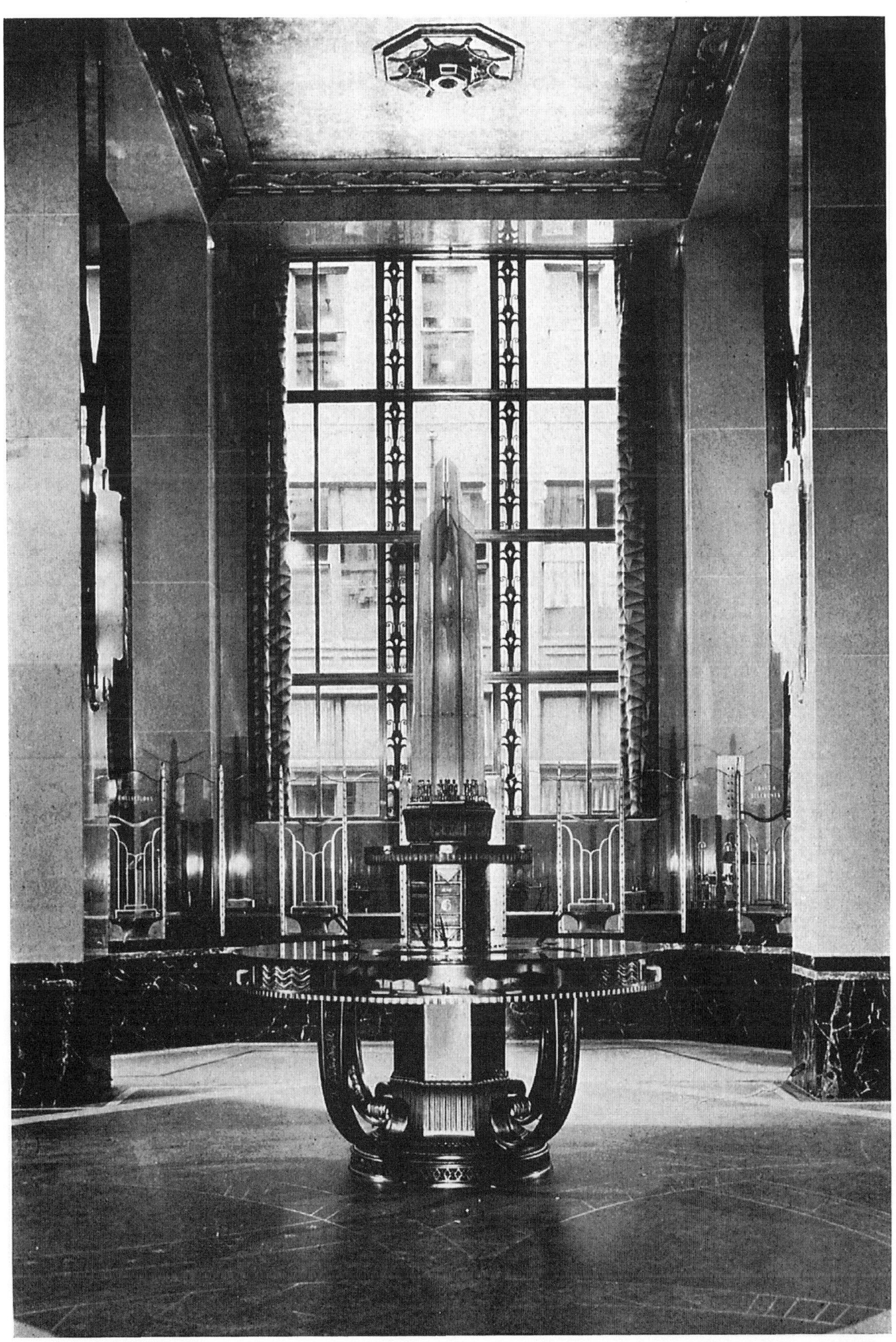

Courtesy The Metal Arts | Paul Philippe Cret, *Architect*

Detail of Main Banking Room, Integrity Trust Co., Philadelphia, Pa.

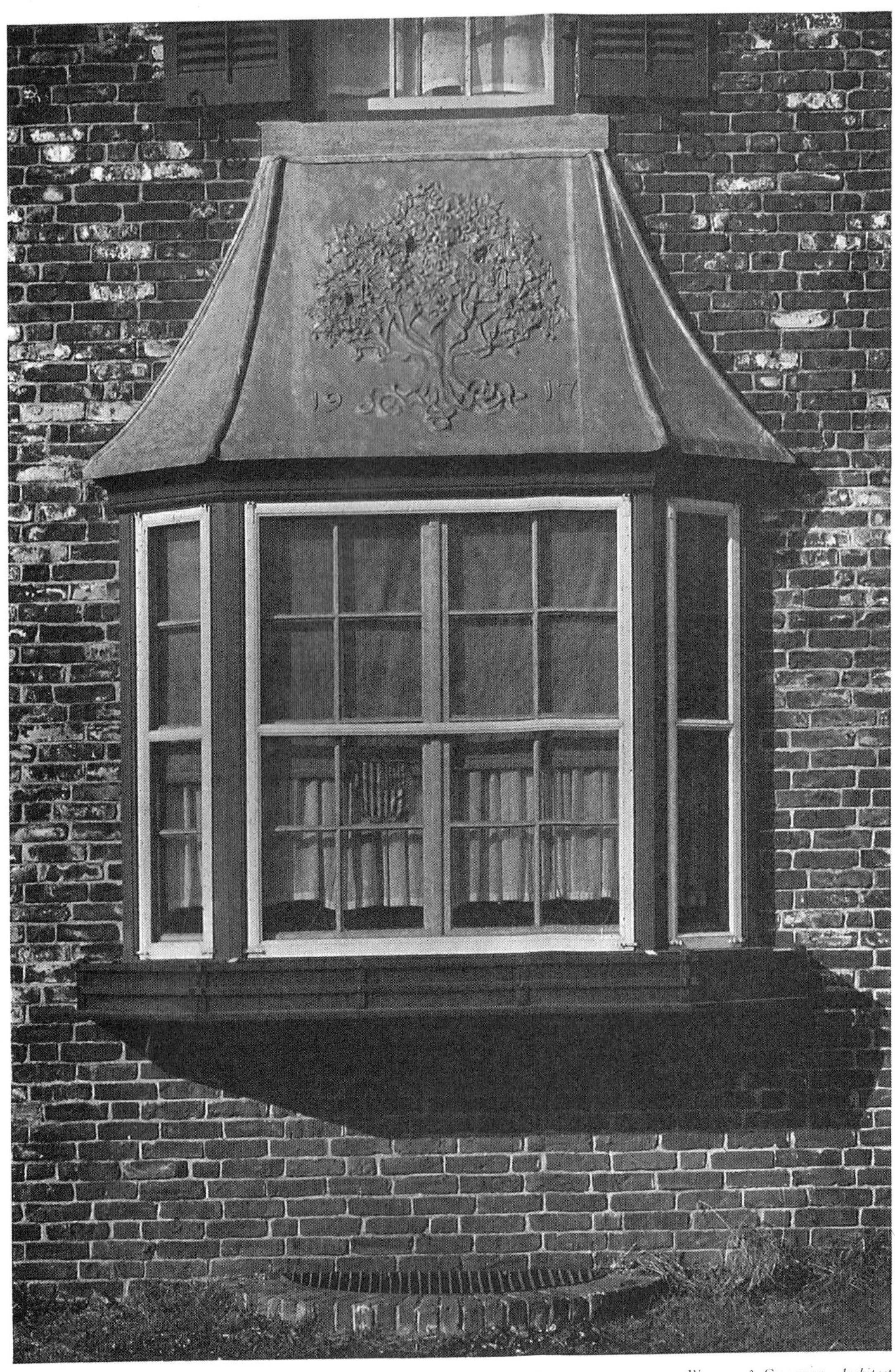

Courtesy The Metal Arts

Walker & Gillette, *Architects*

Lead Roof on Bow Window, Wheatley Hills, New York

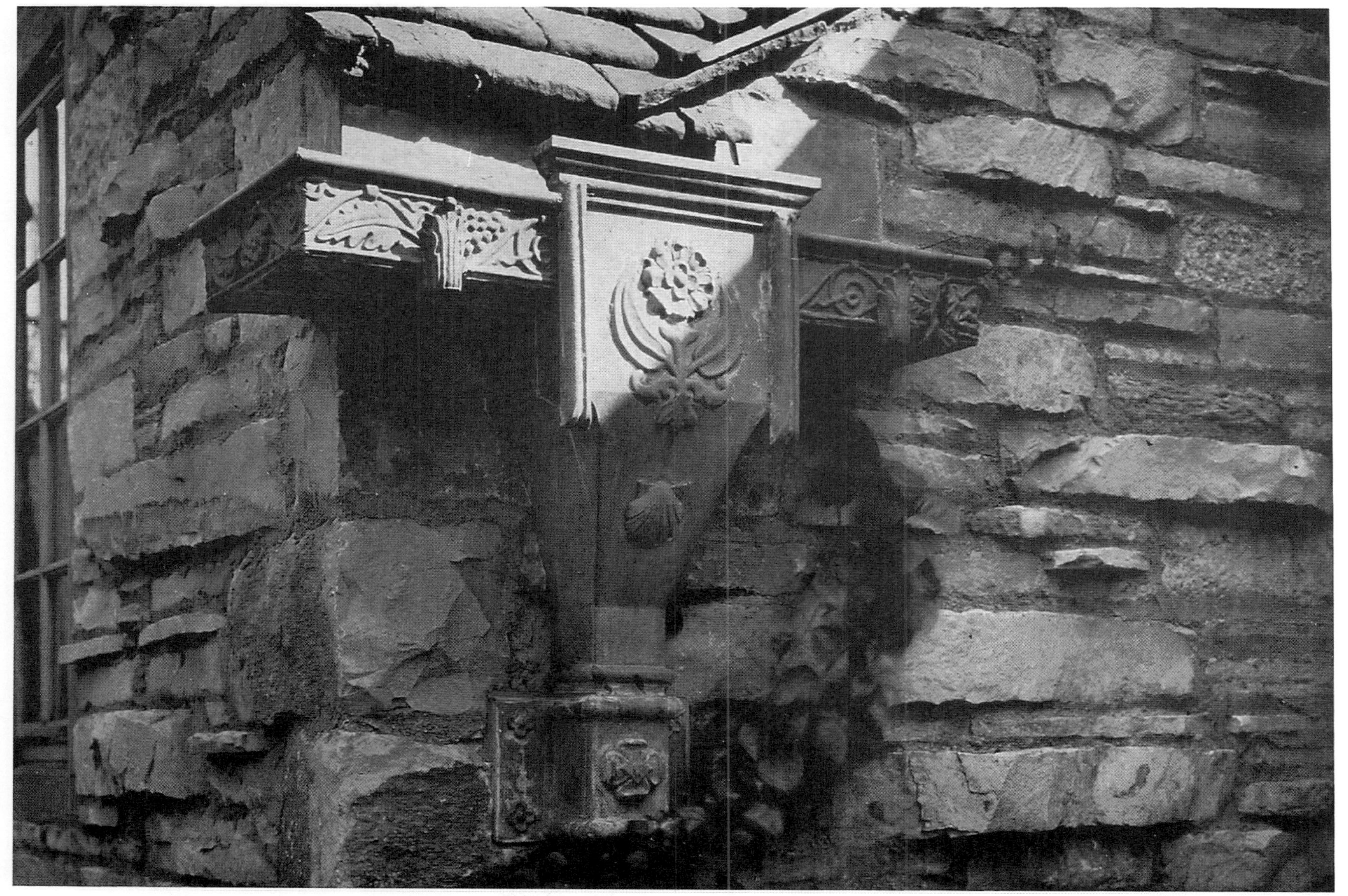

Courtesy The Metal Arts

Richard Powers, *Architect*

Detail, Lead Rain Water Head

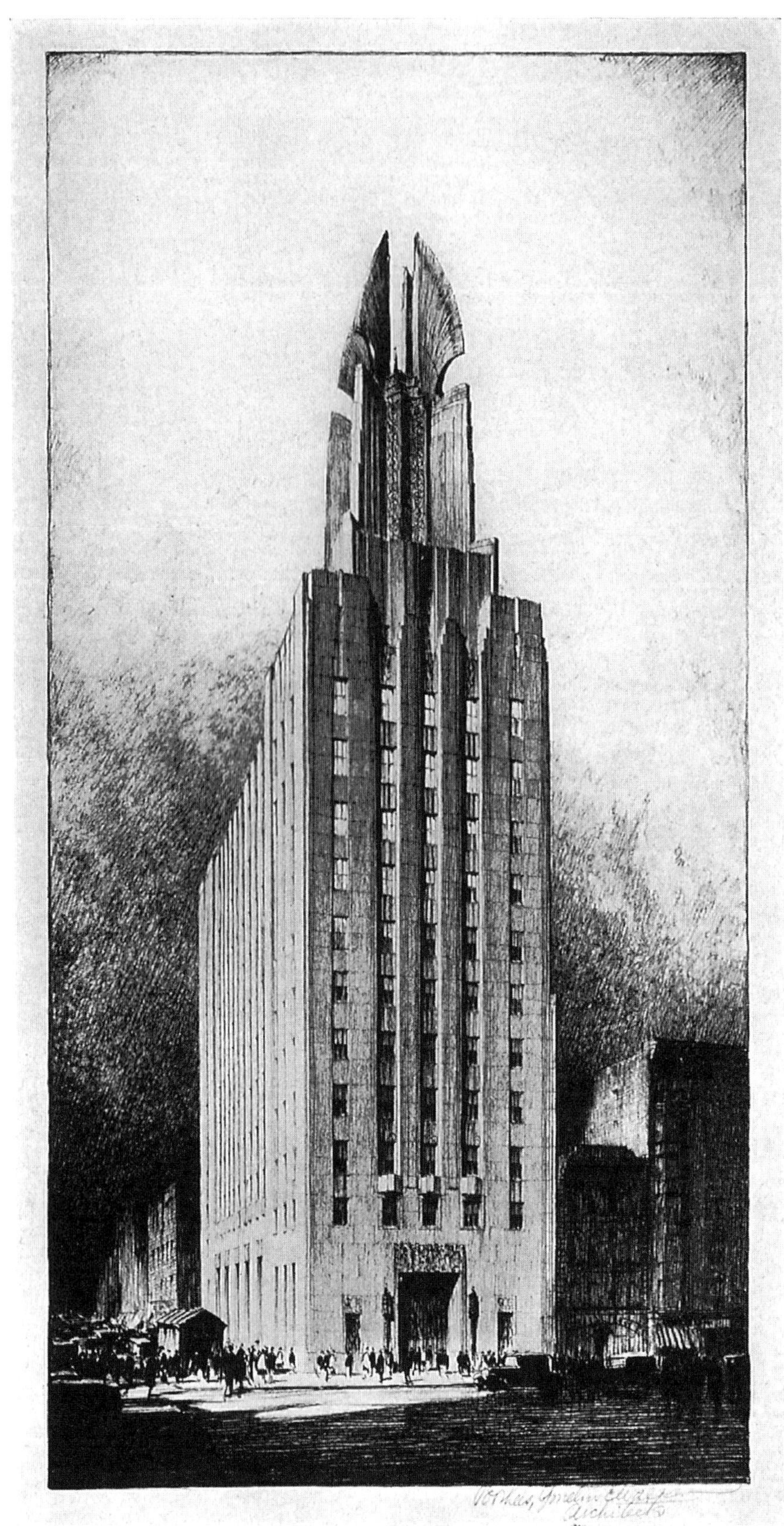

Courtesy The Metal Arts — Voorhees, Gmelin & Walker, *Architects*

Aluminum Cresting on the Genesee Valley Trust Co. Bldg., Rochester, New York

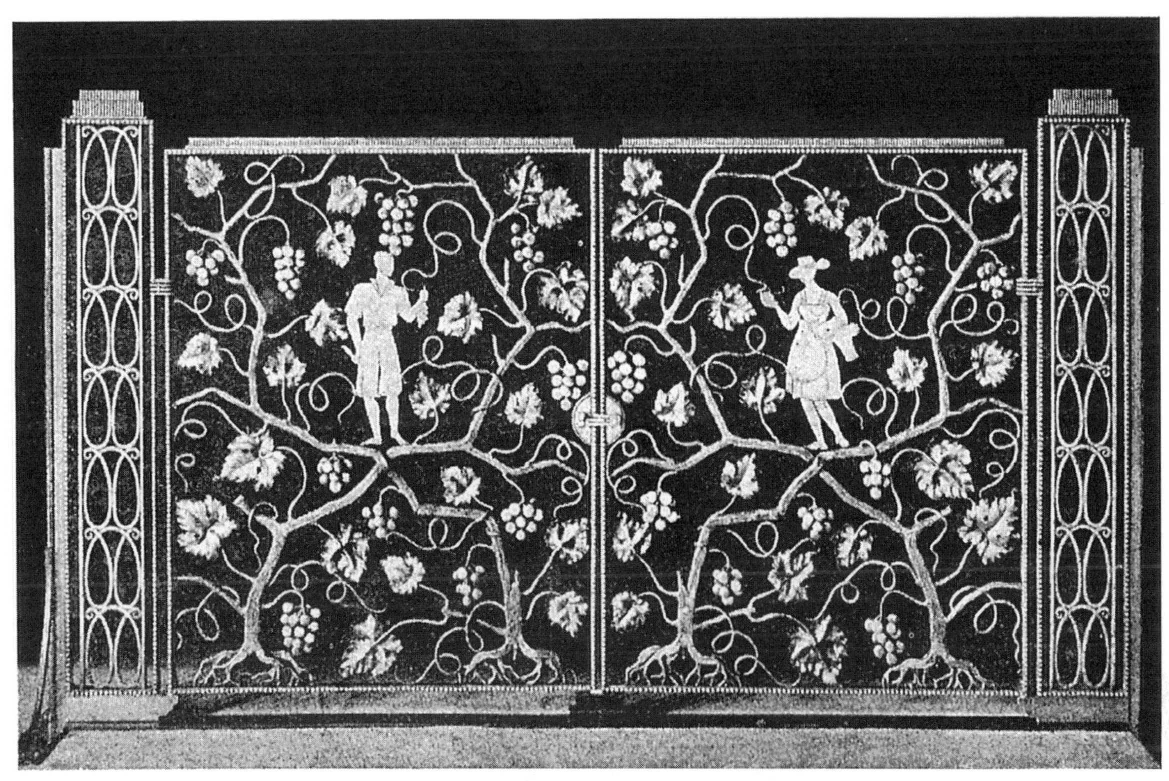

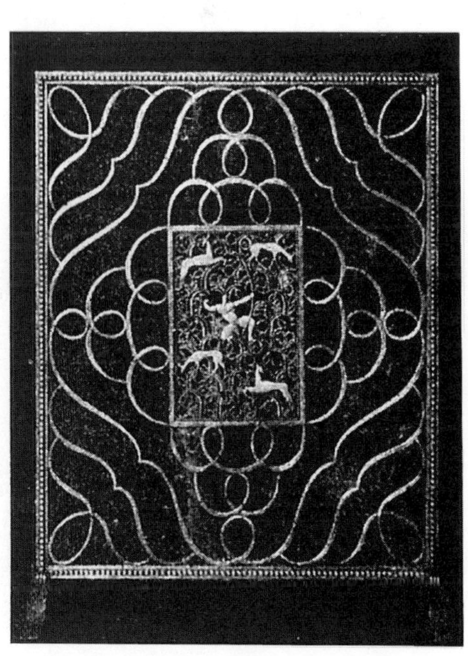

Screens and Grille by Edgar Brandt

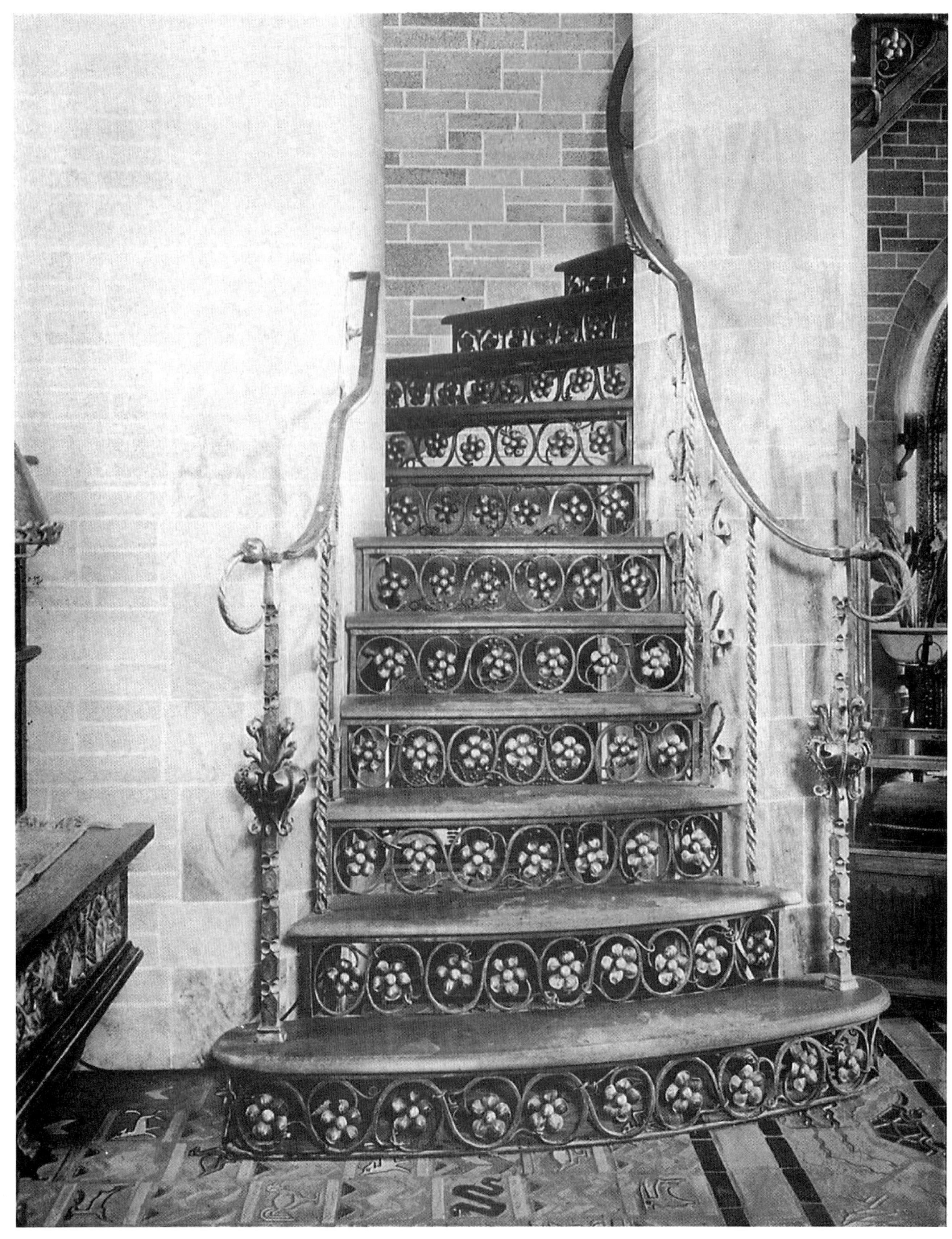

MILTON B. MEDARY, *Architect*

SECTION OF WROUGHT IRON STAIR RAILING CARILLON SINGING TOWER,
MOUNTAIN LAKE, FLORIDA

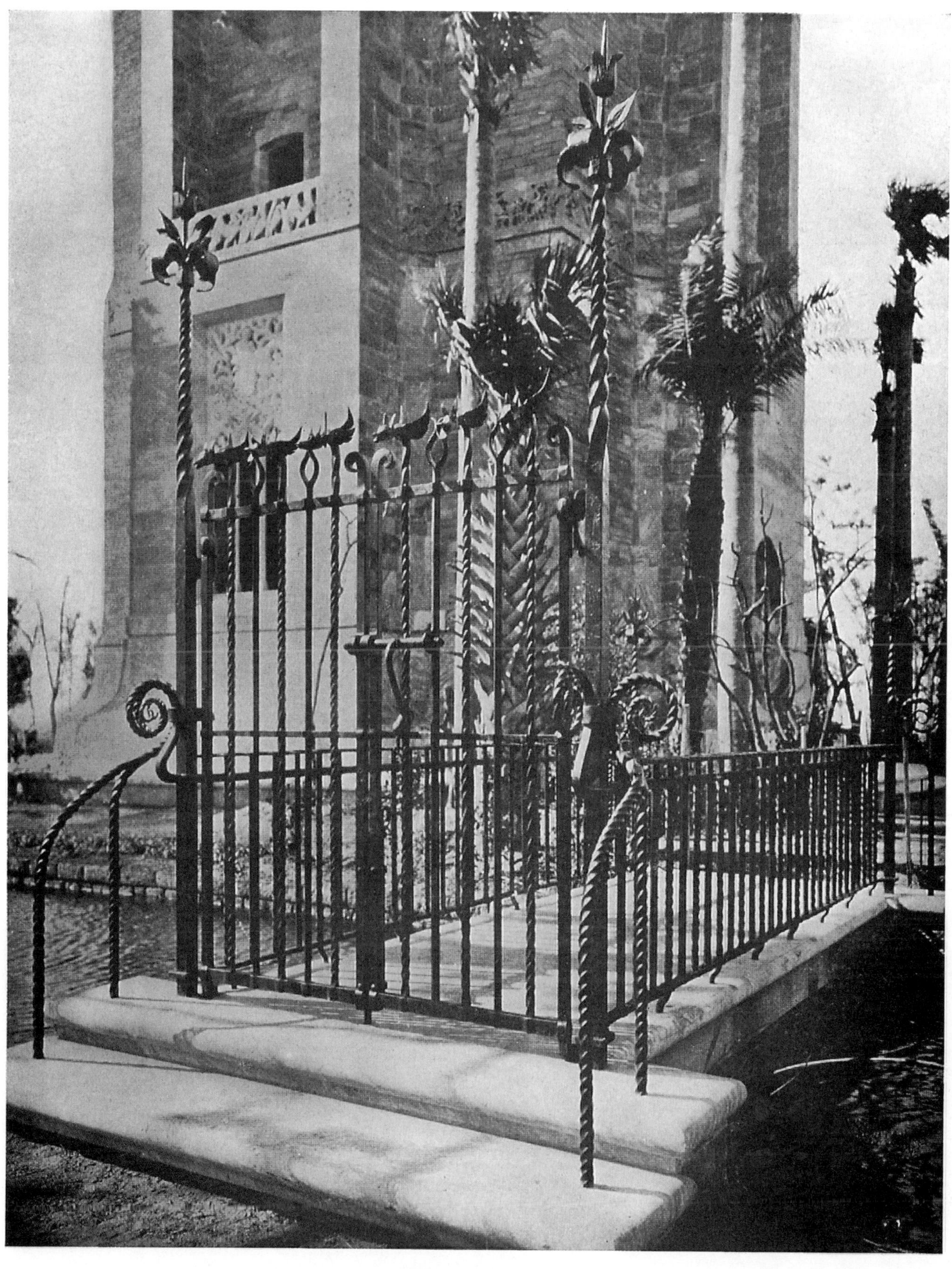

Milton B. Medary, *Architect*

Wrought Iron Bridge Gates Over Moat, Carillon Singing Tower,
Mountain Lake, Florida

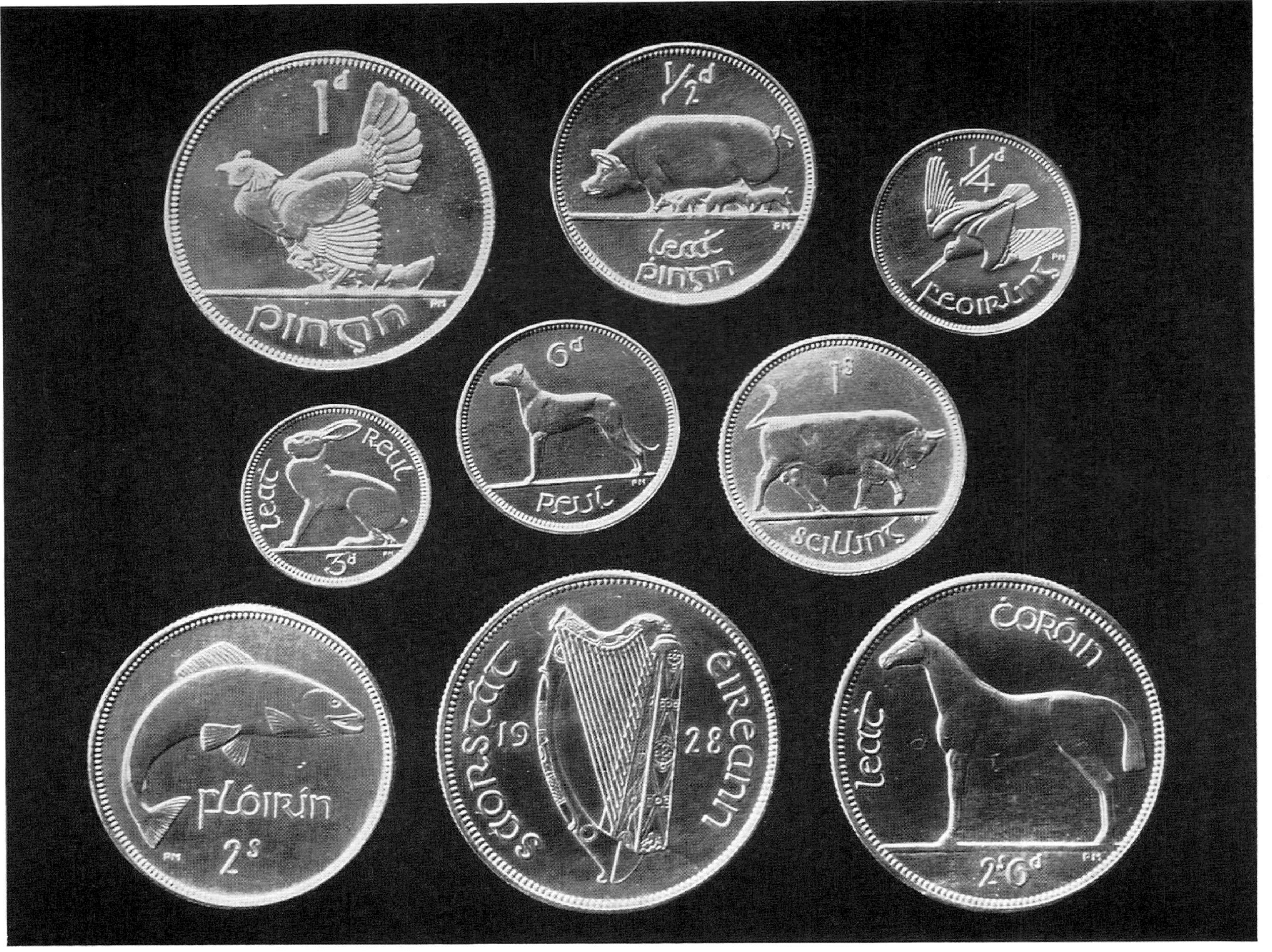

IRISH FREE STATE COINS